POSTHUMOUS PEOPLE

Vienna at the Turning Point

MERIDIAN

Crossing Aesthetics

Werner Hamacher
& David E. Wellbery
Editors

Translated by
Rodger Friedman

*Stanford
University
Press*

*Stanford
California
1996*

POSTHUMOUS PEOPLE

Vienna at the Turning Point

Massimo Cacciari

Posthumous People was originally published
in Italian in 1980 under the title *Dallo Steinhof*
© 1980 Adelphi Edizioni S.P.A. Milano

Stanford University Press
Stanford, California

© 1996 by the Board of Trustees
of the Leland Stanford Junior University

Printed in the United States of America

CIP data appear at the end of the book

Stanford University Press publications are
distributed exclusively by Stanford University
Press within the United States, Canada,
Mexico, and Central America; they are
distributed exclusively by
Cambridge University Press
throughout the rest of the world.

In memory of Ferruccio Masini

Preface

Parts of this book are adapted from articles originally published in *Laboratorio Musica*, edited by Luigi Nono, and in *Nuova Corrente*, edited by Giovanni Sechi, whose memory I honor here with affection and sorrow.

I hope this collection succeeds in breaking fresh ground after my earlier books on similar subjects, *Oikos* (1975), *Krisis* (1976), and *Intransitabili utopie* (1978). I would not have written it if I thought it a mere amplification of themes already covered.

The notes are solely to refer the reader to the body of criticism essential for understanding the text.

1980

Preface to the
American Edition

This American edition modifies somewhat the Italian edition of 1980 as well as the Spanish translation of 1989. In particular, I eliminated sections at odds with today's critical literature on Vienna around the turn of the last century. I have little interest in the amorphous "strudel" made of waltzes, decadence, a carefree apocalypse, and theatrical destinies that in the course of the last twenty years has come to be glorified as "Grand Vienna."

The last essay of the American edition, "Profane Attention," on Robert Musil, is not in either the Italian edition or the Spanish translation. It first appeared in 1979 in *Metaphorein*, the journal edited by my unforgettable friend, the great Italian Germanist Ferruccio Masini, to whose memory this new edition of my book is dedicated.

Attentive readers should recognize that this book is not simply a collection of scattered essays. Its diverse figures and various tempos form what I would rather call a *Liederzyklus*, a song cycle. This quality differentiates it from my subsequent books, *Icone della Legge* (1985), which will appear in English translation soon, and *L'Angelo necessario* (1986), already available as *The Necessary Angel*.

1995

Contents

Sixteen pages of figures follow page 96.

Translators' Note

Massimo Cacciari writes in a rich, allusive style that derives some of its fascination from highlighting Italian with German elements, indeed with German words. The English translation is necessarily plainer than the original and loses much of its Italo-German effect.

Where Cacciari translates from German sources, I have generally translated them anew, based on the original and on the Italian translations. An important exception includes all citations of Wittgenstein's *Tractatus Logico-Philosophicus*, which are taken from the standard English translation by D. F. Pears and B. F. McGuinness. Where references are available in English translations, I indicate so in a note.

It is only after death that we will enter *our* life and come alive, oh, very much alive, we posthumous people!

—Nietzsche, *The Gay Science* 365

Introduction:
The View from Steinhof

This book's epigraph might have been "Wer seiner Zeit nur voraus ist, den holt sie einmal ein" (Ludwig Wittgenstein, 1930), which means, "Those who are merely ahead of their time deserve to have it catch up."

Two symmetrical avenues along the edge of the Viennese woods lead to the church of Saint Leopold. Looking out from the top of Baumgartner Höhe, there must have been a brilliant view over Vienna, like a Bellotto landscape, the city shimmering and sparkling with light. Otto Wagner's church, crowning the grounds of Vienna's hospital for the mentally ill, stood out of the folds of green with its resplendent gold leaf cupola (see Figure 1). It is impossible to say what time this work was ahead of, and impossible to say what caught up.[1]

Four bronze angels stand at the vestibule. They are the *ermeneuti* [interpreters] of the interior and at the same time its custodians. The hieratic rhythm that scans them evidently quotes Ferdinand Hodler's figures. The principles of repetition and symmetry with which Hodler made "bitter and dangerous cracks in the world of impressionism,"[2] dominate the entire structure. Behind the four angels (by Othmar Schmikowitz) stands Kolo Moser's great semicircular stained glass window. The throne of the Father is in the middle, and at its sides are two angels draped in precious mantles, with their wings unfurled above them. Adam and Eve are on their knees at the extreme angles of the arch, practically enmeshed in the fronds of great curving plants. This window and two others on the transept cast white and gold, green and blue light over the interior of the church. Great angelic figures appear in their full glory in the transept windows. The two upper angels, hovering over saints that represent works of charity, have vast, magnificent peacock wings. For the main altar, decorated in majolica, stucco, and mosaic, Moser designed two other standing angels, facing front, exhibiting the symbols of Christ's martyrdom. The large panel between them shows the triumph of Christ surrounded by a chorus of saints, among them Dymphna, protector of fools.

The symmetrical, repetitive rhythm is accentuated from the outside by a revetment of thin marble blocks. The iron clamps and bolts that keep them in place, rimmed with copper leaf borders, give a sense of motion to these walls, yet without any monumental emphasis and without any concession to ornament. Inside, the building's perfect measure of basic forms is joined, without contrast, by the multicolored clarity of light that streams through the stained glass windows. Here is the meeting, never realized so well, of the principles of tradition and quotation on the one hand and the *Nervenleben* [vitality] of the Secession Movement's images and color on the other. *Nervenleben* illuminates the pure basic forms of the temple that constitute the space in which the oscillating Jugendstil tonalities find an order, a clear and comprehensible consistency, however ephemeral it may be. The interior space gathers this meeting into its center. A profound necessity moved Wagner, therefore, to "squeeze" the interior space of the cupola. While the exterior should be visible from far away and dominate the entire landscape, inside a centripetal force should prevail, a "gathering," since the forces that are found here give life to a difficult and brief unity. Perhaps the church at Steinhof can be understood only upon exiting and turning away from it. Then, while studying the various views that open out from the church, we understand the intimate weakness of its extreme theophanies. The infinite coming and going and the interminable crowds that inhabit this landscape began, perhaps, in the utopia that we just now left behind. Here all of them sought a final, impossible resting place. Woods straight out of Alfred Kubin's pictures embrace this church and block out its light. But the greatness of this church lies in its continuous, intentional crashing against the edges of the woods, on the beaches of the night, like one of those falling stars that Georg Trakl talks about.

Posthumous People

The view from this church looks out over a landscape of posthumous people. They haunt society. They go about in disguise, but they are recognized. They are objects of curiosity and interest. But in company—and not in contrast, as Nietzsche believed—they are ghosts. Nietzsche talks about them in *The Gay Science* (365) and later in *Twilight of the Idols.* They pass through closed doors when all the lights are out. Other people may reach out to them, but their hands pass right through them. This is not their only disguise. Indeed, they possess endless stores of masks and alibis. Posthumous people have too many alibis to be satisfied with simple truth. ("Every truth is simple—but isn't this a double lie?") Posthumous people go through an infinite number of masks without ever staying with any one of them. And "this causes fear," it is their *Unheimliches,* their uneasiness.

Since they have no substance, they are misunderstood more than others, more than actual people. And yet they are heard better. "Or more exactly, we are never understood," but the ghosts of posthumous people practically force themselves to be heard, practically cause the dimension of hearing to be rediscovered. Their "authority" is nothing but this solitary, mute invitation to be heard. "We, the subject," is converted into the form, "we, the posthumous people." The cogent force of a decree pronounced by the present and fully productive subject ("we, the subject") is transformed to the dimension of an absence ("we, the posthumous people") that is clearly heard, while it criticizes, deconstructs, and shreds that idea of substance in which the kingdom of the subject resides. Therefore not only do posthumous people indicate the end of "we, the subject," but they are the only ones to survive, as mere phantasms, after the end of the subject. They are the only ones to initiate the hearing of the abyss, the *Ab-grund*, the dimension gaping beyond the foundation of the ground, the *fundamentum veritatis*. They are the hikers in Nietzsche's *Human, All Too Human* who seek to understand how things of the world proceed and who silently collect and maintain their multiple voices. In this way, posthumous people come alive. Only after the death of "we the subject"—and therefore only after death—will they have their lives.

Nevertheless, to call people posthumous is not to call them untimely. The term "untimely" carries, however unconsciously, the possibility of becoming timely. Untimely people can always look ahead to their own time. Not so for posthumous people; they are absolutely protected from the risk of expectation. They cannot be reached, they cannot be understood. Their own lives do not signify their actuality, that is, the establishment of their rationale. They have too many rationales to be able to confirm them. Untimely can still be a value that intends to realize itself on others, a potential subject. Posthumous people have traversed every subject to the end. The lives they protect do not confirm a subject, a presence, but rather confirm the insignificance, the superfluity of the actual (that in which the actual appears truly as "the indecent overvaluation" of itself and of its own language). Thus the dimension of posthumous people drowns out the dimension of the untimely (which many Nietzschean readings understand to be extreme).

Joseph Roth's "Invalid des Lebens" is posthumous. Ludwig von Janikowski is posthumous. He kept himself far from the lying life of writing, and he helped Karl Kraus to compose and revise the essays of his first collection, *Sittlichkeit und Kriminalität*. The most perfect interiors of Peter Altenberg and Adolf Loos are for these posthumous figures, for these strange ghosts. Hugo von Hofmannsthal's Sigismund tends to this very sort of posthumous life.

Hunted, expressed by silence, persecuted by the present and by research into the present, he wants to create a void in himself and around himself in order to listen to its sense, the imperceptible invitation. "We, the Posthumous People" must be the title of Robert Walser's entire opus.

It was Robert Musil, however, who more than anyone else understood the unheard of force of distance that being posthumous allows. The clarity and force of a Renaissance German engraving that underlies a piece like "The Flypaper"[3] comes from this distance. Being posthumous brings the most secret events into brilliant focus. Precisely because he is not only untimely, but posthumous, Musil's eye savors the unreachable gifts of distance, the *Entfernung*, the remoteness of remoteness. (Derrida gleans this notion from Nietzsche.) It is necessary to know how to survive in the most pure and rarified atmosphere so the eye may reach this point of clarity and may reflect images even in their most infinitesimal details—even, finally, to the point of becoming one with them. At the height of distance, in fact, the most profound sympathy opens up. That is why the power of Musil's language is so great. On the one hand, it submerges itself in the distance, but on the other, it captures the event in its most secret fibers. Musil's language "discovers" the event under the masks of truth that pretend to immobilize it and listens to its irreducible polyphony. If this is the poetry of "Pre Posthumous Papers and Other Prose," then Wittgenstein, from whom this work gets its initiative, wrote posthumous papers par excellence.

Sprachliches

In order to understand the crux of the *Tractatus*, it is necessary to consider the fault lines in the universe to which it belongs. If research on two or many Wittgensteins is as sterile as the scheme of a "seamless continuity,"[4] we must ask ourselves what body of problems is contained in the *Tractatus* and if these do not indicate theoretical fractures already existing in Wittgenstein's work. The first myth to dismantle, then, is that Gottlob Frege and Bertrand Russell together prepared its way. In reality, Frege's philosophy penetrates into the *Tractatus* and into its core in a much more organic fashion than does Russell's.

For Russell, there is no description without denotation. Description always has an ontological content, and logic is always ontology. There is no trace of this germ of neo-positivist philosophy in Frege. For Frege, descriptions can have meaning without denotation. I can name everything that I can think, but my thoughts cannot necessarily be reduced to denotations. "Good logico-syntactic forms of expression (in non-formalized languages) give no assurance that the expressions have an object."[5] The notation of "object" cannot be reduced to "direct denotation." Nor do we put names in univocal correspondences with single things. A single name for a single thing does not exist. That is why to Frege natural language never seems perfectly adaptable to logic. Wittgenstein rediscovers its intrinsic problematic nature in the *Tractatus*. Systems of logic do not try to rationalize and remedy such language. There are some languages of which it is senseless to ask if they are "true." The idea of an essential logical framework of language, one that would be the province of evidentiary logic, is not a metaphysical idea, but is metaphysics itself. Profound, radical "irrationalism" is to trust in such an idea and to repeat its failures infinitely, rather than collect the fresh power that it confers upon *ratio*, upon logic, rather than abandon it. Making logic a universal instrument of hygiene and development means to rigorously limit it to the discovery of laws of being true, predictable only through pure thought. Logic is good for much more than sublimating natural languages—or, according to Nietzsche's famous aphorism, reinforcing faith in God with faith in grammar.

There is a fundamental perfection in creatures that in Frege has as its symbol the insuperability of *Dichtung* [poetry]: the pseudo-propositions of poetry cannot be idealistically surmounted. By definition, creatures are beings endowed with fantasy. Logic gives this faculty up, in its grand utopia of annihilation, in order to pursue creatures who "lose themselves" in a fantasy world. Logic limits itself to the most rigorous and restrictive definition: the strong sense of knowing the laws for being true, in the sense of a reality that is independent of our recognizing it as such. This reality modifies the subject whenever it is recognized, but it is not, in any sense, produced by the subject.

The fact that logical propositions may not cover the range of the term "true," as it is ordinarily used in speech, does not lead to the conclusion that the sense of a proposition is supplied only from the possible contexts of occurrence of the proposition itself. "On the contrary, the *concept of proposition* itself should be limited" (De Monticelli). Beyond the "fantastic" polymorphic capacities of natural languages, there is still a "third world," a context of justification for the proposition itself, absolved from the status of the consciousness and language of the speaker. Here perhaps is the most significant connection between Frege and Edmund Husserl. It does not seem that in Frege, contrary to Husserl, the same semantic indeterminacy of natural language is assumed as a condition of openness, of intentional charge. The "paucity" of natural language (compared to the logical precision of formalized language) underlies its intentionalizing power, its capacity to develop itself and enrich itself, constantly determining new ways to refer to the real. That is why the realism of these ways should not contradict the intentionality of the speaker, which is indeterminable a priori. Such manners embody themselves in language and represent human knowledge accumulated in language. Nothing can be expressed except through language and in language. The sense of a proposition is verified on the basis of language. Language is not invented—if it does not manifest a history, a tradition, at the same moment that it transforms history and tradition, then it cannot express anything or communicate anything.

Frege surrenders to a reconciliation of the pure formal language of thought with language in which we often "act against our will in poetry." This attempt at an answer to Frege's problem runs along a thread of paradox. In the semantic indeterminacy of natural language (and for Husserl philosophy was built, classically, upon and in natural language) there appear incarnate ideal ways to refer to the real. These ways have varied across history, due precisely to the formative receptiveness of natural language. Its variability is limited by the entire status of knowledge and by its forms of expression. This variability even presents itself as a kind of progress and development, to the extent that it is determined on the basis of a comprehensive test of inherited conditions. The problem of foundation is thus transformed in Husserl into one of the reciprocal limits, historically experienced, of variance and invariance in the dynamic of philosophical and scientific grammar.

What appears "paradoxical" in this response is, above all, the conversion of the paucity of natural language into the power of its intentionality (which is the perfect symbol of that paucity). The fact that natural language does not speak of simple things, that its meanings cannot be reduced to denotations, does not imply a production of ideal modes of reference to the real. The concept of intentionality establishes, in and of itself, that a meaning (signified) cannot be extracted from the intention of the subject in which it is

expressed: the referent is constituted *only in language*. There is
nothing else to derive from *intentio*. That may suffice to formu-
late as a problem Russell's neopositivism of derivation, but it does
not constitute in any way a new foundation of Frege's "third
world." For Frege, *concipere* means to take up a thought that already exists, independent of the fact that I think it. This thought
certainly constitutes an ideal form of reference to reality, but is not
at all a product of *intentio*. What schema can emerge between the
poverty and indeterminacy of language (this language that *intentio*
opens and transforms continually) and the independence and in-
alterability of the world of the thinking subject's thought? How
can the forms of theory, which seize thought that already exists,
determine the "range of variation of the concepts" (De Monticelli)?
That the range of variability is not free—that it is historically determined by the status of knowledge and by the linguistic compe-
tence of the speakers—does not imply that its limits are frozen by
fixed forms of theory, by ideal modes of reference. The problem
can also be resolved (much more "economically") by establishing
that these limits are made by the procedural nature and communicability of the range of play and by the bounty of their functions.

Affirming the innate forms and laws of the dynamic of knowledge does not resolve the problem of schematism, the Kantian
legacy to the *cupio dissolvi* of subsequent philosophy. Even if we
admit the procedural and self-regulating character of Husserl's ideal
modes, there remains the problem of their proper language, of the
foundation, the *Begründung*, without which, for Husserl as for
Frege, there is no force behind scientific knowledge. This language
appears embodied in natural language and its dynamics—even if,
at the same time, it transcends natural language. The a priori conditions of the possibility of linguistic innovation consist in the
"natural" openness to the intuition of ideal modes. Such modes establish the possibility of variation. They are the site of *Begründung*,
and they transcend the operative dimension of scientific grammars.
These modes describe wholly a priori the limits of variability, and
no single "case" can be inscribed there.

This problem gives birth to the extreme teleology that dominates Husserl's *The Crisis of European Sciences* (the tragedy of which the armies of Husserl's scholastics have always attempted to convert to positivism and rationalism). Philosophical activity cannot concern itself with anything except the phenomenon of natural language. But chased back into the poverty of its semantic indeterminacy, philosophy discovers a new realm there. The realm of intentionality proper to natural language understands how to connect to the world of ideal forms, which describe the limits of variability of those same scientific grammars. Thus philosophy can be an activity that forms the basis of its own dynamics as expansion. Philosophy's gaze on science wants to be anything but "oblique." Not as "oblique" but rather as "interrupted" is how this activity intends to repropose itself as the language of foundation, as the transcendental language that, a priori, can describe possibilities and limits of transformation of play. Finally, either such possibilities and limits are actually inherent in the very dynamics of play, and nothing then can warrant the definition of an autonomous language and a specific scientific discipline (philosophy)—or the flexibility of play is etched a priori onto a horizon of invariance, absolutely objective, unchangeable on the speaker's part. And so it is necessary to deduce the forms of schematism between the speaker and such ideal modes. But how can such modes be "understood" by philosophy that is phenomenology of natural language? And how can such invariance belong to natural language, which is variation? If there is expression of invariance, it would be absolute logic (or knowledge), not philosophy. And if the field of possibilities and limits of variations are determined in the process of variation itself, multiple forms for their analysis and their calculation would emerge. And that is neither absolute logic nor philosophy.

Inquietum Cor
Nostrum

It seems to me that Wittgenstein's research parts company with Husserl along these same lines. It is true that "fetishist" elements remain in Wittgenstein's respect for the rules of the game.[6] The manifest tension in his discourse, however, from the crisis of the *Tractatus* on, lies in his understanding all the rules of the game together as admitting the possibility of their transformation. The game is understood as the content of the participant's *intentio*, proportionately subject to willpower and therefore to the intrinsic indeterminacy of languages. As long as the game remains firmly aligned with its traditions and never destabilizes into mere invention and transformation, *ideal* modalities may not determine its limits unless those limits are understood in a weak sense and divested of any teleological weight—that is, unless their basic promise is not taken seriously. What counts is not so much the discord between Husserl and Wittgenstein over the fact that the processes of transforming the game are self-regulating, but that for Husserl they have a teleological disposition that is absent in Wittgenstein. In Husserl these processes can come autonomously, philosophically, which does not happen in Wittgenstein. Seen in this perspective, Husserl implements a powerful strategy of "reform" on the subject and its theory, conferring sense onto scientific grammar, a strategy Wittgenstein had already abandoned in the *Tractatus*.

The fault lines of the *Tractatus*, fundamental for understanding the later development of Wittgenstein's thought, correspond to the forms assumed by the critique of fundamental strategies.[7] The strategy of logical discourse no longer corresponds in the *Tractatus* to the objectives of making natural language logical or to the pretext of establishing scientific grammars. The strategy of logic is a "degenerate" proposition (Rosso), tautological, not descriptive, and unconditionally true only at great price. The strategy of scientific discourse is a mere image: scientific propositions (from the natural sciences) try "to provide a faithful image of the world, limiting themselves to the most relevant points on a single, homogeneous plane" (Rosso). This plane does not hearken back to any logical or philosophical basis, but to the "reckoning" of the denotative capacity of its propositions. Scientific propositions are wholly denotative. But how can denotations retreat from the absolute contingency of the facts they denote? The first, and fundamental, fault line of the *Tractatus* concerns, therefore, the statute of the scientific *image* as such. The critique of fundamental strategies, as it were, trails behind it.

The first proposition of the *Tractatus* may be translated as follows: "The world is the result of the choice wrought by the case in the realm of all that is possible" (Rosso). That is why whatever can be expressed is absolutely accidental and contingent. "Science reveals itself to be precisely the study of contingency" (Rosso), and that is why hierarchies of bodies cannot exist, every body being wholly and equally gratuitous. The significance of a proposition is the designated object—therefore, the accidental and gratuitous and contingent. But won't the meaning itself turn out to be contingent? The *Tractatus* turns—and *stops*—around this question. Wittgenstein means to withdraw scientific propositions from the radical contingency of their objects. He finds the logical and fundamental route blocked and interrupted. He tries to make an ontology of it: there is a world substance that cannot be further broken down, and every proposition is a function of it. The world is an accidental configuration—but of objects that are simply not accidental. That is why images of science contain not only the contingency of the configuration, but also the substantiality of the objects or simple entities that form the basis of the configuration. The theory of representation or of meaning native to the *Tractatus* makes an ontological question of *Begründung* [originating].

Is this ontological realism truly immune to the many aporias the establishment of unchanging reality encountered, independent of being true? Is it immune to the conviction that truth and falsehood *exist*, independently of our recognizing them? The ontological foundation of the *Tractatus*, in order to verify itself, ought to permit a reduction of the names of propositions, not to things that stand before it (*Gegen-stände*), but to simple objects that are *not* givens. Natural language, like scientific language, describes situations; it does not name objects. Even the most simple atom of language will end up always complex and contingent from the point of view of the demand for ontological foundations postulated in the *Tractatus*. It is impossible to name a simple object; it is impossible to describe the totality of the world. Language can only denote situations or construct tautologies—that is, logical propositions. All that can be sensibly expressed resides within these limits. Thus the ontological foundation's demand is established in the *Tractatus* with a fundamentality that condemns it to failure. Not for one moment, in the *Tractatus*, does *intentio* exhaust the intended or contain symbols of direct relation with it. *Intentio* is prefixed to an unreachable goal, and it does not depend for an instant on the reduction of meaning to simply-given, as will take place in the scholastic version of the Wiener Kreis, Vienna at the turning point.

If the problem of ontological *Begründung* is revealed clearly in *Philosophical Observations*, it was already present in the *Tractatus*. The images it speaks of cannot be analyzed as linear functions of simple objects or given data. The images (*Bilder*) of facts surely derive their inspiration from the work of Gustav Hertz and Ludwig Boltzmann much more than from Ernst Mach and the Wiener Kreis.[8] That is why every proposition endowed with sense is necessarily closed in by the inexpressible. The substance of the intended meaning is, in fact, *inexpressible*, along with the world in which the contingent situations that we intend take place. It is a myth that linguistic configurations contain signs of a direct relation with the objects they depict. The "substantial" necessarily evades the relationship of atom to totality. The expressible perseveres against its limits without being able to ever get through them.

Even through this line of reasoning we can see how the mystical (*das Mystische*) makes up, not an equivocal atmosphere in the *Tractatus*, but rather its necessary conclusion. It describes the limits of meaning for the propositions that come afterward. It is even their inherent law. It prescribes their rules, routines, and operative conditions. The mystical indicates how the world may simply show itself. "Let the world exist; let the possibility of the possible be given" (Rosso). That is the mystical. Facing the problem that comes before all problems, in the glow of all questions—"Why are there things rather than nothing?"—Wittgenstein does not flee into the passive voice of scientific equivalence or into visions about the totality of the world (*Weltanschauungen*). "To reawaken understanding of the sense of this question" (Heidegger) would be superfluous in comparison. But no discourse answers, except the ineffable showing itself. The problem becomes one of the meaning of the verb "to show," and we shall return to it. Is it not possible now to confirm that the parabola of Heideggerian thought intersects, in the end, with this "answer" of Wittgenstein's? Does not the history of metaphysics, which is Heidegger's subject (to the extent that it too is channeled by the space of history and criticism), also show, at its conclusion, the ineffability of being, the why of being?

In a note from 1931, collected in *Culture and Value*, Wittgenstein wrote, "The inexpressible (that which seems mysterious to me, *geheimnisvoll*, and that I am not capable of expressing) provides the ground upon which all that I am able to express acquires meaning."[9] The inexpressible exercises what amounts to a gravitational force on logical propositions and keeps them thus within the limits of "sensibility." This is its operative facet, merely self-evident. In terms of *Culture and Value*, we can say that the possibility of "liberating" the proposition from contingency has become in-

expressible, as have reconnecting the sign to the world and onto-
logically establishing the relationship between *intentio* and intended. The problem of the inexpressible initiates the dissolution
of *Begründung* in the analysis of language's intrinsic limits and the
certainties they offer, and this dissolution will be completed in
Philosophical Investigations and, above all, in *On Certainty* (*Über
Gewissheit*). The foundation is convention. The inexorable tight-
ening of rules that we cannot logically refute is essential (Franck).
That is not the only reason why logical and mathematical formalism is an "inexorable" game. Being certain means "to belong to a
community that is held together by knowledge and education."[10]
This certainty however has no psychological or sociological impli-
cations; it is composed of accumulated knowledge in language, in-
herently historical. "Certainty is not synonymous with a 'spiritual'
attitude; it is the articulation of a grammatical procedure"
(Wittgenstein). The "beginning" is not "*Ego cogito,*" but the mass
of historical thoughts that are transmitted to us and that we know
how to engage and re-engage. Everyone postulates, decides, and
makes changes within the scope of these thoughts. They define the
limits of their grammar's variability. The operative nature of our
discourse has the fact of this action or play as a condition, as the
situation that it determines.

This reasoning assumes the inexpressibility of the existence of
the world. If the existence of the world could declare itself, our
language would have the power to render it. The world would be
our phenomenon. Philosophy's madness, its rite, resides in this
pretext. Here is philosophy's vain attempt to deduce the existence
of the world, or rather to attack its manifestation in order to dissolve it, in order to substitute it with philosophy's own phantasms.
Philosophy appears either as the cutting off of the world, which is
absurd (*un-sinnig*) discourse, not meaningless (*sinnlos*), or as logical
tautology, or indeed as a radical calling into doubt of the world's
existence and its transformation and sublimation into a mere phenomenon. Philosophy cannot resist the ineffability of the existence
of the world. The utopia of *Begründung* (whether logical or ontological), the "empty ceremony of doubt" (Franck), the desperate

search for an answer to the Heideggerian question, are aspects of its "demented" rite.

Is it necessary to recur to this rite in order to avoid fetishism with regard to the world as it is? The mystical does not cut itself off from the world as it is. The mystical never speaks of an objective world, but limits itself rather to *showing* the world. The "fetishism" of verbalizing the world (as opposed to showing it) belongs to philosophical discourse and has nothing to do with the mystical, to the extent that the mystical indicates from within the limits of possible propositions (possible in the reductive sense of empirically possible). Propositions about the historicity and changing nature of action, of play, also belong to this field. The possibility of variation is inherent to play—otherwise the rules of the game would be replaced by new ideal forms, ideal invariance. But such possibilities cannot be described a priori. They proceed in the dynamics of the contingent language of the *intentio* of the speakers, *intentio* that appeals to accumulated knowledge, that tastes it, that experiences it, that plays with it and changes its rules. There is no metaphysics that can describe a priori the possible directions of change. But to be in an effectual sense practical and communicable, it has to be rooted in language and in knowledge accumulated in language. Only one general limit can be expressed a priori. Thus there is no "fetishism" in our game's linguistic situation, of which its *intentio* is a part. The awareness of limits of language is not fetishism. To be ignorant of them, rather, is consummate fetishism, since it signifies turning away, not from the world, but from the very contingency of situations of things as they are, preaching their dissolution, foundation, and sublimation. Wittgenstein's silence is not opposed to changing the game. It is opposed to preaching that comes from the realm of the expressible and with empty ceremonies proclaims its own powerlessness to be free.

The New Domain
of Trauerspiel

Behind the mirror of this thinking about language we find the problems we have confronted up to this point, along with more characters from the *serious* (as opposed to merely academic) Viennese turning point: "It is impossible to lead men to the good; it is only possible to lead men to some place. The good lies beyond the domain of facts and data [*Tatsachenraum*]."[11] This proposition from 1929 unfolds 6.4 of the *Tractatus*, "Alle Sätze sind gleichwertig"—all propositions are of equal value. All propositions endowed with sense have equal value, since they necessarily refer to that domain of facts and data. No hierarchy of them can be established. No value can be placed on the events of the world. If there were value, then it would be found outside of any event or development or state of being, since any event or development is a case (*Tractatus* 6.41). In Wittgenstein, the relationship between proposition and fact is transformed (and profoundly so in the *Tractatus*). The action or play of certainty is transformed, the norms are changed that define the utterable, but the axiom never fails that propositions endowed with sense, propositions on states of being, on cases, are of equal value. Such a "solution" arises with the force of ripping, irreversible experience. Whatever would render the world non-accidental—*nicht-zufällig*—cannot be found in the world, since, if it were found, it would be in its turn accidental—a case. The occurrence of the world, and the world is necessarily an occurrence, means that the world is like an accident. Reading the parts of *Nachlass* published so far bears witness to how deeply essential this thought was to Wittgenstein and to its continuity through Wittgenstein's work.

Finding the good through the accidentalness, the *casualness* of happening is inconceivable. If chance, through some hidden force, were to intend good, it would no longer be chance, but value. The force would have to come out of hiding and reveal itself as other than chance. If chance remains unutterable, the propositions continue to exist anyway in a state of perfect equivalence. If their forms take on meaning by chance, it is possible to lead only *irgendwohin*, to some place. From this case, here and now, I can foresee other possible cases, I can construct their possibilities, their intentions, and so on infinitely. None of these cases would be the home of the good, surmounting the *casualness* of happening. The leitmotif of the English Conference on Ethics was already in the *Tractatus*: the ineffability of Ethics. If language has chance occurrence as its contents, the possibility of new configurations of cases is implicit in its very definition. If a case were *the* case, that possibility would cease. The possibility of leading *irgendwohin* (of being unable to do anything but lead somewhere) is therefore written a priori into the confines of this language. The good exists beyond the domain of data and facts and beyond the limits of propositions of equal value, that try to express their configuration. To want to express the good is *Missbrauch* [abuse] of language. More than mere bad usage, it violates its form. Language can lead, but not to the end, to the goal. It can only lead from chance to chance, from event to event. What inexorable forms of understanding can analyze this chance and this inherent leading without resorting to impressionistic relativism? How do we know that the rules of the game do not appear less "inexorable" (in their rules of transformation) because they concern a game?

This radical surrender is the basis for meaningful language, for the equivalence of its propositions. Transferring it would not lead us beyond the limits of such a language, but to the abuse of its possibilities. Rather than learn to see the event clearly and to construct new cases, understanding the unutterable rapport between case and possible (a possibility that offers itself only because "the world is all that is the case"), we would build vain and contradictory rhetorics of the unutterable. Certainly one can always try to escape from the limits this surrender traces (specific, determined, not in the least "romantic") and from the despair (in the literal sense of the term) that indicates the experience of it. This is rather "evidence of a tendency in the human soul . . . that I really would not want, upon my life, to make fun of" (Wittgenstein). The ruin into which this tendency continually falls bears witness to its authenticity. The tendency and the ruin exist as evidence of an unsupressable component of language itself, enabled by the constant work of surrender. But is this enough to define it? Is this surrender, ever present, enough to make it a "master" of its limits?

What is the *Tatsachenraum* that precedes everything in Wittgenstein? *Tatsachenraum* is the space, the domain, of *Trauerspiel* [tragedy] in the pregnant symbolic acceptance that Walter Benjamin analyzed on the basis of German baroque drama.[12] This drama, with Hofmannsthal in particular, finds the limit of its metamorphosis in the *Tatsachenraum* of the *finis Austriae* [the end of Austria]. The Adolf Loos house in Michaelerplatz stands consciously before the Hofburg, as Hofmannsthal's *Der Turm* stands before Calderón de la Barca's *Life Is a Dream*. The consciousness of belonging to this Romania is shared by all the Viennese dialects of the turning point. Where the order of the *verum-bonum*—the true and the good—collapsed, there is the space of *Trauerspiel*. It is found in the area divided between signals, indications, traces, formation of personae, of the *entity* definitively emerged from its own "subjectivity" and from being a "translation" of substance, of the entity that is no longer a subject, and the area of chance crossed by the infinite passages from case to case, from form to form, the domain of the saying and leading of *irgendwohin*. This is not the domain of the pilgrim. Its personae happen like the things of the world, and these things want to see well. There is no light that can save the chance in value, but that does not mean chance is a fog, an indistinct opacity, which pilgrims must pass through until they come out on top. The equivalence of creaturely propositions is constructed according to rules and is changed in a clearly defined way. Cases have form. The desperation of resigning is fixed, almost frozen, on the scabrous terrain of facts in the logical domain of the utterable. Here the personae of *Trauerspiel* hold out.

To this domain belongs the "nihilism" in Loos's house at Michaelerplatz. Inhabitants surrender themselves to all allusivity or to every metaphor of the *verum-bonum* on the foundations of this nihilism. They do not "substitute" the absence of truth and the good, and that is why they can construct new linguistic possibilities, new combinations, from within their own history, within tradition, playing and replaying their game. Ornament is an extreme form of decadence in the metaphor of the *verum-bonum*. The tendency to render our propositions as propositions of value lives out a final, indecent day in ornament. This tendency, however, is no longer the tragic evidence of which Wittgenstein spoke. That is protected at all costs. It seeks to avoid ruin, to accommodate itself beside the propositions of sense (ornament and functionality, utility and beauty). As opposed to *Trauerspiel* that takes place in the *Tatsachenraum*, ornament is the light comedy of ruin, a homemade tendency to transcendence. It aspires to furnish the temples of the tragedy of ethics.

Peter Altenberg's *Extrakte des Lebens* also belongs to the new domain of *Trauerspiel*. The desperate holding out in surrender is founded in the *Extrakte des Lebens* with the perfect emergence of the subject, that is, with its radical critique, with its end as a subject. The subject transferred is no longer a subject—what is left of it speaks and transmits *irgendwohin*, it *happens*, and in happening it opens extraordinarily to all cases, its brothers, the things of this world. It loves them coming and going, and it heeds, in telling them, the limits of telling, since the *Missbrauch* of words would seem almost to harm their tone, their voices. Thus cases are chopped up very neatly in their language, harvested from a look that is part of them, that does not "comprehend" them, that does not judge them, that does not illuminate them. The cases are given to this look without fear. They believe in it.

But why should the new domain be that of *Trauerspiel*? Why is it impossible to settle in the absence of order established by the utterability of the *verum-bonum*? Wouldn't the language of equivalence, of equality of values, detached from any metaphysical pretext, disenchanted, be able to find its own place in this *Tatsachenraum*, in the measurability of its being present, right at hand— *Zuhandensein*? And why couldn't even Wittgenstein be read in this sense, in the sense of the totalizing destiny of technology, of its productivity, that knows nothing except phenomena compatible with its own ends? Wittgenstein's *Tatsachenraum* can be the scene of *Trauerspiel* because in tragedy words never exhaust deeds, names never exhaust things, and language never exhausts situations. If the idea of *adequatio* is already present in the *Tractatus* in a problematic and contradictory form, the idea emerges in the following works, in *On Certainty* and *Culture and Value* (which has the inflections of a diary), of certainty as construction and process. Not a utopian advancing over the world's contradictory being-thus in philosophies of foundation, it is a certainty of the present ability of rules that we do not succeed in refuting, of conventions that satisfy us because they work, a certainty of grammatical operations (which belong to tradition, community, laws of life) that succeed in seeing here and now, without pretending any invariance.

And yet the question comes up again: Isn't it possible to feel at home in this procedure? Precisely in this interminable building up of certainty? What could be less paradoxical and more domestic than convention? Of course, a similar practice of convention is always possible. But why do we believe that this one, far from representing the fulfillment of liberation of language from metaphysics, as its apologists claim, cheats with its own limits? Why do we believe that the expression of *Tatsachenraum* as *Trauerspiel* is the logical and necessary consequence? The *Gottlosigkeit* [godlessness] of language—language abandoned by *verum-bonum*—does not lead to a happy and unstoppable progress toward conquest and comprehension of the world, as if surrender were worthless except as a sort of strategic move to gain the absolute power of technology over and within *Tatsachenraum*. Nothing changes if we call the "search without end" the solution, if we establish that it answers all possible or anticipated questions, as long as no other utterable question remains. The disenchantment of interminably building up certainty is then mere publicity, since its practice is understood to be *effective* and it is the very idea of effect, of solution, that displaces that of substance: either the particular substance of fact or the substance of the subject that comprises it. One cheats with the meaning of convention whenever the limits of the assertable are traced down from above or, likewise, the limits of the arguable, of whatever it makes sense to ask, of whatever can be conceivably pronounced as a question. When operating thus in the building process, the process is in reality a solution, a domestication of the *verum-bonum* into *Tatsachenraum*, a domestication that falsifies both of them.

In the *Tatsachenraum* there is no language of solution. Any solution is structurally bound to the *casualness* of happening. This means that the new domain of factual data cannot present itself as the space where everything assertable and arguable is resolved—and this is so in spite of proclaiming research "without end." And it means, additionally, that language does not proceed in its quest progressively "recuperating" from its problems and finding its solution. Not only is it difficult to distinguish between "the cases in which I cannot, and the cases in which I can hardly make mistakes," not only must one always guard against the "spell" of word knowledge;[13] but it is necessary to argue against anyone thinking they have found the solution to this problem. It is enough to demonstrate that there was a time when that solution had not yet been discovered and that the solution discovered in that time now seems merely a case. And again: if someone were to predict that the next generation will learn to solve the problems that wear out the present, it is enough to show how the next generation will struggle with new problems and not solve the problems left unsolved by their parents. Roberto Bazlen seems almost to be thinking of these propositions from *Culture and Value* when he writes that there are only ways, and no way out; or where he says that we look for a way out only to build a new way, *irgendwohin*. We do not build this new way because we know where it will end, just as we do not know some things because everybody knows them. But the road is no less defined for this, and the rules of its construction are no easier.

The *Tatsachenraum* is the domain of *Trauerspiel* because that is where every solution takes shape in the questions of the here and now, in the questions formulated by this present entity. A solution could arise precisely in the measure in which this entity recognizes itself and accepts itself *wie ein Zufall* [like an accident]—does not pretend, that is, to go beyond its own world. A solution can only reveal, never unveil. From solution to solution is a matter of incessant revealing. Every generation lays its own veils on the problem, and none takes up the same problems as their predecessors, thus building what seems a sort of sacred chain wherever earlier solutions appear to have remained unfinished. But the pure despair over the limits of language negates the form of *Trauerspiel* as much as progressive metaphysics of the solution does. (Pure despair that not only does not belong to Wittgenstein, but does not even belong to Heidegger, despite what Hermann Weyl thought: radical perfection and pure despair are not analogous expressions, and Heidegerrian perfection does not at all exclude the interminable constructiveness of technology.) *Trauerspiel* does not mean to trace the limits of the utterable a priori in such a way as to impose or enjoin the domain of silence, but to understand language as a revealing ensemble of solutions and certainties. In the space of *Trauerspiel*, the annihilating confirmation of despair finds no place. It is rather the domain of revealing people interminably, of renewing problems profoundly (even as they seem to stay the same while time passes and people change) and, finally, of the showing of the other-than-utterable, and of the possibility of this showing, since an "endless quest" could never be authentic if it dressed itself in the logic of the solution.

"Wir stehen in Kampf mit der Sprache"—this struggle with language is endless. The new space of *Trauerspiel* is the field of this struggle. In the domain of facts and data, the limits of language are not providentially assigned to simplify internal order. We "frequently beat our heads" (Kraus) against the wall of language. Clarity of expression is not prepared for its limits. "The philosopher is a prisoner in the web of language" that Nietzsche spoke of, struggling with language to be able to constantly reveal, but in this struggle infinite documents are accumulated from that profound dedication to surpassing limits. Without that dedication, no revealing, no transforming game would be thinkable. To this same practice of linguistic revealing belongs our hurling ourselves "against the walls of our prison." Simultaneously quoting Nietzsche and Kraus, Wittgenstein can thus clarify that if language did not dash itself against its limits, we could not know what these limits were and therefore we could not even speak sensibly within them. This wreck is necessary to the very definition of the utterable, but, at the same time, the domain of the utterable appears thus absolutely foreign to that of dwelling.

There is no desire in this language—and nothing adorns it. It shows every intention of transcending the same limits as structural components of the same syntax, critical of the idea of solution and indefatigable revealing. The domain of *Trauerspiel* is that of our struggle with language and of language with itself, and not of the desire of language to surpass itself. It is the domain of words, perfectly defined and limpid in their despair, that know how to recognize the silence of ruin as essential to their uttering. The essential does not reside in avoiding it, in exorcising it, but in repeating it differently, ever in new places, since the answers are always different, since the problem is always different: "True life means: to invent new places where we can be ruined . . . ; every new work is only the invention of a new death."[14]

A Critique of
the Modern

The new domain of *Trauerspiel* is defined in the tension of a double antithesis: an opposition to the modern and the impossibility of the tragic.

The opposition to the "originality" of modernity appears in Wittgenstein as a radical separation, a metaphysical gap. In a draft of the preface to his *Philosophical Observations*, written before the published version and published separately in *Culture and Values*, Wittgenstein wrote, "This book is written for those who look kindly on the spirit in which it was written. This spirit, I think, is different from that of the mainstream of European and American *Zivilisation*," from the spirit that finds its expression in "industry, architecture, and music, in the fascism and the socialism of our age." That spirit is "completely alien and *unsympatisch* to the author." But this assessment, Wittgenstein warns, ought not to sound like a "value judgment" upon the age. The fact that *Zivilisation* is opposed to the idea of *Kultur*, where every element has its place, and where everyone can work in the spirit of all and measure their own success in the sense of the whole—the fact that these times are the age of *Un-kultur* ought not to lead to effete pessimism, but uniquely to the recognition of the radical transformation that humanity's means and forms of expression, and very existence, have undergone. Wittgenstein views *Zivilisation* without "sympathy."

He writes only for "friends scattered to the ends of the earth." In order to measure Wittgenstein's "ascents" out of the philosophical and cultural habitat of modernism, it is enough to compare his words with Rudolf Carnap's preface to the first Viennese edition of *The Logical Structure of the World*, dated May 1928: "We discern an intimate consonance between the basis of our philosophical work and the spiritual attitude that permeates every field of life today. . . . The conviction that the future belongs to this way of seeing supports our work." In a 1931 note we read the names of those in whom Wittgenstein recognized—sometimes sadly—the force of influence. Next to Boltzmann, Hertz, Frege, and Russell (not Mach), not only Kraus, Loos, and Piero Sraffa, but also Otto Weininger and Oswald Spengler. What "form" unifies these friends scattered to the ends of the earth? What is the essential difference between this diaspora and European and American *Zivilisation*?

Zivilisation, for Wittgenstein, rests upon a word and is bewitched by a word: *Fortschritt*, progress. It is nothing but the historicist secularization of the idea of a solution. Progress is the same as the idea of an ongoing, continuous, dedicated solution to problems. Its form is *typisch aufbauend*: *constructive* in its most intimate essence. This is realized by making structures that are ever more complex, in a constant growth and complication of the "perimeters" of the world. Therefore, Wittgenstein's disengagement from the idea of progress represents a disengagement from the reasoning behind it: from its essential constructivity or productivity. Already this definition is in itself alien to the varicolored traditions of European pessimism in the Age of Decadence. It does not oppose *Zivilisation* as something destructive and unorganic; on the contrary, it denounces precisely its constructive and productive aspects, its characteristic of reducing things into objects and objects into structures (structures that are ever more formalized and complex, noeses, mathematics). The essence of progress consists in building the world. Therefore scattered friends desire their own diaspora, not in order to flee presumed irrational and destructive forces of *Zivilisation* (a fatal destiny celebrated in the success of the

Faustian man), but in order to preserve their roles as the other, as foreign to the constructive essence of Western rationality, to the productive epos of its *Gedankenwelt* [ideal world].

What can "the friends" put up against this epos? They begin by asking themselves: The system of rationality represents itself necessarily as an *Aufbauen,* as a working edifice—but on what basis? The basis of this constructivity is the original "destructive intention" of the logos, whose dialectic can demonstrate that every sensitive or abstract object that can be expressed in a judgment can be proved to exist and not exist at one and the same time, possible and impossible.[15] This foundation returns as a *problem* in Wittgenstein, and it is its incessant return, its continuous reconsideration, that comes up against the epos of typically constructive reasoning (*typisch aufbauend ratio*). No amount of progress can ever resolve such a predicament. The path of history resembles the path of a cloud, says Musil—but of a cloud blown to *some place* by the incessant wind of this problem. It is *here* that things return. While the dialectical logos, believed to be resolved into constructive and productive forces, lines up its *Gebilde* or structures, one after another, almost like going from step to step, others remain where they are and insist on considering the same thing: the original problematic foundation of the destructive intent of this *ratio.* "The labyrinth of reason," writes Colli, "only seems an edifice." Already in Zeno "the cheerful aspect of dialectical reason" was transformed into "a harsh, hostile, dangerous, and devastating frown." Both of Parmenides' roads are passable by now, and the very heart of *aletheia* falls victim to the logos. But the world of representation, having reached this climactic moment, unveils its "inconsistency," so that "it betrays itself as self-destructive, in a nihilistic and at the same time cathartic push." "Reason's trust in being constructive" is brought into question and annihilated right from the start.[16] In building stairways toward determined objects (which constitutes progress), it is precisely this origin that must be sublimated. Nothing may ever go back there. But anything that can be "reached by a stairway does not interest me" (Wittgenstein). We should already be where we really must go.

The basis of dialectic's destructive intent shows the sense of the equivalence of the propositions in a perspective that cannot be reduced to a function or a construct. It demonstrates the unutterability, the impossibility of representing a content of propositions, a wisdom or a gnosis of them. The destructive intent radically demonstrates a metaphysical difference between the logos-that-speaks and the what-has-been-said. This ends up with dialectic turning against itself: it breaks down its own form, unveiling its unbridgeable distance from the thing in itself. The constructing and transforming of *ratio* rests upon complete comprehension of the thing in itself. In terms of "origins," the logos means something other than itself, a place, *aletheia*, whose form pitilessly contradicts the merely revealing form of dialectic. *Ratio typisch aufbauend* [constructive reasoning] of "mainstream" *Zivilisation* is nothing but the extraordinary sublimation of this original metaphysical difference. Constructivity and productivity do not occur without such sublimation: to surrender to it is impossible on the stairway that pretends to lead beyond "endless research" as a solution.[17] It is never possible to create authentic clarity in our language until it connects to considerations of this basic enigma of our *Gedankenwelt*, until it shows it can consist of *this same thing*, which comes back in every affirmation, every development of formalism latent in the logos.

Ratio typisch aufbauend sees this radical *Andenken* of the basis of its own intentionality as a disease to cure or "recuperate" from. Difference is itself a sign of sickness by its dialectic. In order to give up sublimating the basis it is necessary to place oneself under the sign of the fool. In order to understand something one must go mad while keeping one's head straight.[18] Madness embraces our thinking as death embraces life.[19] Clarity here means: to understand ever freshly our abiding in the sense of the basic problem, under the sign of its unresolvability.

But why do we say "clarity"? What word could seem more coherent with the idea of progress in our *Zivilisation*? Doesn't *Zivilisation* pit clarity victoriously against the dark background, against dialectic's obscure motives of destructive intent? *Zivilisation*'s clarity is not an end in itself, though. Its visibility and its brightness are only functional. It is the clarity of constructive calculation, production's necessary brightness. On the other hand, Wittgenstein's *Klarheit* is purely "in honor of God." The motto of *Zivilisation*'s own clarity sounds like this: *simplex sigillum veri* [simplicity is the seal of truth], where "simplex" does not at all contradict the complexity of the structure, of the construction, since this is precisely the result of the "simplicity" of calculations and logic with which the subject succeeds in reducing and governing the entity. While the "simplex" clarity of *ratio* is functional to the structure that it intends to produce, Wittgenstein's *Klarheit* means to render transparent the very foundation of construction, to constantly return to that same thing, constituted by its problem, to render its nonconstructive foundation evident—the intrinsic, reciprocal affinity between nihilism and the metaphysical gap that is its sublimated content.

It is only the clarity of the simplex that dominates the modern. Certainly not the modern that Loos talks about, flinging itself against a nostalgic soft spot for the past, nor that of Klee, whose time belongs, as we shall see, to Rilke's magic marionettes. Their illusionless gaze on the modern derives (as Benjamin saw, and Stefan George before him) from that supreme moment of urban intellect that the lyric form intuited between Baudelaire and Mallarmé. Alongside and against the modern there is the "avant-garde" that, in the apparently disenchanted exaltation of the machine era, ignores the backward gaze of Benjamin's angel and the "eternal return" of its problem. Such an "avant-garde" is productive from the start: it is the utopia of the full resolution of any problem in building, in the "simply" constructive end that surpasses (perfect *Aufhebung*!) the original destructive intent, the utopia of the omni-mastery of language, of unending amplification, the unstoppable utterable. The aspects that are most clearly functionalistic and constructive are nothing but the most esoteric aspect of the whole matter of the avant-garde (at least of its public matter and of the "culture" that has flowered around it). It is rather exactly there, where it seems to excavate the dark background of the signified, the *Hintergrund der Bedeutung*, that its *ratio typisch aufbauend* appears with the most evidence. Everything can be produced, uttered, and made manifest. Everything can be made transparent. A feverish *horror vacui* torments it, a will to show all that it often interprets, nonsensically, as a direct affiliate of Nietzsche's *Wille zur Macht* (the will to power as art).

Wittgenstein's *Klarheit* is defined, on the contrary, precisely by confirming that the *Hintergrund der Bedeutung* is *un-aussprechbar*, unutterable, since it refers to the metaphysical difference between word and thing. And this difference brings with it a continuous return into our struggle with language and language's struggle with itself. *Klarheit* can emerge in Wittgenstein only by lacerating the certainty of the simplex, of construction as bringing every problem progressively into the evidence of the utterable. The "avantgarde" looks to the basis of meaning in order to discover the essential word, the word buried in the impersonal passive voice (in German, *man*), unconsumed root and content. *Klarheit* in Wittgenstein resides in the most pure surrender to this desire and thus preserves that basis as *un-aussprechbar*.

The clarity of *Trauerspiel* has the identical form. This is indeed the great form of the critique of constructive and productive rationalism. This reasoning becomes transparent in its dialectic. It argues with the semblance of progress, it slashes at its claims with pure crystal, until it reveals a dark, remote motive. The desperate analysis of this intention belongs to *Trauerspiel*: its place is defined by its metaphysical difference from the other, unutterable, unrevealed *aletheia*. The clarity of this form is essential. It is manifest in the perspicuity of relationships that are established in it, the evidence of its critique, the force with which it knows how to deny images of nostalgia, with which it knows how not to wander.

Klarheit is opposed, finally, to *Aufklären* [gloss]—and in order to elucidate this point it is very important to keep in mind Wittgenstein's critique of Freud (Wittgenstein's interior motives, rather than the direct pertinence of his critique to Freud). For Wittgenstein, the work of analysis tends fundamentally toward a "primal and essential sense" and a "latent thinking." At most, a "reality" is discovered that is completely different from appearance and is the reason that appearances are deceiving. The *Aufklären* of analysis—and *Erklären* [explanation] in general—always presupposes that objects signify something other than their appearance. But is this interpretation really necessary? Is it really necessary, in order to produce clarity, to "translate" these appearances into some other reality? And if the dream were nothing other than "a sort of game played by the dreamer"? Can we not produce clarity just by asking ourselves if by chance the dream that we now consider didn't inspire some of its images, without there being some causal connection between a "before" of the dream and the images that it now inspires in us? Or again, could it not be that only some images of a dream can be explained according to the methods of analysis? Wittgenstein viewed the form of *Erklären* as intimately involved with the solution, with a clarity that is essentially constructive and productive "simplicity." The *Klarheit* of *Trauerspiel* describes the revealing mechanisms that are part of the metaphysical gap between logos and *aletheia*—a gap whose continual reformulation as a problem is a critique of *ratio typisch aufbauend*.

Where Wittgenstein speaks of "order," it is unrelated to strategies of simple linguistic tidiness. It means to render clear—willfully and before God—every relationship in the tangle up to now: the basis of *ratio* as *the* problem to which there can never be *the* solution. Constructive and functional "simplicity" is reached through "clean" speech and the power of expression—*Klarheit*, the perfect analog of the most terse writings of Musil or Schoenberg, only reaching, and maintaining, their depth of meaning as an unutterable background. And it is against this background that language proceeds, amid the continuous course of events that its pure crystal reflects and recomposes in infinite ways.

The Impossibility
of the Tragic

The impossibility of the tragic is the other horn of the dilemma that defines the new domain of *Trauerspiel*, and it too is a leitmotif of *Culture and Value*. The equivalence of two propositions depends essentially on a surrender of the tragic form, and this surrender is suffered by no author in "Wittgenstein's" Vienna as deeply as it is by Wittgenstein himself.

There can be no tragic form in the new space of factual data, since tragedy is speculative and its development has been a circuitous return from the apparent multiplicity of a conflict to the conclusive unity of its metaphysical significance. Such a conclusion is denied to *Trauerspiel*, to its worldly aura. In this light, the speculative point of view could only reappear as *Werturteil*, as an assessment of value. Value judgment is nothing but an indecent substitution for tragic speculation in the world of the *Trauerspiel*, an ethical and constructive "translation" of the Tragic. But even more interesting is the explanation of the impossibility of a tragic form on the basis of its incongruity with the Judeo-Christian God. It is as if the metaphysical difference we explained above had returned here as the difference between Tragic and Romantic, in the Hegelian sense. A sense of names "archaically" conjoined to things belongs to tragedy, while the Judeo-Christian God imposes a difference between names and things as his law. He orders man never to make a tragedy of himself, for he has reserved heaven and hell for him alone. Earth is the site of our labors: pure and insuperable *Tatsachenraum.*

The infinite is unutterable. Earth is *eine wüste Gegend,* a desert without images. Jews are prohibited by law from making images. That is why tragedy, which is essentially symbol of the infinite, is itself essentially non-Jewish (*un-judisch*). The contrast that rips across Schoenberg's *Moses* and that appears in the same terms in Wittgenstein's reflections develops in a direct form—opposed to the circuitous form of tragedy—that concludes with the command to hold out in the desert, since the unfocused mass of spirit can only run *under* the desert. Nothing possesses this spirit, since nothing can possess the name that it has as a thing. And Wittgenstein quotes Goethe and Max Stirner, saying, "der Jude muss im eigentleichen Sinn 'sein Sach auf nichts stellen'" (Jews have to base their destiny on nothing, in the most radical sense of the term).

A bi-directional motion comes out of this condition of the Jewish spirit. From one side, the centrality with which it insists on the unrepresentability of the infinite, on the absence of a name, completely impedes its productivity; on the other, this very distance from productivity permits it to understand more deeply the products of other people's creativity, to better analyze their limits and their aporias. Wittgenstein characterizes the Jewish spirit as a peak of analytical capability, of self-reflection. He discovers himself completely aligned to this power/powerlessness. Self-reflection is, for him, absence of creativity, and capability is absence of "health." And this is a disease that cannot be "analyzed," much less cured: a radical otherness of character and of destiny.

One also needs to speak about Christianity in light of *Trauerspiel.* On this subject, too, Wittgenstein gives an important, ulterior explanation on the theme of certainty. There is a sense of certainty at work in Christianity, in fact, that has a completely different nature from the certainties before which "we are obligated to bend our knees" (Wittgenstein) in the various activities of life. This certainty has a *Glauben* for its content, a faith, a belief that is radically opposed to every form of self-assurance as a component of *Weisheit,* of wisdom. In *On Certainty,* the de-sublimation of

Logic does not lead anywhere except to the complexity of worldly conviction, to *Weltweisheit*. But Christianity establishes a certainty that divides itself *by the sword* from this *Weltweisheit*. The paradox consists in the fact that, while according to the logic of *On Certainty*, nothing can stop the ratification of certainty *even* of *Glauben* (it is not possible, that is, to prohibit such certainty), the "reasoning" behind this *Glauben* condemns all philosophy and all *Weltweisheit* to radical fallacy. This paradox cannot be resolved— but here too the essential consists in maintaining the form of this pure difference, without turning to edifying syntheses or compromises. The conciliation of the two forms of certainty belongs to the unutterable.

Christianity orders life to change, orders the completion of a global *metanoia*. Its belief is a scandal for the certainty of *Weisheit*. This change of life cannot be made rationally, but only *leidenschaftlich*, with passion and sorrow—or more precisely, with *enthusiasm*. *Weisheit*, adds Wittgenstein, does not know *Leidenschaft* (it is not enthusiastic, although it is worldly to a radical degree) while noting, "Kierkegaard calls faith *eine Leidenschaft*." Perhaps in no other passage is Kierkegaard's influence on Wittgenstein made apparent with such clarity, even if the Kierkegaardian concept of Christianity figures here in a cultural frame that is profoundly distinct: in Wittgenstein, in fact, contrary to Kierkegaard, this metanoia is absolutely unutterable; the fallacy of *Weisheit* that it confirms is unutterable; and this judgment is "senseless," as is any judgment of *Weisheit* upon faith.

Like Kierkegaard's, this concept of Christianity is opposed to Pauline synthesis. Wittgenstein believes he notices an irreducible difference between the Gospel of Christ and Pauline dogma. This difference, as is well known, had already been underlined by Nietzsche. Belief, with Paul, seems to want to confirm itself as positive certainty, like *scientia*. This dogmatic pretext makes it necessary to have hierarchies, honors, officers. The Gospel contains the scandalous, "senseless" obligation to change one's life. In Paul metanoia becomes method. And the method coincides with the Church. And the Church ends by opposing itself to the very *Richtung des*

Lebens [course of life], to the evangelical form of existence, to its "tents in the desert." The Church tends to dampen enthusiasm; this too, like worldly wisdom, becomes *leidenschaftlos*: in fact, the overcoming of "fear and trembling" constitutes its objective. Anguish derives from the reemergence of that unresolvable otherness between faith and wisdom that constitutes, for Kierkegaard as for Wittgenstein, its *own* Christianity. But the tradition of Christianity is the nationalizing of faith and wisdom in the form of Pauline doctrine.[20]

But why is this Christianity of Wittgenstein's essentially "Romantic" and anti-tragic? Because the imperative to change life means looking *directly* at the world, and looking at it directly means understanding that "absolute judgment is out of place before the facts of the world."[21] The gospel is self-assured—assured of its certainty—that value lies outside of the world and therefore outside of the propositions that describe it and construct it. That is why the Christian is prohibited from judging the world in the perspective of its value. The Christian does not judge, since "human language cannot express absolutes" (Vannini). The Christian's faith *never* changes into a foundation of knowledge, never betrays itself into judgment of value—even if it calls on wisdom and its judgments to change life. The contents of this metanoia consist in ceasing to betray the absolute into judgments of the world.

As Hegel had already seen, Christianity and *Trauerspiel* belong to each other reciprocally, since the *original* Christianity (the importance of seventeenth-century baroque drama, *post* Reformation, pertains here) recognizes the impossibility of value judgment for equivalent propositions and it reserves the contents of its faith in pure unutterability and unrepresentability, while *Trauerspiel*, against a background of the unutterable, expresses only the conflicts and the struggles that happen in language. The unutterable cannot however be "forgotten" in the space of the *Trauerspiel*, since the same equivalence of its propositions and the impossibility of Judgment begin to make sense only on its ground. Equivalent propositions have *nothing* to declare about the possibility of metanoia. But in the space of *Trauerspiel* the unutterable can nevertheless show itself. It does in fact show itself: but transcendence, the event of transcending equivalence, cannot ever find words there. This event is the Messiah of *Judentum* [Judaism]. (See "The Star of Narration" below.)

The final words of Schoenberg's *Moses* ("Oh you, you word, that eludes me") contain perhaps the secret reason for Mahler's farewells and for the silence of the unhappy Lord Chandos—they express without doubt the bidirectional motion of both the unutterability of the absolute and the equivalence of the powerless propositions on Judgment. This vision of evangelical *not judging* seems almost to reunite the Christian faith to the interminability of the Diaspora of *Judentum,* to the infinity of its *undichterisches Leben* [life without speech].[22] But it also means that in the desert there are no victors, that in the desert we can recognize and love our limits and our anguish as our own character and destiny.

Visit the Serraglio!

Perfect figures of *Trauerspiel*, symbols much more than inhabitants of its new domain: Wozzeck and Lulu.

Pierre Boulez refers to the development of compositions like Alban Berg's as "novelistic development,"[23] continuous change without return. Extremely stable forms reclaimed from tradition are inextricably mixed, giving life to figures of extreme complexity and ambiguity. Such disquieting ambiguity derives from the fact that the various forms are themselves stabilized idioms, in and of themselves, and not material for a collage. There is thus a nonstop interaction between the intention of the compositional work and the autonomous sense of those forms that are reactivated or recalled in it. It is not at all a matter of the destruction of these forms, as Boulez seems sometimes to think, but a Nietzschean refusal to surrender to the "so it was," to "paying off" the past. Berg's work proceeds, in a way that recalls Walter Benjamin, to the discovery of the many pathways to the "beyond" that are hidden among the ruins, and to conferring upon the ruins the sense of such pathways. Mahler's compositional dialectic acts the same way toward traditional forms.

The labyrinthine qualities of Berg's work elude Boulez's definition of the "universe in perpetual motion" or "the ever-expanding universe." It eludes those commonplaces about the Viennese maestro's complex and contradictory variety of styles. The "severe logic," to use Berg's own phrase, that orders such variety is that of *Trauerspiel. Wozzeck* and *Lulu* are its models. The fact that Benjamin's notion is realized in the most finished way in a musical structure is deeply significant. The most authentic human sense is in fact the sense of hearing. To live is to listen, life is heard. But hearing cannot produce images. Nor can the sounds that it hears and constructs be described or replaced with images as consolation for lost nature.

Misunderstanding thus belongs to allegory, inasmuch as it is opposed to tragic seeing, to *theory*. But lies are exposed by severe logic. A being's self-contradiction, self-wounding, and confusion, its nothing-other-than-being-here is exposed, not as a root multiplicity, but as the actual form, available only as sound, of Hölderlin's no-more and not-yet. Allegory transposes, and in transposing, it necessarily destroys and betrays. It recognizes the no-more. At the same time, in this never-ending labor through tradition, the ways of the not-yet also emerge. Tradition is never available in the reassuring neoclassical framework of simple ruins. Allegory uproots tradition's no-more response to the not-yet. It turns that which has been heard into a herald of that which can be heard, of the purely possible. The sound of the not-yet seems able to manifest itself in this unending movement. Continual metamorphosis thus excludes either a return to origins (to the very principle of origin) or the discovery of new compositional orders leading to true peace. One order: the clarity of metamorphosis, the intelligibility of *Trauerspiel* as the essential musical architecture.

Ambiguity of form is the essential groundlessness of beings. This principle excludes all naturalism of the soul, to use Georg Simmel's expression. There is no "nature" where there is only translation and transportation of forms in their insuperable historicity. Berg is the negation of every *Urschrei* [primal scream] expressionist. Creaturely exsistence is intrinsically composed, irreducible to an origin. It is possible to enlarge, transform, and continually traverse the allegorical forest where creatures live speechless (*undichterisch*). Composition works it and re-works it, without ever being able to come to a conclusion, without ever being able to clear away the ambi-

guity. Even before Benjamin thought about it definitively—
roughly contemporary with *Wozzeck*—this compositional principle had already been in some way prefigured by the great Viennese
art critics, and in particular by Alois Reigl. For Reigl, the art of
decadence is not negatively defined as a loss or absence of the classical, but as an event apart from classical in a new severe logic of
essential historicity, of allegorical ambiguity. Berg's compositions
belong to this universe, not to seeking native forms of *Urschrei*
against it, which is characteristic of expressionism and modernism.
Decadence here expresses the conscious disenchantment of the twilight of the age of *Kultur*, and no vague sense of derivation. Decadence is the non-representability of the whole, the elusiveness of
the symbol. It is knowing oneself apart from the symbol and thus
knowing the obligation to venture into composition, into saving
and transforming the fragments, sacred in themselves.

Here the deep influence of Nietzsche acts on the "language's
great Viennese," as Roberto Calasso has called them. Mario Bortolotto has correctly understood how Nietzsche speaks of Wagner-
ian leitmotifs as a prefiguration of Berg. "Wagner, maestro of unstoppable speed, intangible nebula, crucial fibrillation, chromatic
collisions, microcosms suspended in a symphonic magma, resembles Berg too closely, and is even closer to the Berg of Adorno's essays."[24] This affinity is rooted in an analogous decadence that assumes its full meaning between Riegl's idea of expressionism and
Benjamin's notion of *Trauerspiel*. In light of what has been said, a
laughable reductionism ought to become evident in commonsense
interpretations of operas like *Wozzeck* and *Lulu*: social protest, condemnation of authority, and so forth. A tendency to reduce Berg's
allegories to expressionistic naturalism of the soul shows up again
in these categories. Not that such motives could be absolutely absent, but the true problem has less to do with the social criticism of
these operas than with their logical and compositive sense, in the
severe logic of the language of *Trauerspiel*.

Even insisting—mistakenly in my opinion—on the term montage (montage has as its transcendent condition the reduction of
material to semantic indifference, which should *not* happen in

Mahler's and Berg's assumption of the tradition), Bortolotto gave us a splendid gloss of *Lulu*. "The parts build up, starting with the Prologue, into impossible piles. Pieces on top of pieces." From the illustrious as well as the plebeian topoi of musical theater to the colors of the Prater, from Mozart to *Singspiel*, to the "inexhaustible incarnations" of *Biedermeier* down to Brahms and Strauss, it defines "an enormous structure, made of minutiae (Wagner's 'minimal transitions'), a baroque volumetric made of cuts and *bibelots*." The grand form consists in composing this multiplicity of parts. Grand form is not, however, a style, but an *excess* of style.[25] It is impossible to reduce to categories of style the overabundance of languages that strike us like "vagrant" quotations from Benjamin. ("Berg's quotations, like Benjamin's, reveal themselves to be vagrants off the street that jump out with a weapon and demand the lazy to form an opinion" [Bortolotto]). The grand form is the enormous composition of minimal transitions. The excess of style creates the compositional principle: the adventurous and problematic unity of composition, opposed to the static and formal unity of style.

The grand form means "to comprehend" the world as the totality of cases, as everything that is the case. In *Lulu* this principle reaches perfect *Klarheit*: it lives in every fold of the opera, like a presupposition, a precondition of its language. The scene of its *Trauerspiel* is precisely that of *men without qualities*, of the purely possible. But men of possibility are simultaneously absent. Pure possibility causes all who encounter it to vanish, rendering them liquid and spectral. As Bortolotto has already pointed out, it is this quality of the absent that renders the characters of *Lulu* beyond the reach of style. In *Lulu*, the domain of *Trauerspiel* combines itself, beyond style, with the logical space of the *Tractatus*. Lulu is the angel of this combination. She is music beyond style; she refuses the principle of style. She transcends it in the dimension of pure possibility, and she finds grand form in this dimension, in its compositional structure, and in the severe rules of the logic of her game. That is why this figure of possibility can become the idea of an aesthetic *intentio* at the same time that she reaches the bedrock of profane vulgarity. This figure passes through *every* possibility, uncontrollable, irreducible. At the same time the language of equivalence, its premises radically questioned and applied, connects to the problem of manifesting the unutterable—to the problem of the limit that turns the composition into a grand form.

Lulu is the angel of possibility or, better, is the angel of the music of possibility. The angel is the face of unconsumable possibility. Without this, there can be no images or sounds. Lulu the angel is a divine vision captured in profane lights. A similar profane illumination agitates that most pure eros of Geschwitz. She knows that only Lulu's music can fulfill once again the dreams of the imagination, and it is to such dreams that her love tirelessly tends. But an angel that manifests the purely possible arouses an interminable love, attracts all the figures that she meets in a vortex that turns eternally in upon itself, like Geschwitz's waiting, beyond all jealousy and possession. This figure's peculiarity consists in having understood what Lulu says—not that Lulu is Music (everyone knows that), but that her music is an angel. It accompanies the facts as their insuperable limit. It expresses the ephemeral, and at the same time it expresses the illumination (the *Klarheit*) that issues from the ephemeral as *composition*: a paradoxically divine vision of possibility (far from the bourgeois "sublimation of sex" as Adorno, incredibly, misunderstood it).

As much as Lulu the Angel exceeds the stereotypes of the florid femme fatale, that is how much *Wozzeck* is irreducible to a category or metaphor of the unified organic world damaged by social oppression and by the authoritarian norms. The immense presentation of forms and motives makes the first act of *Wozzeck* an extraordinary universe of traditions and events. This same labyrinthine multiplicity rejects the myth of origin. It promises no methods for overcoming or getting beyond alienation, which is defined in terms of Nietzschean "decadence" as the logic of allegory. To such logic belongs the language of Wozzeck. To abstract him from the complex dialectics of the opera would be to place him in the glacial solitude of a tragic character, to make a tragic hero of him, turn him into a theory of the events that swirl around him.

The dramatic force of this most pure persona of *Trauerspiel* consists precisely in his desperate belonging to the allegorical ambiguity of the work. Wozzeck never penetrates his belonging, exploding into a naturalism of the *Ur-schrei*, of the primal scream of the soul. The persona's importance in this context does not derive from his being the bearer, to whatever extreme, of an origin or of a category that intends to reform him, but from the fact that his very existence, his very corporeality, expresses the creaturely nature of the work and its language with maximum tension and desperation. Wozzeck always hears the *Abgrund*, that point in the totality of cases where a vortex opens up and sucks everything in (the vortex that Hofmannsthal pictures in *Der Turm*). In Wozzeck, the multiplicity of voices and categories reaches an authentic sense of decadence: he shows how they pass through to the *Abendland* [land of twilight] and how they belong there inexorably. Wozzeck hears, already from the heart of the *Abgrund*, the voices of decadence, of the *Abendland*. As he hears them, those voices forgive their trite, quotidian surface, not in the sense that the music transfigures or redeems them, but in the sense that they lay bare the irreconcilable maze of their most secret and intimate nerves.

The importance of *Wozzeck* in context reaches its diapason in the second scene of Act I and in the extraordinary passage that accompanies the death of Wozzeck. Here the tension of that which cannot be heard (with hearing the voice that speaks in Wozzeck, with the sounding rod of the *Abgrund* where twilight occurs, with the intuition of the *Gebild am Himmel*") displaces the already-heard, crashes against the limits of the already-heard. But this breaking against the shoreline of tradition is the force that continually transforms it, is the crisis that changes its borders. Perhaps no other contemporary work portrays with more dramatic clarity the fact that the authentic nature of *Trauerspiel*'s persona, of all creatures, lies in being in constant struggle with the limits and history of language.

It would be a grave error, however, to assume dramatic *intentio* as an index of the solution or of the method for solution. Berg speaks of a "Piano-Oper mit Ausbrüchen"; the tone of the opera is "piano," which combines participation with estrangement. The intensity of participation is a condition of the acuity of intellectual understanding and vice versa. On the other hand, this tone is continually shattered. The entire architecture was reached by solutions of continuity, explosions. The principle of interruption dominates that of conclusion. There is no solution. Every motif is taken up again and varied, never followed through and developed in all of its possibilities. Every motif remains a possibility, holding out in the dimension of the possible. The metamorphosis renews itself by incessantly interrupting itself. The opera presents itself as an extraordinary universe of fragments: extraordinary because such fragments are not neutral shards in a collage, but entire traditions, forms, and languages. Every motif is continually revealed and reveiled; its surface and its sense are transformed—but never resolved, never presented as a whole that has finally been achieved. There is no method that can lead back from the fragment—from this idea of the fragment—to the symbol. Architecture-by-fracture in *Wozzeck* means precisely the impossibility of the symbol. This is the very language of nature, the logic of its allegorical nature. The disturbing passages from the second and third scenes of Act I and, above all, the screaming crescendo in A major that collides with the tavern dance in the interlude between the second and third scenes of Act III do not serve at all to isolate the various parts impressionistically. Instead, they clarify the logic of allegorical architecture as opposed to synthetic and symbolic architecture. Paraphrasing Heidegger: every pathway is interrupted, but these constant interruptions do not merely diverge through the forest, they lead to multiple centers, to multiple clearings, to innumerable discoveries. Multiplicity experienced, multiplicity interpreted, but never exhausted, is the source of *Wozzeck*'s sense of misunderstanding.

This is not aphoristic writing. Aphorism seeks definition, seeks to circumscribe microcosms with all the parts strictly and organically connected inside. The writing in Anton von Webern's *Six Bagatelles* Op. 9 is aphoristic, for example. The bagatelles are seeds of microcosms. The intuition of their *free* inner connection is *Er-*

lösung [redemption]. Aphorism in Webern defines the *necessity* of composition. Redemption consists of nothing other than embracing that necessity, in loving it, like Nietzsche. In Webern, the microcosm is finally the single sound itself in its purity, just as it echoes in the silence-within-us. As such, the aphorism is inseparable from the tragic form and the metaphysical opposite of the uncompromising movement of Berg's *Trauerspiel.*

Not that movement and transformation are missing in Webern, but his philosophy of time is different. Continuous variation attains, in Webern, a principle of non-repetition. The aphorism cannot be repeated precisely because it is complete, because its arrow has hit the bull's-eye (which is the silence-within-us, inasmuch as the target is the archer's heart). Any repetition would be ornamental. Continuous variation in Berg, on the other hand, derives from the opposite principle of the impossibility of tragic aphorism or, better, from the nonexistence of a center at which to direct the aphorism, from an inherent ontological poverty. While Webern's brevity is the symbol of the essential nature of the microcosm compressed to its limit, the compositional fracturing of Berg indicates allegorically the essential historicity of nature, its desperate productivity among the shifting facts of the world. Webern's intuition of the perfect annuls the linear dimension of time. In Webern, there returns with unequaled clarity the Nietzschean problem par excellence, which is the problem of liberation, of *Erlösung* of time. Webern's ascesis turns each fragment into a unique, unrepeatable microcosm. Certainly uniqueness can never be construed as a resolution, but it is in itself perfect and unequivocal. The *Abgrund* of Berg's *Trauerspiel,* on the other hand, grasps the same fragment, with its same intimate structure, in an unstoppable metamorphosis, where redemption is not possible or else appears like the light of a star extinguished since time immemorial.

For these metaphysical differences, there is much more significance in the sisterly relationship between these figures of the Viennese "school" and the names and motifs that together make up the culture: Trakl and Webern's Op. 14, for example. It is the song without words of one who has no country and who passes by the moribund city of *Abendland*. This song of Webern's is a mistake in Berg's terms, for *Abendland* is tinged with decadence and at the same time lit by raking sunlight. Trakl's poetry, that of a soul estranged from the world, is necessary to understand the very structure of *Wozzeck*. The motion toward the silence of this soul in Webern's Op. 14 finds its analogy in Berg's *Altenberg Lieder*. Here too, the structural function of silence in the composition, which is the deepest lesson of Mahler, seems to allude to the possible *Erlösung*. It is a matter of the tranquillity that follows snowstorms and long delays, of peace full of the gestures and pains resolved in that time. It is the silence of a long sigh, aware, beyond the reach of consolation, like the farewell at the end of Mahler's song-symphony *Das Lied von der Erde*. The snow that plays lightly on the lake of the heart (in Altenberg-Berg), the falling stars that inflame the rosy evening (in Trakl-Webern), the sea of the sky where the moon bobs in the waves (in Mahler) are voices brought together by differences. As productive as they are in developments and discoveries, they are that successful in justifying their diversity, as happens in the vocal and pianistic lines in Webern's Lieder Op. 12 or in Schoenberg's George Lieder. Moreover, to learn to hear the affinities among the diversity, like learning how languages develop and are transformed within family groups, is to learn how every family is a multiplicity of fragments wholly in themselves: this was the very principle of Schoenberg's teaching.

Music, Voice, Text

Since the order of musical composition cannot be "invented," but comes from an enriched transformation of inherited traditions within new, distinct configurations of signs, the relationship of music with text becomes a fresh problem, one of extraordinary complexity.

The way Schoenberg confronts it in his famous essay on "Der Blaue Reiter" could give it a reductive cast, with regard not only to Schoenberg's "philosophy" of composition, but also to those of Hugo Wolf and of Mahler. Schoenberg's essay brings a subtle equivocation into play: the text, as a denotative system, as discourse that directly signifies something, adds nothing to our understanding of Schubert's Lieder. The problem is even more radical: Why does the text exist? What structural function requires the presence of text? What compositional problems does it trigger in the entire Viennese "tradition" from Schubert to Webern? It is not possible to respond to this question as Schoenberg does in "Der Blaue Reiter" only by showing the ability of text to determine the formal articulation of a piece of music. That is true perhaps only at an elementary level of composition, where the text stands out against an extremely regular melodic structure, built of brief symmetrical phrases. It is evident that the procedure that results in maximum clarity and comprehension of the text in Schoenberg's or Webern's Lieder is completely different from the *radikale Re-*

produktion that Goethe praised in Carl Zelter. But the presence of text as a structural element, one that participates as sound and sense in the compositional form or, put more generally, the importance of the *verbal* element in composition holds not only for those forms that would seem to have a natural predisposition to that relationship, but also for Beethoven's great romantic symphonies.[26]

What is the meaning of the verbal element, as such, in composition? Why is it called a necessity? Because that is exactly what it is: text is necessary in a Schubert Lied, but not to be better "informed" about what the music "means," not to get the "program." Rather, text is necessary in order to understand the entire composition clearly, within a framework that is not merely formal, indeed is not even as formal as it is cultural and philosophical. A fresh dimension of the necessity emerges along the entire Schubertian line. The problem is not "what is said," but the clarity of the emergence of the voice. "What is said" could perhaps be entirely removed without reducing the intelligibility of a Schubert Lied—but this would certainly not remove the problem of the voice as the emergence of a new compositional subject. The voice is not used up in reciting a text; rather, the text appears as a mere material vehicle for the voice. It sustains the voice's place as an uncontrollable force within the entire instrumental composition. This force stands out more and more sharply from the whole. It is not a simple instrument among others in the language of composition. It contains infinite games, relationships of growing complexity. But it always emerges as the specific subject, and for this reason its emergence unfolds the indicated structural function. It actually points out the whole of the composition as a problem that cannot be reduced directly to its coordinates. The *voice* breaks through this composition. And not the voice that is articulated in discourse, that appears directly as a simple means of communication and information. Schoenberg was right not to pay attention to the words in Schubert's Lieder. The words, in fact, were not essential to their compositional structure; what mattered was the presence of the voice. The usual approach has been notably reversed. While the

voice is usually understood as the mere medium of significant discourse (usually spent on verbal communication), here it is the text
that seems to serve as a vehicle for the appearance of the voice, and
the text that furnishes to the voice a mere means to manifest itself.

Schubert's Lieder are constructed around the utopian presence
of the voice. The location of the voice, in fact, is *no-where*. For us,
the sound of the voice is only the sound of the *signifying* voice.
Ever since Aristotle's *On Expression* (which remains too deep in
spite of Giorgio Colli's commentary), we disregard the voice as a
simple sound in favor of a true science of logos, in favor of expository discourse that connects us to the world only. It is as if this
discourse had no sound or the sound of the voice were completely
superfluous for it. Such a sound returns in Schubert as the pre-
ponderant problem facing the grammatical and syntactical line of
musical composition, and that is why it determines its entire sense
and structure. The composition pulsates in attendance of the unattainable sound of the voice. Surging from the head—indeed confined to the head—the voice breaks out of the compositional fabric as if in search of its native presence. The voice is intrinsic not
only to the text that embodies it, but to musical language itself.
True discourse here is that which the music develops, and this in
turn defines the voice. Beyond the verbal text and within musical
language, the problem of the voice imposes itself. That is, the voice
becomes a problem, after the long history of its sublimation, of its
"victory" in discursive structure. Indirectly, it is precisely this situation that Schoenberg underlines in his essay: the "what" of the
text of the Lied is truly and completely disinterested—but the
voice that manifests it is far from disinterested. The text is, literally,
the utopia of the voice.

All the subsequent literature of Lieder develops along this track.
But the problem of the voice and of its unattainable origin, which
confers authentic metaphysical content upon the *Sehnsucht* [long-
ing] of the Lied, is linked finally with the problem of text, in its
semantic value. To complete the preceding design, there is another
structural element: the clarity and intelligibility of the text as such.
If this is not the logos that "takes away" the voice, that removes its

problems, neither is it the simple pretext for a "heavenly" manifestation of the voice. The utopian attribute of the voice is clearly
recognized here. This attribute appears precisely with the manifestation of the indomitable autonomy of the text from the voice,
with the irreversibility of the process that leads from the voice to
meaningful discourse, to the syntactic order of language. In order
to manifest the "body" of meaningful discourse, it is necessary to
put it in clear phonetic and semantic terms. The voice alone appears on this rugged terrain. It has no place of its own. But that is
exactly what it shows: that the place of the text does not use it up,
that the text is by no means its origin. The voice is not at home
in the text, but only in the text can it "go on."

All of which changes not merely the quality of the relationship
between text and voice, but also that of the whole relationship between text and musical composition. Diverse ways of rendering
come to light. Where the music reproduces or follows the text, or
where it turns back on itself as a disinterested vehicle of the voice,
this diversity cannot appear. There exists, then, only the order of
musical language, or the relationship between it and the utopia of
the voice. On the other hand, whenever the presence of the text
becomes a meaningful semantic presence, the relationship between
this presence and that of musical language is a relationship between two autonomous forms of connecting to the world. Connecting to the world is irreducibly complex. There is no idealistic
dialectic, no solution, that can resolve the complexity of it. It can
only be compiled: the order of composition is the order that reveals and renders comprehensible the diversity of elements. It is
the order that works on that diversity and transforms it, along with
the complex relationships of its elements. Various combinations
and configurations of signs appear in the composition. Metaphysically, these take on the value of various possibilities of thinking or
of connecting to the world. None is a mere vehicle or pretext for
another—no one is the true sense of the other.

Thus even at this new level, it is not the "what" of the text, its
informative content, that really counts. Rather, it is the general
presence of another system beside the musical signs, of expressive

signs which are also thoughts. It follows that such a system has to be presented as fully organized in itself, fertile whether from an intrinsically musical point of view or from a truly semantic one. The inclusion of "babble" reveals the scope, which is to show a natural diversity of ways of connecting to the world. The presence of a particular text alongside the voice forbids musical language to delude itself with new universality, while it rigorously defines the borders of its possible domain. There is no clarity or intelligibility without defining limits, and the particular text becomes the symbol of the presence of limits that permit understanding and clarity. Between music and text a relationship happens: a relationship between two languages not dialectically surmountable in "higher" syntheses. The text poses a limit, but, in posing it, it questions. The relationship does not happen between two languages at peace with each other or on parallel tracks. The text is radically assumed as an interrogating presence, to which the response is—diverse, not neutral.

That is what happens between Hölderlin and Brahms in the *Schicksalslied,* and between Brahms and Goethe in the *Alto Rhapsody.* At the end of the *Schicksalslied,* the return of the conciliatory motif of the introduction is clearly an answer to the fall into *Ungewisse* [uncertainty], to the absolute loss of God on the part of Hölderlin's *leidender Mensch* [suffering humanity]. Likewise, the connection between poverty and utopia in Goethe's poem constitutes the unifying inspiration of the final section of the *Alto Rhapsody,* until it ends in silence, in *der Wüste* [the wilderness]. In both cases, the text is *presence*: a motif of order and articulation of the musical form. But much more, it is a problem for that form, the limit of its language, an interrogating *Gegen-stand* [subject].

Just as Peter Altenberg's essays are *Extrakte des Lebens,* Hugo Wolf's Lieder are "Extrakte der Seele." But how to manifest their distance from every late-Romantic *Zerrissenheit* [striving]? How to order and articulate the completed loss of ego? How to keep from getting lost in interminable allusive chains? If the problem of Wolf's musical language consists in rendering the *Extrakte der Seele* intelligible, this was also the profound intention of Eduard

Mörike's poetry. The relationship between music and text is truly essential here. Wolf captures definitively the problematic nature of the text, and he throws himself against it with abandon. He knows infinite ways "to go outside the stable structure of the strophe and bring out its most central nucleus." He "is the first to treat a poetic text with absolute indifference to its preexisting order,"[27] even while exalting every moment in it, so that it independently takes up and presents anew the most secret themes of the musical idea.

The autonomous text survives, even saturated with the problems that musical language confronts; not a text of music, but a question and answer directed at the articulation of musical form. After the "visionary" Wolf (Bortolotto), this relationship reaches its most complex expression in Mahler's *Rückert Lieder*. Ladislao Mittner criticizes too hastily this figure of an erudite poet. Friedrich Rückert's formal virtuosity, his historical and linguistic awareness of India and oriental civilizations in general put him in a precise cultural and aesthetic region: that which passes from Goethe's utopia of "universal literature" to the philosophical and artistic concepts of Schopenhauer. His language game is contemporary with Schopenhauer's pessimism about classical and romantic conceptions of art. That is, by now art can be nothing but cultural reworking, virtuoso philology, a linguistic game—despairing, finally, of any ethical or existential content ancillary to Nirvana. It is this *essential* despair that Mahler finds in Rückert's poetry. It is not by accident that Schoenberg speaks of Mahler "in the name of" Schopenhauer.

But here, too, the assumption of the text takes place in full freedom, criticizing its sense. In the five *Kindertotenlieder*, Mahler annihilates the elements of consolation present in Rückert's text. He dissolves their metrical assonance and their closed rhyme scheme to bring out of them two fundamental motifs: the simplicity of pain (withheld constantly in its pretense to declare itself) and reawakening (the impossible resurrection, powerless to sound here as in the finale of the Second Symphony, in spite of a mysteriously leavening utopia that embraces each word and each sound of abandonment and solitude). The slow rhythm, barely interrupted by brief cries of the voice against the limits of the form, indicates the irreversibility of time. The reawakening does not announce it-self beyond such time, but appears rather as the experience of the eternal return *in the irreversible*, as "the joyous light of the world" that repeats itself in the irreversible. The farewell does not free one from the earth; it does not free one from its light. "Farewell" is bid to friends, to children, but not to the earth's light that illuminates irreversibility and poverty. The joyous light of the world turns the poverty of passing time into clarity (*Klarheit*).

An identical *itinerarium* is found in Mahler's *Five Lieder* with text by Rückert, composed almost at the same time as the *Kinder-totenlieder*. From the springtime beauty and melancholic irony of the first three, it proceeds to the abandon of the fourth (which draws everything back "inside" the Lied). It then proceeds to the desperation of *Um Mitternacht*, where full defeat looms paradoxi-cally and scandalously in the majestic passage from A minor to A major at the end ("in deine Hand gegeben . . . "). The finale links death and resurrection together, joins time to the final farewell and to repetition, joins the misery of time passing and the joy of the world's eternal light, the perfect void of Nirvana and the "sweet scent" of the first Lied. The multiplicity of language, the profound misunderstanding of the relationship between music and text, has perhaps never found a fuller expression than in the *musikalisches Denkmal* [musical memorial] that Mahler brought out of the words of the erudite poet—or rather, from their Schopenhauerian substance.

The text is a problem that musical form finds intrinsic to the compositional process. The text is a complex of signs, indices, memories, and facts that the music has to digest and rework; in turn, the text must manifest the *intentio* of the musical form. In this sense, a continuous thread connects Wolf and Mahler to Schoenberg. Not so much to Schoenberg's expressionistic rework-ing of Richard Dehmel as to his crash encounter with Stefan George.[28] Hofmannsthal said George subjugated life "to such a de-gree that he breathed an incredible calm and the freshness of a deep temple into our senses, which are used to confused noise."

Dehmel's position is far more complex than Schoenberg understands it to be, and the literary historians—even Mittner—have noticed as much. Not only is Dehmel's presence at Darmstadt colored by the original anti-Wagnerian intonations, but even his so-called "symbolic naturalism," above all in *Weib und Welt* (1896), enters into dialogue with motifs from Arthur Schnitzler to Otto Weininger, far from unknown to Schoenberg. Nor should we forget Dehmel's reading of Nietzsche—for example in *Nachruf an Nietzsche*—where he refutes the myth of a Nietzschean "school" and acutely captures the true sense of the *Wille zur Macht* [will to power] as the subduing of the True One: *I, God*. Dehmel, finally, is no "accident" for Schoenberg and cannot be reduced to the "spirit of '14" of his *Kriegs-Brevier*.

Only George's *Book of Hanging Gardens* could accompany Schoenberg in his approach to "an expressive and formal ideal that had already floated before me for several years." The extraordinary essence of George's poetic "music" recalls that of the piano literature, in which every note is stripped in its uniqueness, liberating it from all tonal *religio*. The voice, which preserves Schubert's secret intact, connects to the text in a more pregnant and incisive manner. The melodic construction lies, as Adorno noted, "in the use of minimal values, in the subdued declamation of legato notes detached from the conclusions of phrases, in the chromatic conversion of all central sounds."[29] The melodic construction transcends the space of floral imagery, of all the Jugendstil sensual sonority. But this transcendence is exactly George's problem, the roots of which are not to be found in any mythic Prussian esotericism, but rather in Mallarmé and in the great "metropolitan" French lyrics. Schoenberg's music confronts this whole aesthetic and philosophical problem in George's text. The dialogue between music and piano, "made of extreme subtleties, of subterranean connections, of projections at ever-recurrent intervals yet hardly noticeable at first,"[30] possesses nothing of the simple rapport between two players, two "instruments" in a cycle. It is rather a closed musical interrogation of George's text to extract the trace of the path from lyric naturalism of the soul to the absolute measure of an intellectual *imaginatio*, capable of plastic, objective strength.

The complex network of allusions, of cultural and formal meanings that constitute George's cycle of 1895 is not immediately recapitulated in the music. Only the fundamental metrical values—the text as a creator of order—are assumed in the music. For the rest, the music recomposes and reorganizes the sense or tendency of the text. In fact, the almost explicit objective of the rapport between the two players is that of rendering evident the idea that music and text do not form a totality, do not constitute a synthesis a priori. What is this fundamental textual tendency that the music must draw out and express? It is the tendency toward *form* that Hofmannsthal emphasized. The music's assumption of the text's metrical values is essentially a reading of the deep strata of George's work. The music freezes, in its own meter, the symbolist residues of the text, the flowery exuberance that shows through, and, above all, the exasperated, pale, and highly refined chromaticism. The fundamental tendency of the text (on which Schoenberg constructs his cycle) is death, the end of the brilliant insight, of the poetic possibility of voicing sentiment as nature, of expressing it as an object, a situation, a game of appearances. That which lives in the text as only an inaudible tendency becomes the explicit sense of the music. It is the collapse of the extreme naturalism of the soul, and finally the impossibility of poetry as a producer of images, of beautiful images in a brilliant intuition. "The images always flee . . . when the clear cold morning draws near." The morning of the music freezes the symbolic naturalism of which the text is already a contradictory witness. Read and listen to the eleventh poem in Schoenberg's cycle: "Ich erinnere, dass wie schwache rohre / Beide stumm zu beben wir begannen" (I remember, we both began to tremble silently like fragile reeds). What could be more clearly Jugendstil, or even more flowery, than these trembling reeds? But what logic can be more severe than the perfect meter that scans them? And here is how *this* tendency is comprised and is recomposed in Schoenberg, beyond any possible intuition or image, in the design of a unique line that voice and piano pursue independently, in "a solitude and a stillness full of continuous events of pure crystal" (Musil).

The text therefore is *other* material. It has its own strong principles of organization that the music assumes and considers as such, without reducing their complexity, without posing a solution to their problematic nature. But the presence of this other in the musical deed is destined to reconstitute its very form, since it defines, on the basis of this limit, its own non-universality and, at the same time, its own effectual "domain." As in the examples already cited, the relationship between music and text develops a complex logic of relationships, a network of intrinsically problematic relationships that are founded on the history of the respective languages, on the awareness incarnate in them, on their sense and their tendencies and their crises. Music and text constitute, relating to each other in this way, "prose" relationships, affinities, families of sense, conflicts, and contradictions. All of which prevents *a single* language from pretending universality, impedes an accord that presents itself as a synthesis, as *the* tonality. "Are dissolved patterns privileged in the structure of the accounts, in the formal systems, or in the theory of harmony, criteria that are proposed in order to choose the dissonance . . . ? For Wittgenstein, the formal proof is a paradigm, a harmonious figure. . . . Schoenberg—having rejected the formal responses of technique, the naturalistic privileging of tonality—assumed as his criterion of legitimacy of dissonance the perceptibility and perspicaciousness of the dissonant accords" (Gargani).

In this logic of relationships, every sign, every form, every movement consciously avoids the presence of the other. Within these limits they are organized, they are developed, they seek to become more powerful and more intelligible—within the silence that embraces them and that they need to demonstrate or allow to be demonstrated.

Wonders and Marvels

Equally complex is the composition of Musil's "Into the Millennium," the story he should have told but that escaped all his writings. In *The Man Without Qualities* Ulrich and Agathe begin from a premise of resignation.[31] They belong to that facet of desire that torments Margaret and Faust and whose motif runs from Goethe through all German literature. Severe rules of abstinence and self-imposed codes enforce separation, impede desire from being recognized, allow the lovers to be *pure*, and allow their quest to remain disembodied. Woman's beauty "evaporates" the obstacle of the human body, that "third thing" that Andreas-Salomé saw as the soul's tragedy in passion and that incites chastity.[32] Beauty attracts desire and keeps it from turning elsewhere. And yet, since it is ideal, it cannot be reached. It can only be contemplated in a platonic sense. This theme of passion crowned in resignation can express itself in the characteristics of incest that every couple ends up redressing.

This has little to do with generic asocial interactions or with philistine calculations intended to guarantee the survival of desire for the sake of continued abstinence, as Lemoine-Luccioni seems to believe. To the simple dialectics of the analyst nothing is more refracted than Musil's millennium. From the perspective of the finished novel, which sees the "wisdom" it expresses and communicates, the encounter of the two siblings happens at the peak of the explosion of the subject as ego, beyond the limits of order and beyond the rule of ethical discourse. The *ekstatische Sozietät* of brother and sister goes beyond those limits, and only its own internal sense can give it the force of sharing, of mutual assurance about what to call their actions. As Emanuele Castrucci has demonstrated,[33] Lord Chandos, who exceeds those very limits, finds his exact double behind him in Benito Cereno (not by accident a key figure for Carl Schmitt) and before him in Musil's couple. Ecstasy has therefore a precise foundation: it sends up the individualistic and possessive sphere of the liberal age. In his relationship with his sister, Ulrich attains the full absence of possession; he frees himself from the category of possession.

This category is organized around the problem of property, of appropriation. The history of truth, says Jacques Derrida, is "a process of appropriation." To seek truth presupposes a fundamental *proper* to which it belongs and supposes that "the value of belonging has a unique sense and its own stability." Now it is exactly this metaphysical stability that the man without qualities adulterates and corrupts (without *Eigen-schaften* [qualities], and therefore foreign to the "family" of *Eigentlichkeit* [reality], and even to the Heideggerian family of *Being and Time*). The man without qualities always leads from the immutable preference for the proper "to the abysmal structure of the proper," a non-fundamental structure, superficial and bottomless at the same time, the structure of the abyss that reveals the event detached from ontological consideration.[34] Musil's novel connects to the most subtle games in Nietzsche's thinking: the debasement of the basis, of the *Grund*, of the structure that constitutes the very possibility of appearance and appropriation. Any gesture or style opens onto the abyss (*Abgrund*) of an event that can no longer be appropriated—onto the *marvel* of the strange happenings of *Geschwisterliebe* [a love between brother and sister].

The outer stillness of solitude that this resignation of the proper is called upon to create ought to correspond to an internal *Gelassenheit*, to an emptying in oneself, to an abandoning of oneself. Only such a radical dispossession can fully show the meaning of "without qualities." Ulrich is certainly the language of equivalence that dissolves value judgment into the facts of the world. But since Ulrich matures in the lunar light of his sister, he is the one "without propriety," he who seeks an interior dimension of emptiness in the surrounding stillness. There is a rapport between "without qualities" and *Gelassenheit*, but they are not identical. "Without qualities" remains within the limits of a critique of the possessive and acquisitive ego and its body, of the conservative power that it exercises. The idea of *Gelassenheit* indicates, rather, an *ecstasy* liberated from relations and conflicts with "property," an end to the very problem of possession. Language changes color from expository tones of irony and critical judgment to tones of enlightenment.

In the novel there is a double unwritten story. The first was not written because it already existed. It is the story of Lord Chandos. Many dare to interpret *The Man Without Qualities* as if the only story it contained were that of the unhappy scholar imagined by Hofmannsthal. The novel has more than just the desperation of Lord Chandos in its past—it also has the formation of syntax and language of equivalence that moves in that "common nutritive liquid" produced by dissolving the ego. From the first instant, Ulrich is language "without qualities," and it is absurd to imagine his route as a return to the original conditions from which he had detached himself. His route is rather to go beyond "without qualities." "Without qualities" is complicated by a radical "without property," and this figure, in turn, connects to the interior *Gelassenheit*—and still further beyond that dimension lies the story not narrated and impossible to narrate.

The opus that Ulrich wants to initiate with his forgotten sister turns out to be the redemption of time. The sacred dialogues that the couple embroider together tend imperceptibly, by minimal and musical transitions, to abstract her from the *mundus situalis* [the mundane], to vaporize her concerns, to refine and purify her material, as if in search of her invisible star. This star speaks in Agathe: "We have to break away from knowing and wanting, and free ourselves from reality and from the desire for reality. Draw into ourselves, until mind, heart, and body are all one silence." Brother and sister cultivate an extreme *attention*, sharpened against every sensation and thought. San Giovanni Climaco speaks of attention as an angel that stands guard at the gates of paradise. Everything that comes to the gates of the heart gets interrogated, in order to determine whether it comes as an enemy seeking to destroy the slow work of emptying, of *Gelassenheit*. The sacred dialogue tends evidently to a sort of interior prayer under the watchword of "attende tibi ipsi" [heed yourself].

The "arcane perception of something happening without anything happening," of "a solitude and an immobility full of continuous events of pure crystal," of time as the unending repetition of clouds in the sky, is a possible redemption of time that nevertheless takes place in time. This is due to the transforming of words *and their speakers* in the sacred dialogue, in the opus that it symbolizes. The dialogue has the rhythm of a slow and difficult decantation: Ulrich and Agathe raise themselves up, ever more pale and "dispossessed," from the critical and interpretive melancholy where their souls "hide." Here all the themes of the great novels return, as if in midflight, unable to be held. Critical judgment (Ulrich's native language and mother tongue) has dissolved, decomposed, and has demonstrated the groundlessness of vanity's attempted syntheses. It killed the mortal. That is why all of its themes must return. The dialogue between brother and sister would not even be conceivable without this dissolving of the stability and durability of appearances. The dialogue initiates another phase: nostalgia for the soul, which the material, dissolved at last, had kept prisoner. It is nostalgia for the "being that, behind appearances, thought and felt," and through which the "bodies transformed themselves into cruel prisons."

Meditatio and *imaginatio* are the terminal points of *Geschwisterliebe*. The conversation between brother and sister is above all an intimate conversation. It does not consist in an exterior dialectic, but in the attention that it develops and in the *Gelassenheit* that it produces and nourishes. As in the opus, here the value of the conversation lies in its speakers far more than in its results. It strips

brother and sister of their ephemeral bodies for the Millennium of
the immortal golden Eros. Behind the apparent dialogue, a true
metalogue, there lies the intimate conversation between spirit and
spirit, as with Hofmannsthal's Sigismund or, to use the words of
the *Lexicon Alchemiae* cited by Jung, a conversation with someone
"who remains invisible, even such as God, after having invoked
him, or with one's own self or with one's good angel." Behind the
apparent dialogue there lies, finally, "a living relationship with the
voice of the other."[35] *Imaginatio* blossoms out of the intimate conversation. It is the imaginative faculty of the soul, capable of conceiving things that the world cannot conceive: the consonance between the star from which the *spiritus sydereum* emanates and our
own souls. Paracelsus says that when man succeeds in freeing himself from the body, as happens in dreams, then the soul can "*fabulieren*," or converse with its star. In the solitude that they create
around themselves, it is as if brother and sister were searching their
sleep in order to dream the dream of God. If Ulrich and Agathe
are nihilistic and atavistic together, they are so under the sign of
imaginatio that flowers from *meditatio*. Their nihilism resides in
the intimate conversation with one's own good angel, which is the
symbol and image of the conversation between the soul and its
star. It was by imagining the universe that God created it. To
dream the dream of God means to dream a magic production, and
in the form of this dream, in its clarity, one is reborn from the dissolution of any quality or property, from the darkness of being
"without."

More than intermediary faculty of the soul, a bridge between
sensation and idea, *imaginatio* appears in "Into the Millennium"
as a point of arrival, the recurring and unattainable goal of intellectual intuition. It guides the conversion from corporeal to spiritual (a still shadowy movement toward stability and the light of
ideas). Its airy or fiery puff increasingly seems to be the only force,
the unique *spiritus*, that is capable of perceiving divine inspiration.[36] It is as if the extraordinarily problematic nature of these relationships were incarnate in Musil's "style." *Imaginatio* can no
longer be understood as an intuitive pass, a stairway that leads to

the contemplation of God, failing completely to define the love between brother and sister, or even its possibility, within such an "ascensive" scheme. *Imaginatio*'s *umbra lucis* refines the corporeal and changes its colors in dreams. There is no light except in the *umbra lucis*. Brother and sister reciprocally transform their images into a continually changing chiaroscuro, as unpredictable as a dream. Like flashing wingbeats they fracture the darkness momentarily and reveal instants of light that are difficult to remember. Brother and sister are seen in waiting, ever ready to take hold of each other, to stop each other in memory, and ever in pain from the apparent vanity of this hope. Even in the repetitive pattern of "Into the Millennium," there is the constant and unstoppable change that results from this struggle between shadow and light, from which it is impossible to disengage. Clearly this moment consists of an infinity of colors, sounds, voices, and dreams. It is the irregular motion of the *spiritus phantasticus*.

Agathe is the mystical sister who, together with her brother, holds the key of this work. But the relationship between sister and *artifex* represents how much happens in the work itself. In their dialogue, it is as if brother and sister were animated by a nostalgia to blend together, to pass into each other—that is, to reproduce or reformulate their common single embryo. They are, it is true, separated and abandoned, but their unity has not been lost, and they seem drawn to it. Brother and sister need to *join* each other. In the marvelous vehicle of their dialogue, they tend to produce this conjunction. That is why calling each other brother and sister is not enough, nor is it enough to call each other twins, or even Siamese twins, in order to express the dream of "being two creatures and one," to express this quintessence of *imaginatio*, whose effect "was no different from that of a dream escaped from the confines of the night."

Only for a marvelous and strange instant does this dream of unification appear to be realized. "When Agathe had overcome her fright, . . . by one of those cases that no one can control, she found herself marvelously satisfied and indeed undisturbed by any earthly anxiety. He carried her, holding her sweetly close, across the dark-ening room to the window, and he placed her down next to him in the mild darkness of the evening that washed over her face like a flood of tears." Here it seems the *attention* succeeds in becoming truly free of disturbance and that the dialogue is transfigured into pure, interior prayer. This instant surprises the couple and reveals their love to them. It seems strangely distant from the pure force necessary to the development of the work. "They shared the fraternal figure of their own bodies, as both had grown from a single seed." Musil clarifies the symbolism even more directly with Ulrich's closing words: "Ulrich said foolishly, as if speaking into the void, 'You are the moon . . . ' Agathe understood. Ulrich said, 'You flew to the moon, and the moon gave you back to me.' " Silly lunar clichés? "Ulrich said, 'It is an *image*—we were outside of ourselves. We exchanged bodies without touching." What does *image* mean? To exaggerate reality? But reality here had been grand! Image is *fabulieren* with the star, and here the star indicates the twins' shared roots. "What brought us together from the very first could well be called a lunar lifetime of moonlit nights." Agathe resembles Pierrot Lunaire, who certainly has nothing to do with the romanticism of *Claire de lune*, but "must be the fragment of another life." Then Agathe truly understands—her attention opens the gates of her heart to the meaning of her brother's words: "he probably wanted to say, 'Why don't you know a spell that would keep all that from dividing us at the last moment?' "

The "last love story that could ever be" (Bazlen hits this nail on the head) ends on this note of disturbing proximity to the *coniunctio*. Even so, questions do not cease: "Toward what direction do our feelings turn? Toward what transformation and transfiguration of the real world and real people?" Does this questioning of attention sustain the heart and its *Gelassenheit*, or is it rather a discussion with the enemy, not knowing how to disengage from the struggle and passion of the dialectic? Does that strange and marvelous moment become truly "imagined" or, rather, pinned down anew in the vortex of the discussion? The "great truth" that is perhaps hidden behind the "common" truth remains an impossible question. The *imaginatio* that the conversation unfolds does not succeed in producing the Millennium. Making the dialogue deeper, opening the abyss to its common roots, emptying out the diabolical *Selbstheit* [selfhood], it seems to encounter ever renewed resistance or new points upon which it needs to rest and reflect. Infinite arguments appear, disappear, and reappear in the light of the sister's lunar beams. They seem to pour out interminably. The essay form returns, but as if in an atmosphere that ignores its critical arrogance. The opposite is also true. In conversations of love, agonistic forms of critical discourse return. The story is interrupted by the inseparability of the two dimensions. To conclude it would be to decide an ending, decide a solution that seems undecidable: either killing the voice of the twins, that singular language in which they had grown and in which they had found each other as the original One or—in the nihilistic negation of the *imaginatio*—dissolving that experience, the strange, marvelous event that happened in the mild darkness of the evening, in exaggeration, emphasis, and fantasy. The novel ends instead on a perfectly suspended note. On that note, it is definitive.

Every experience lives and becomes significant only upon the point of dissolving into the void, of being as if it had never been. But this experience, in its turn, dissolves ever anew the mere nihilism of reflecting and doing. We only have the endlessness of the relationship—therefore, not the perfect conjunction, and even less the child that it promises. We can ask what is the *imaginatio*, but the *imaginatio* remains sterile. The untold and untellable story is that of the conjunction and its creation. The image of *Geschwisterliebe*'s sterility transcends the space of mere dissolution of quality and of the typically constructive (*typisch aufbauend*) reason that emerges from it. The facile disenchantment and the simplex figure of "no illusions," are, once again, the distant past of Ulrich's story. His ruin is an absolutely new development: the symbolic creativity of *imaginatio*. The *Geschwisterliebe* is sterile when it comes to shedding light on an answer that touches all of life's problems, that combines the deepest forms of attention to every trifle with the feeling that "nothing is important." But *Geschwisterliebe* was able to plumb the depths of this problem. These two stances toward reality partake of each other reciprocally only once in a while, "in a propitious moment," secret and fundamentally incommunicable. The node that links brother and sister is the repetition of these moments and of the contradictory pathway that leads to them and forks off from them again toward the Millennium. The untellable story is the end of the story, where the end should be reconciled with the beginning. The untellable story is the point where the end reveals itself as the beginning. But it is this that constitutes the authentic sterility of *Geschwisterliebe*: that the circle is broken forever, that once broken it can never be critically or reflexively made whole again, that whoever has no home now can never have one. Many marvelous things can happen to Ulrich—troubled love, of course, "anything but simple." Profane illuminations can surprise him, coming out of the intricacies of facts and conjectures, like a flame that "dies down and droops, holds its breath, and then flares up even higher."

The Misfit

Hugo von Hofmannsthal's great *Lustspiel* [comedy] of 1920, *Der Schwierige*,[37] takes up the problem of language at the point where the *Chandosbrief* had left off. What happens to someone who snaps out of the illusion that words possess denotative ability? What happens to someone who stops believing the myth of the ontological foundation of language, or the pretext of the perfect transparency and communicability of all nouns? In other words, what happens to someone who emerges from the "war" of the *Chandosbrief*, from physical collapse, from *finis Austriae*? What happens to someone who "privately" keeps a memento of reconciliation and agreement among people?

In comedy no relevance is accorded to things; there is no "landscape." The protagonists are condemned to words—but words do not work as communication. They merely inform. To communicate is impossible, because where there is a failure of the ontological relationship between sign and world, communication can happen only through "tone." But the range of tones is infinite and infinitely varied—the length of a pause, the intensity of a single pronounced syllable, the context of a word, the sound of the voice. "Tone" is incommunicable: it is a gesture, whose connection to fact, plain to all, is a priori unexplainable.

So, if conversation, which is the beginning of comedy, is articulated only as information, which consists of signs and gestures that are denotative only by convention, then misunderstandings are organically laid into its development. To speak (and it is necessary to speak since we are fixed in a universe of *Konversation*) is "to present images." But nothing attests to the descriptive and denotative "truth" of these images, of these *Bilder*. Presenting images, as Emil Staiger demonstrates, is inextricably connected to misunderstandings and mistakes.[38] Comedy shows all the possible gradations of misunderstanding, of *Missverständis*—tricks, slapstick, situations, incomprehension. Even the blank page of silence, as the negative side of language, is a source of error. Misunderstanding appears with every line of speech or its opposite, reticence. The "ideological," in other words, cannot be extricated from the very act of self-expression. A perfectly transparent and perfectly communicable language is an impossible utopia. The notion that natural language could be logical or could be reduced to a logical unity is an impossible utopia. The will to be "definitive," the pretext of using language in terms that are non-illusory and categorically univocal, is implacably parodied in the figure of Stani, Hans Karl's nephew. And it is not as if he had no memory or experience of fracture.

Misunderstanding has an even more essential foundation. It derives from the primal tragic condition of speaking. As Staiger explains in his fundamental essay, speaking means *not* being unified with things. Speaking is not, as it might appear to one with a naive faith in language, the apex and synthesis of things, but on the contrary, departure from them, from their *Wesen* [essence]. Here is the radical metaphysics of misunderstanding: it is impossible to speak without "presenting images" of *Wesen*, without "giving the impression" of naming it—and even the very act of speaking demonstrates the fallacy of the image and the impossibility of the name. The character of Hans Karl connects to this stinging contradiction. He recognizes it and he *lives by* it. It remains hidden to the others, and they merely *live in* it. Hans Karl recognizes the indecency of faith in words as an expression of *Wesen*. That kind of faith is possible only to those who are dominated by an *indezente Selbstüberschätzung* [arrogance]—to those who believe their own linguistic conventions to be the Name of the Spirit of Time. There are no *sacred* words. It is indecent to presume that one's own words can be torches to light others' deeds and inevitable "conversations."

If words cannot possess things, they are even less able to possess the essence, the soul, of the speaker. Hans Karl cannot "explain himself." Not a misfit, but a man for whom nothing fits (Mittner), Hans Karl does not succeed in explaining and understanding the factual situation in which he finds himself, the *Gegen-stand*, or in explaining and understanding himself. "But really you do *not* see the eye" (*Tractatus*, 5.663); "The subject does not belong to the world: rather, it is a limit of the world" (5.632); "The self of solipsism shrinks to a point without extension, and there remains the reality coordinated with it" (5.64). *De nobis ipsis silemus. De re agitur.* [We say nothing of ourselves; we stir things up.] But which reality? And how coordinated with our signs? Can only propositions in the natural sciences be utterable? But then, wouldn't they be illusory, *Konversation* dreams? Isn't natural language perhaps connected to the conventionality of conversation? No decree can ever remedy it. Its misunderstanding cannot be eliminated. Its fault is independent of my willing what-the-world-is. That is why Hans Karl must speak, independently of his will, knowing that he brings to consciousness only misunderstandings, "in spite of all and everything." Speaking is hesitation, silence, gesture, and tone, with the burden of possible, inevitable, desired misunderstandings, with floods of senseless words. Hans Karl is condemned to speak. And the deep, tragic paradox of Hofmannsthal's work consists in its being a comedy—a *Lustspiel*, a work "made to be spoken" and even structured around a persona that points to speech as a disgrace and silence as the only (yet impossible) decency (Staiger).

But this is exactly where a miracle seems to happen. The universe of mere signs and blunders, where all is *Konversation* and *Konvention*, seems finally to "redeem" itself. The conclusion of Hofmannsthal's paradoxical *Lustspiel* diverges profoundly from the negative closure of the *Chandosbrief* and from the unnavigable labyrinth of *Andreas* as well. With no explanation, the misfit suddenly succeeds at something—and it is something that concerns "our vital problems." The possibility arises of being understood, of being revealed, of a relationship that arches beyond misunderstanding. Nor does this relationship resemble Musil's *Geschwisterliebe*, since the latter presents itself as the possibility of real, everyday communication, aesthetic even prior to being ethical. The last scene between Hans Karl and Helene indicates, in Hofmannsthal, the outermost edge of a radically contradictory utopia: to find a place in the world, within *Konversation* and *Konvention*, to succeed in communicating—to find the essence of the relationship in common words. This utopia has no foundation in the severe logic of the work. Certainly, it is not Hans Karl directly who converts the meaning of it. It is Helene. Hans Karl wants with all of his power to find himself in his friend's words. "Do you understand everything?" "Do you know all this?" And then, "You knew it all . . . " "How well you say it!" But neither does this moment come near the case, which practically delivers itself from all distress, from *Geschwisterliebe*. The tragic paradox of *Lustspiel* is betrayed in this conclusion. Hofmannsthal will no longer have the "courage" of such conclusions. Inaccessible, *Der Turm* and *Andreas* will resist the "indecency" of lighting pointless candles of hope at the end. *Der Schwierige* truly ends not in a marriage ceremony, but in a spoken marriage in the stupendous scene of Hans Karl with Toinette. Hans Karl speaks about marriage as a case where timing and necessity converge, as a case of reconciliation, forgiveness, and resistance all together. He *must* speak of marriage as the unspeakable paradox that Thomas Mann also described in the same period, although without Hofmannsthal's sad awareness. "It is a matter not only of locating the flesh in spirit, but also vice versa, locating the spirit in flesh: Indeed, this above all, given that there is nothing sacred that is purely spiritual." How can Toinette understand him? She interrupts him, misunderstanding him completely. In the words of Hans Karl, marriage (which in Mann is still, however paradoxically, an institution) is represented in the farewell, which is the very essence of the term "sacred": separated, distinct, divided off, alone. In the end, however, Helene's courage and force of desire seem to be enough to get him back, as if Hans Karl's refusal were the result only of his existential condition and not of the metaphysical complex of relationships between words and world. Certainly the others—Stani and Crescence—see only convention in marriage, but that is not how it is. Hidden behind this aspect, protected from misunderstanding like Kierkegaardian knights of faith, Hans Karl and Helene are *pledged* to each other. They *believe* they are pledged to each other, to have quieted their own silence. And this faith consumes the most extreme, deep, and painful *Missverständis*, so essential that not even Hans Karl can admit it, from which Hofmannsthal himself pulls away. But for the last time: the "sacred" of *Der Schwierige* is represented in *Die Frau ohne Schatten* only as a perfect utopia, to be lost, finally, in the labyrinthine sign of *Andreas*. The misfit is the bridge between the immediate negative of the *Chandosbrief* and the awareness, already implicit in *Andreas* and in *Der Turm* and total only in Musil's novel, that the story does not function to say (which would be impossible) or even to hide, but to demonstrate that which cannot be said.

Acheronta Movebo

I shall stir up hell: "Acheronta movebo." Freud used this epigraph (the fury's oath from *Aeneid* VII) to seal his own work, and Hofmannsthal has the Doctor swear it to Julian at the end of Act II of *Der Turm*.[39] "I shall unclose the gates of hell and shall employ the lowest of the low. . . . Mighty is the age that wishes to renew itself through nobility." *Acheronta movebo* is an oath "to free the forces." This falls to the Doctor: "in the end there is a higher judge." At the beginning of Act IV, in the first version of 1925, Julian, in a stupendous dialogue with Sigismund played entirely upon misunderstandings, now becomes a full dramatic figure and takes up the Doctor's words: "It is true what someone said, that we need to uncap hell." And again when he begins to understand Olivier's betrayal and when the revolt of the *Namenlosen*, the No Names, begins to spread, "I unchained hell and now hell has free passage. So I must look it in the face."

The motif has a double personality, and this indicates the specifically equivocal nature of Hofmannsthal's late work. Julian misrepresents the hermetic figure of the Doctor. The Doctor is a psychopomp: he wants to ferry Sigismund's soul toward the light of awareness and the dignity of man. But Julian wants to free him in order to have him and put him into action. The Doctor leads to complete dispossession of the sacred dialogue between spirit and spirit; Julian, to the renewal of the terrestrial realm. Both of them

1900

1925

lead, both assume in a certain way the figure of the psychopomp—
but their alliance is a hybrid, a diabolical amalgam between two
forces of the soul that inhibits the success of the work just as it will
inhibit John Dee, as imagined by Gustave Meyrink in *The Angel of
the Western Window*. The misunderstanding, in fact, is not Julian's
alone. The Doctor joins Julian and consents to his plans. He
speaks of spiritual rebirth and of a new Adam, but he never opposes Julian's profane designs. He limits himself to recognizing
them, which is what takes place in the dialogue in Act I, without
impeding or combatting them (as the Beggar, by contrast, does
with King Basilio in *Life Is a Dream*). Julian and the Doctor ac-
cept misunderstanding, and they pursue their own works along its
fault lines. The figure of the psychopomp becomes a double figure, and its two faces seek in vain to reconcile themselves. The
Doctor himself, in fact, is a strange and disquieting hermit: he does
not guide beyond the material realm to a symbolic death that
promises resurrection into a divine state, nor does he approach the
divine, but he causes one to wake up in the world. He is the magician who puts Sigismund to sleep, who closes him into a hermetic dream, but only until he is carried into the presence of the
King and into a vortex of power games. It would be possible to say
that the Doctor tends dangerously close to the profane in mistaking his mission and that Julian (as Sigismund constantly reminds
him) also misrepresents his own most intimate and hidden voca-
tion in following the mirage of power.

To which of the two figures, or to which of the contradictory
tendencies that they express, does Sigismund belong? He confirms
that Julian is his teacher. But his teaching was involuntary, or
rather, Sigismund deluded himself about what it meant. Julian
taught Sigismund that "wir sind aus solchem Zeug, wie das zu
Träumen," that we are such stuff as dreams are made on, but he
meant, in reality, to mold him into "no illusions," ready for orders
and for action. In the first version of the play, it seems in some way
that this teaching is realized. Sigismund assumes power and learns
"in haste the language of the world," even if he is only an *interré*.
And yet, he still wants the Doctor beside him, whose wisdom he

loves. ("Wisdom isn't merely renting space in you; in you it lives in its own house.") In the first version, Sigismund seems to collect himself at the point where the Doctor's and Julian's paths of destiny cross. But in reality it is nothing other than a crossing of misunderstandings, which renders Sigismund's material extremely weak, too mortal, and makes the conclusion of the work "unacceptable" to Hofmannsthal. It is no accident that, in the last acts of the 1925 version, the figure of the Doctor appears faded and insignificant, while in the final version he holds the key dialogue with Olivier.

In the final version, Sigismund does not belong to either of the two faces of the psychopomp. He remains uncollapsable before Julian's misunderstandings, and he alone recites that prayer that the others refuse to say, right to the end. Not even the Doctor, who had procured a symbolic death for him only to bring him back before his earthly father, can "comprehend" his horizon anymore. Both give Sigismund "words of comfort in this desert of life," and now these words flow in him with no obstacles. He is *alone*, freed from both of them—from Julian's "nothing" and from the Doctor's imposing speeches to Olivier. He knows what neither Julian nor the Doctor knows, that "the tongue is too thick" to say what is truly worth saying. He has taken a lesson from both of them that they gave involuntarily. A reversal therefore takes place: Sigismund becomes the psychopomp. It is he who carries Julian's hidden soul to light, and the Doctor's as well. He carries souls with him on his way to his own destiny, while he abandons the "body" of his teachers to the "cold and sober" daytime of the No Names.

The Doctor is never on the same plane as Julian, even if, in the final and (in my opinion) truly definitive version, Sigismund disentangles himself from the misunderstandings underlying his relationship with the Doctor and Julian and between the two of them with each other. What underworld does the Doctor want to stir up? The first act gives no cause to doubt the intentions of this hermetic figure. He rises up against the monstrous crime "that cries to heaven," committed in the person of Sigismund in name of the interests of the state. Wherever these crimes are committed, they open a vortex that carries everything down, because "everything holds together," and it is not possible to fix a part without renewing the whole. Only charlatans, he says, responding to Julian, can pretend to heal the body while the soul of the world is sick. The Doctor announces the need for a *renovatio*, the very stamp of which is on Sigismund, on Sigismund the victim. This idea of the whole, this ideal of a consonant universe composed of different worlds and disparate elements, is evidently derived from hermetic and Neoplatonic traditions. Strains of Paracelsus and of Pico's *De dignitate hominis* can be discerned in the figure of the Doctor. In other words, the Doctor is the image of the "unfinished dawn"[40] destined for ruin in Olivier's here-and-now, in this "naked reality" that holds many prisoners. With an extraordinarily keen cultural sense, Hofmannsthal captures in *Der Turm* (in the final version) the complex image of that utopia and the cause of its impotence.

The symbols are easily decipherable and send us back to the ones we already saw in the analysis of Musil's married couple. Raw material is locked in the "oven," where no artifice may free its soul. The Doctor bears light into the midst of this material, and he discovers that a ray must have already penetrated there and roused its "most profound essence." In the depths of dejection, the Doctor discovers this imprisoned ray and learns that his task is to free it, purify it, and pour it forth. Even in the midst of filth the possibility of a quintessence is hidden, and the entire work appeals to quintessence. A "gold" that is formed slowly, through nature's design, is hidden in the depth of misery, just as "alcohol appears in our muscles as soon as putrefaction emits its first breath. From mortal poison the energy of health." (This, of course, is the basic principle of Paracelsian medicine.) The Doctor discovers Sigismund the animal, pure material, abiding in his lair, and the Doctor needs to flush him out of this "abiding," and make the material volatile. This is also Julian's objective. But Julian seeks fool's gold; his intentions are evil. The Doctor, consenting to Julian's plan, becomes an accomplice. He catches the disease of the tower guard. He can succeed in no undertaking where the *intentio* is not perfectly direct. He must fail—for reasons that are different from, and yet secretly complementary to, those that render the distress in Agathe and Ulrich's love insurmountable.

Let us say that impure *artifex* is the flip side of the figure of the Doctor and that it reveals itself precisely in the motto, *Acheronta movebo*. This slogan expresses the aspect of hermeticism that comes closest to *hubris prometeica*, a gesture of challenging the Olympians (in Virgil, the fury's "flectere si nequeo superos, Acheronta movebo"—if I cannot sway the heavens, I shall rouse up hell). The price of this gesture consists in ignoring the end of the work. It does not end in the hands of the Doctor. He penetrates into Sigismund's lair and is able to bring him out; but that is the extent of his science. The possibility of misunderstanding everyone and everything rests on this essential ignorance, from which Sigismund is freed only in silence and in a death that is nothing more than a symbolic voyage. The Doctor's Paracelsian magic is, in effect, interrupted. *De dignitate hominis* is seen from the standpoint of its failure. The "fallen" psychopomp brings Sigismund out of his past, from the dark forces that imprison him there. He wants to heal him of the insupportable weight of his relationship with a father who did not know—because of the blow that paralyzed him (he cannot even move in his cell)—that the son had killed his mother coming into the world. But this cannot be understood as *renovatio*, nor can it hide the vortex that "carries everything down." Doesn't Sigismund give the Doctor's work back to the King? Or to Julian's designs? Or to the nameless power of Olivier? The figure of the Doctor is torn and his most profound calling seems incomprehensible and incommunicable in Olivier's world. In their dialogue with the No Names, the Doctor cannot even pronounce it. He seeks in vain to demonstrate to the new power the height, the purity, and innocence of the creature that he has raised up out of the muck. His language appears to Olivier a mixture of doctor and priest and his world "a truckload of walking clowns." The intrinsic groundlessness and negativity of the "Olivierian Principle" is not revealed—as I have already demonstrated in "Intransitabili utopie"—through the words of the Doctor. It is revealed in the solitary figure of Sigismund, who finally overtakes his teachers.

This is also what happens in the utopia of the children who are called upon to make new laws (clearly modeled on the esoteric accents of Shakespeare's later plays).[41]

There is no *symbol* that can hold together the hermetic magic of Paracelsus, the unfinished utopia of consonance, and the Freudian analysis of dreams; Pico's *De dignitate* and "the language of the world"; the meeting of youths in Shakespeare's *The Tempest*, the *Kinderkönig* of *Der Turm*, the utopia and the earthly *renovatio* that Julian pursues and that the Doctor, torn within, should sustain. All of these unresolvable contradictions intersect in the image of the Doctor. Hofmannsthal infused him with his most erudite and disparate knowledge. The "Doctor of Dreams" knows better than anyone that "the powerful bosom of a man who dreams, who creates his own world," is a candidate for the stars, beyond the reach of the torments and overpowering forces that bring down "obscure" men. And yet, it is he who leads Sigismund to his reawakening, into the cold light of the dawning day that dissolves dreams, that reveals the impotence, finally, of *imaginatio*. The memory of the hermetic psychopomp may be kept in the here and now only in a figure that inverts its *itinerarium*.

The Private Adolf Loos

Another misfit, in those same years, experienced Hans Karl's contradictions. Another master of the German language, Adolf Loos, could not resist the perfect measure of the sign and the perfect ineffability of the sacred. He let himself be tempted by the indecent self-love (*Selbstüberschätzung*) of believing, in spite of everything, his own signs to be *more* than signs and their power to be the expression of laws based in aesthetic, ethical, and ontological foundations. Temptation erupted in him, not merely to show, but to *speak* das Mystische, and he could not stop it.

In order to understand the extent to which Loos's temptation ran counter to the artists of the period, it is enough to observe his smile when he visits the "invented" artist colony on Mathildenhöhe in Darmstadt. "Of Behrens's house Loos said, 'It would make a nice design for a necktie,' and broke into a laugh."[42] It was modern, certainly. But the modern is contingent, current, quotidian. There is no value in the modern: its aim is far from the necessary or the good or the more "advanced," as the self-styled avant-garde's nineteenth-century rhetoric of progress would have it. Change? You want to put a *modern* face on this antique building? Ask Loos and his bunch. You want new marble and wood walls to mess up the marvelous landscape that you see from this window? Don't you understand that it is precisely the simplicity of these walls that reinforces a hundred times the impression made by this interior?

Love of materials is one expression of this culture. It expresses the impossibility of conceiving material egocentrically as a simple medium at the disposition of the artist. Moreover, it expresses the impossibility of assuming the perspective of the ego as the only organizing language, as the only word of power. Note the relationship of Loos with the marble of Casa Müller: he uses imperfect marble that he found in storage, forgotten, set aside. Note his work on the ceiling of the American Bar: the Italian artisan whose job was to mount the slabs of marble was certain they would fall down, and Loos answered him calmly, "Just put up the ceiling." "And the ceiling is still in place, after more than twenty years." And once, interrupting his wife in the bath, "You want to be my wife? You, who care nothing for material? You have no idea how I fought my entire life against senselessness (*Sinnlosigkeit*), against *das Ornament*, against squandering forces, against wasting material? And you, my wife, you don't care at all if that excellent soap comes to ruin *sinnlos* in the water?" Loos's care for material and struggle against the principles of ornament is accompanied by a veneration for tidiness. It permeated him to the point of mania for the smallest details, even of his posture. This aspect could not be preserved by the "modern" historians of constructive functionality and transparent simplicity. Loos would have replied to their laughable and persistent progressivism with the story about Reb Hirsch the Servant. Rabbi Mendel's son was surprised to see Zvi Hirsch the servant cleaning the shul with his customary enthusiasm the very morning after his wedding. Disturbed by this, he went to his father and said, "It is not right that your servant neglects his wedding celebration and busies himself with such vile work during the seven-day feast." Rabbi Mendel of Rymanov answered, "My son, with this news you bring me great joy. I was very worried, wondering how we might be able to pray today if the servant Zvi Hirsch had not cleaned the shul, since cleanliness chases all the demons away and brings in pure air, so we can pray."

Loos's difficulties emerge, as we shall see, in the relationship between the image of the building and its interior, between Hans Karl's *Konversation-Konvention* and his holy ineffable. Function is the architect's business, simple functions, those that are possible to classify, according to the *Tractatus*, as the poverty of the utterable. The kitchen is utterable: the little kitchen in Casa Müller, for instance, small, narrow, practically a dining car. The staircase is utterable: like a stepladder on a boat. ("The ship is the model for a modern house.") The exterior, the façade, is utterable: its language should be the language of the street, of the square, of the city, in that infinite and variable chain of elements that no serious architect can ever dream of reinventing, constructing, defining, or reforming (that immortal, indecent *Selbstüberschätzung* of the architect/artist). But the house is not merely the utterable. With no dialectical bridge, it nevertheless exists and *becomes* the *intérieur*. It is pointless to pretend that the language of architecture is complete, that its word is definitive. Its word is powerless to measure experience, to foresee the future, to represent tone and gesture. All of which is concealed to the utterable in the utopian space of the *intérieur*. "The head of the household has an entire life ahead," in order to grow within and together with the house, and to put everything pleasing into place for the future. The architect should "make an empty space" within the house, in its interior. There is an article of faith about houses that will never be spoken in architecture, much less "resolved," that composition is powerless and the majesty of the artist is silence. "The bedroom, Lerle, is private and holy—no stranger can defile it."

And yet even this private Loos, a misfit, composed of quick jabs and unheard one-liners (the veins of the imperfect marble, its minimal, invisible depth, the classic quote about Haus Rufer) seeks finally to go beyond the limits of his own language. Hans Karl's marriage celebration is "haphazard" (in comparison with the paradoxical logic of the *Lustspiel*). Loos's urban pretension, his later projects for systematizing and ordering life according to values, is "haphazard" (in comparison with *Nihilismus-Haus*, with the unresolvable tension of interior with exterior). And the fall of Loos is far more strident and painful than Hofmannsthal's ephemeral decline. "Every man ought to have his own little house and his own garden. Rentals ought to be for commercial activity only. In England there are entire commercial neighborhoods, and the people live in cottages outside of town." Incredibly, the blind philistinism of an intellectual faced with a crowd reappears, a thousand miles this side of Nietzsche. It is philistinism that brought Wittgenstein to the point of disgust. It is the impossibility of any great intellectual of crisis, of any misfit who has ever known how to manage his life, seeing it through to the point of having it in retrospect, to tolerate the logic of the *Tractatus*. But to have foreseen it, and to have begun to write it down, is too much. "Wer gross denkt muss gross irren"—whoever thinks grandly must make grand mistakes.

Lou's Buttons

The reflective "stroll" that Lou Andreas-Salomé proposes in "Zum Typus Weib" begins with a story of buttons.[43] The buttons represent the quintessence of all that is "not given away but rather collected," the quintessence of the inalienable, of the non-equivalent. In this sense buttons are the opposite of coins: they oppose division, circulation, and exchange with the principle of the secret and the hidden. Coins exist exclusively in an external and public dimension. Buttons, on the other hand, are an unattainable maternal relic, kept in the innermost part of a virgin mountain. (Lou makes the association with the Jungfrau.) Coins are collected as values to be spent, and spending brings about in turn an acquisition, a possession. Buttons are put away as *unicum*, as treasure. Coins are intrinsically productive. They are never left out in the open, but they open things up in the sense that they carry everything into the domain of the merely acquirable. Coins turn all things into possessions. Buttons jealously guard their own unproductivity. They flee from sight and hide themselves as much as possible in a "box of wonders." It is easy to see how Lou connects univocal masculine aggressivity to the coin's productivity, as well as the unhappiness of man's "hurried step." The peculiar lingering of women at the original communion of spirit and sense (to whatever extent this image is increasingly "obscured" by the very progress of the spiritual, by the *Geist* considered in opposition to the *Seele*) seems to rest in the marginal, apparently derelict and insignificant figure of the button. Buttons represent the rest of productivity, all that remains and resists its typically constructive (*typisch aufbauend*) language. Resistance to the universe of equivalence takes on the form of reduction to the margins of insignificance.

How to collect buttons? And where to find them? Does the possibility still exist for a "collection zone" removed from the market of visible things? This zone is interior, but not every interior can be a collection zone for that which survives in the unproductive. The difficulty of defining such a zone results from the fact that it must appear in relationship with the unhappiness of the productive, with the sacrifice that it entails. If this dimension were ignored or removed, the figure of the button would have to be relegated to a simply chronological past, to absolutely lost time, of which it would be false even to speak. If the childhood of buttons exists and works, it ought to appear in the here-and-now, in connection with the domain of coins, the market that trades and exchanges money, the street where it circulates. The "collection zone" should exist *in* the productivity of the metropolis. But how is this possible?

Lou does not get the most out of this problem, since the details of her buttons' childhood are unclear. She appears to believe that childhood can be preserved as such, that a "box of wonders" can protect childhood as childhood. But if buttons are not marginalized into small change by the metropolis, they are fetishistically transformed into closely guarded treasure, and they cease to exist as an authentic childhood. They return to being a possession, albeit an unproductive one. Unproductivity is not enough to "go beyond" the language of the metropolis. Childhood must find its own interior within its relationship to the metropolis.

Not every interior is a "collection zone." Bad poetry (*Heimatkunst*), for instance, that exalts home as protection from the metropolis is the opposite of a collection zone. The home wants to be seen as a treasure chest, but that very desire exhibits its own interior and makes it visible. What is brought out and made visible while pretending to be a place of non-equivalence is a travesty of the coin, not its opposite. And vice versa, the perfectly metropolitan home has no interior. It assumes programmatically that internal structure and arrangement are transparent, that they are clearly and simply understood in the vision of the whole. Between interior and exterior there is nothing but an insoluble functional bond. The metropolitan home (the building) correctly criticizes false childhood in the "box of wonders," while unknowingly representing its simple reverse, its exact counterpoint, in the space of *Modernität*. Even in that box, there is nothing hidden or secret. Its plan tends to the same pure visibility of the metropolitan home. That is why the treasure chest is truly nothing other than a tattoo image of the metropolis. Nothing more than its presence in the metropolitan fabric can render evident its intrinsic tendency to liquidate any possible collection zone.

An interior that protects buttons can only exist in a metropolis, and in absolute contrast with its exterior. The exterior should not betray the things collected in its interior. The exterior resides in the same dimension and sense as coins, should, in fact, be worth pure and perfect money, should *function* in the universe of circulation and trade. This universe should not be adorned, it should just work. If there is an authentic "collection zone," it can only be found within such a language, the unproductive flip side of the perfect coin. This is not to say that the exterior may be treated as a sort of obstacle or material impediment to *Seele*. On the contrary, the reified purity of the exterior is the very factor that permits an authentic interior. If the exterior were to be treated in allusive forms or were to be forced to indicate its interior metaphorically or, again, were to be understood as an obstacle, as not-I—if, that is, the awful late-Romantic ideology of the purpose of building were to prevail again, we would necessarily sink into ornament (which has its own a priori conditions in the dialectic of allusiveness). We would then conceive interiors as imperfect unless expressed, turned into language. It would be impossible to conceive any interior as childhood. There can be no interiors except where the exterior is felt purely and perfectly—studied, analyzed, calculated, and realized with maximum rigor in its own rhythm and relative to the rhythm of the metropolis. Only where the exterior is

adored the way Kraus adored language can another dimension of it
show up, as inalienable as it is unproductive, an *internal* childhood
of language. That is why the "collection zone" is not exactly the
"poetic ensemble" of interior and exterior (the "box of wonders")
or the harmony of the two, but neither is it simply the interior in
and of itself. The "collection zone" is the *difference* between interior
and exterior—this impalpable *utopia* that separates them metaphysically at the same time that it renders them inseparable.

It is so difficult to understand these rambles that Loos can still
pass for a pioneer and prophet of modernity, while the calculated
perfection of his exteriors is a Krausian *pietas* for language, stripped
of the totalizing and patriarchal ethics of *Die Fackel*, intent upon
reducing things to the transparence of linguistic order. The exterior
of the possible "collection zone" is pure language, charged with its
history, with its difficult links, with its inertia that requires such
tireless patience, but not transparence. Certainly there is nothing
(like a shop sign) to indicate from the exterior that there is an interior to this language. But neither should anything indicate that
there is not, as happens with the treasure chest, with allusive ornament, or with the "virile statements" of happily metropolitan
buildings. This exterior does not express, does not produce, has no
transparence. And for these very reasons it can perhaps safeguard
an interior, an authentic "collection zone." It "leaves room," so to
speak, for the possibility of an interior.

This matter of Loos "leaving room" for a "collection zone" in
the midst of (coolly recognized) "metropolis" conditions and his
concern for the possibility of such a place, without nostalgia for
the impossible negation of the exterior—this could be called Loos's
deeply feminine side. In the interior of his house (now, alas, "visible" only at the Museum of the City of Vienna) all of this is made
clear, even formally. But this is not the essence. The essence is the
gulf of difference carved out between exterior and interior, not the
formal solution discovered in the composition of one or the other.
This gulf is the secret of Loos's house: the measure of this difference is the measure of Loos's concern for Lou's buttons, that they
should have a place outside of the treasure chest.

In a fine passage, Eugénie Lemoine-Luccioni writes of the "intimate bond between a woman and her things." Without things, women are lost. Their things inhabit an interior, and they cannot be transformed into coins. The house where they are collected should be inhabitable, not visible from the exterior. The act of seeing a house is fundamentally different from dwelling in it. To define the possibility of dwelling in a house by this difference and not abstractly in and of itself, as if dealing with a question of style or furniture, is, I would say, Loos's feminine greatness. He is concerned with a space where things are safe in their intimate associations with our experience, where things are infused with those *Extrakte des Lebens* that form life's experience. To continue in Altenberg's line, such things are invalid for going out and producing, but they are not therefore a literary protest against metropolis, technology, and *Zivilisation*. In fact, the retreat into the interior means perhaps that the world is by now "simply full of things (an indefinite plural"; Lemoine-Luccioni) or, in other words, that things are by now only perfectly manipulable, alienable, destitute of any consistency, and separated from Being. These things merely exist, are seen, are spoken about. The things that Andreas-Salomé mentions hearken, rather, to a forgotten dimension of dwelling and of experience connected to dwelling. The difference in Loos between seeing and dwelling, between exterior and interior, seeks to provide a space where this dimension can be collected. This difference is the *extreme interior*.

Rilke's dolls stand metaphysically opposite the soul of Lou's things.[44] Impenetrable, rumpled, damaged, impure, "privy to the earliest unutterable experiences of their owners," and even mistreated in some of those first unquiet moments of solitude, the dolls surrender to every tenderness, yet they remember none and are grateful for none. If now we take up a doll "from the cumulus of things that have become part of us," it practically revolts us with its "crass dearth of memory," its disproportionate lack of imagination. We are disconcerted by the sight of this "horrifying alien body, to whom we have given over our most genuine warmth." We wouldn't have traded that senseless bundle of material for anything, heavy and dumb, "stupid as a peasant Danae who is insignificant except for the golden rain of our unending inventions." Lou's buttons resemble rather "things that are part of us"—not only the flash of gems, but also domestic linens, the fingering of a violin, the most simple things that sink their roots in humanity: the "simple and condescending" soul of a ball, the inexhaustible soul of a picture book, the "surd, funnel-shaped soul of a bold tin horn." These are the things that aspire to the otherness of the interior and that render an interior necessary. The doll inhabits places of oblivion, remote hiding places, and when it re-emerges by chance, then our hatred for it erupts, unconsciously developed in the long hours in which we sat with it and pointlessly waited for a response.

The unresponsive doll still does not pass by in vain. Not only and not so much because "we had to have things like that, things which put up no resistance," but because the doll teaches us silence, "life's greatest silence, that always reappeared in our breathing, every time and in every place where we came to the edges of our existence" (*unseres Daseins*). The doll teaches us to recognize the soul's inclination, left over from childhood, toward all that is impossible and hopeless. The doll's absolute lack of imagination points out the silence that envelops us. And in this perspective, the doll's affinities with Lou's buttons emerge once again. The objects without which women seem lost are at once "things that are part of us" and dolls: Lou's buttons respond to the overflowing affection that cares for them, defines a dwelling. That affection points out the silence that this dwelling embraces and points out the soul's unstoppable inclination toward its own abyss. That is why the space of Lou's buttons resembles the hidden and forgotten space of the dolls. Something like the essence of the dolls is preserved in Lou's buttons.

At the crossroads where a doll's silence brings on an awareness of language in the dimension of "things that are part of us" and where those "things that are part of us" not only return our affections but also reveal their metaphysical tendency to silence—that is where the soul of the marionette appears to take shape. "Dolls are as in-

ferior to things as marionettes are superior to them." "A poet can
fall under the spell of a marionette, because a marionette has nothing but imagination." But a marionette's imagination is not simply
the quintessence of "things that are part of us." It compels us to
pose our inclination "beyond hope." The marionette is not the
pure and simple negation of the doll, just as Lou's buttons were
not.

This quality "beyond hoping" had already been indicated by
Kleist: to find the "brightest and most majestic" grace after having
traversed infinite consciousness, infinite reflection. The totally un-
conscious grace of marionettes seemed to Kleist characteristic of a
utopian grace available only after having tasted anew the fruit of
the tree of knowledge. This no-place is where the marionette is
hooked. The strings that animate it are like the long staircase the
gods used to descend in order to speak with humans. A bridge that
to us seems rickety is mysteriously solid for the marionette. Kleist's
nostalgia for marionettes is the nostalgia of the figure Plato speaks
of in the *Laws*, who is still "intertwined" with the cosmos, an ensemble of threads and interior strands that the gods use to pull him
and drive him. Marionettes keep the memory of the golden chain
that unified the universe with insoluble bonds.[45] Dolls have lost
this memory completely. Dolls, in fact, are characterized precisely
by their state of dejection, of collapse, of radical historicity. But
since the marionette is a utopia today, to rediscover its figure is
possible only by filling up the absolute void of the doll's silence
with nostalgia. If such a void were not formed in us since childhood, the marionette's quality "beyond hoping" would not have
been able to appear.

Klee's work is interlaced with these fleeting relationships between coin, "things that are part of us," buttons, dolls, and marionettes. Difficult affinities, paradoxical theophanies, ephemeral orders of movement and flight express themselves in these relationships. The figure of the Angel seems to sum them up and keep
them within itself. Its gaze is turned upon these things. It has to
compose them and put them in order so that it can save their essence from imminent fragmentation and contradiction. The angel

of *things* intuits the necessity of the process that leads from the soul in simple conversation with "things that are part of us" to naming, finally, the empty silence of the doll and from there to the divine figure of the marionette. The angel prevents the marionette from collapsing, as Hofmannsthal understood on that December evening in 1918 of which Burckhardt tells us. It prevents the marionette from retreating into an unutterable past. Klee's figures, Benjamin wrote, "are, so to speak, projected onto the drawing surface, and as a good car, even in the factory, obeys the necessity of the motor above all, so Klee's figures obey, in the expression of their forms, their 'interior' above all." So, these figures are essentially marionettes. The angel is the prince of marionettes. Loos's interiors would seem to be designed for such figures. In the compositional clarity and economy of these interiors, everything achieved through greatest exercise is made to appear natural and necessary. At the end of the road that brought us from coins to marionettes, we must try to imagine the pose of the latter, as if we had discovered it by good luck.

The Glass Chain

At the beginning of *Infanzia e storia*—a work I frequently refer to—Giorgio Agamben analyzes Walter Benjamin's extraordinary short essay of 1933, "Experience and Poverty."[46] The decline of experience or its current poverty (which, according to Agamben, the various philosophies of life affirm rather than refute) finds its exemplum in the presence of the "modern movement" in architecture. Functional architecture of "glass and steel" represents the programmatic liquidation of the very conditions of experience. Its stated goal is to make it impossible to leave a trace, to produce a hidden place, to macro-visualize the house as a mere edifice—not only its individual physical structure, but its relationship with the entire urban organization. For this idea of "pure transparence," glass is the building material par excellence, the prince of materials. Glass is the very principle of transparence. Benjamin quotes Paul Scheerbart, saying, "we can well speak of a *Glaskultur*. The new environment of glass will completely transform humanity. And one can only hope that the new civilization of glass will not run into too much opposition."

But glass is not merely, as Benjamin seems to believe, the enemy of all "auras." It attacks the very idea of interior. That is why Loos can never be confused, from any perspective, with Scheerbart's *Glaskultur*. Glass is only indirectly opposed to ownership. The essential objective of its *Kultur* consists in opposing whatever underlies a place where a "collection" becomes one's own inalienable experience. Glass is not opposed to ownership per se, but to the idea of an *inalienable* ownership. Displaying every possession, glass wants to turn it all to coin, to put it all on the market. *Glaskultur's* critique of ownership follows the lines of circulation and exchange exclusively. The uninterrupted flow of stimuli and insights in the glass and steel metropolis, the continuous "enrichment" of "spiritual" life,[47] profanes more than the ancient "aura." It desecrates the very possibility of experience. It brings out the poverty of experience. In a universal transparence, all things are assumed to be equivalent. The transparence of glass bares every interior, betraying it and delivering it to the equivalence of the passerby whose mourning dress Baudelaire sang about (in "A une passante"). This is the source of the names with no past in Scheerbart's novels, his "completely new creatures" (Benjamin), with their radical lack of an interior. These characters live in the open, but like Hofmannsthal's No Names, they are prisoners of Olivier's disenchantment.

We know that Loos's interiors are far from that plush furniture that even Benjamin seems to foist on him. An interior by Loos expresses a principle contrary to a nostalgic resistance to current developments, on the grounds of his energetic acceptance of the age, the visible sign in any society of its "best and brightest." From this point of departure, though, it is possible to render transparent the "aura" that is still dominant in *Glaskultur* and in its rhetoric of modernity. *Glaskultur* passes a death sentence over past experience. Its windows *reflect* current poverty. In spite of its gesture toward the avant-garde, which rejects inherited language and remains aware of its arbitrary (and not organic) structure, *Glaskultur* belongs to a perfectly logocentric civilization. Its will to bare, "demystify," and render everything transparent expresses a utopia of full, progressive identification between human and linguistic realms: every secret is told, every interior shown, every childhood exposed. Here language, and the power of language, is absolute. Its new ability to form free constructions is precisely what permits it to take full command of the subject/self. Freed finally even from the *intentio* of subject, language speaks, grows, and transforms itself. Man is the animal that language possesses, but it is a language of transparence, exposition, and production. It is a language of technology. It means concluding the very metaphysics of the self that says, "I think . . ." *Glaskultur* is only one of the forms such a conclusion may assume.

To *criticize* the limits of this power fails to express the power-lessness to endure it, but expresses rather the desire to traverse it and to manifest its organic ties to current poverty. *Glaskultur* uses every means it can to mystify its part in the current poverty. Consider Bruno Taut, who is broadly influenced by Scheerbart. When he illustrates his *Glashaus*, a model or platonic form of the glass house exhibited at Cologne in 1914, he speaks of a kaleidoscopically rich architecture, varied and fascinating. The principle of glass is here embellished and gilt with every word. Even the connection between intensity of urban stimulation and poverty of experience, highly present in Georg Simmel, vanishes. Every effort is made to harmonize the irresistible surge of *Glaskultur* with nostalgia for the soul and *Erlebnis*. Loss of experience is cosmogonically sublimated in that ingenuous facsimile of an alchemical experiment, the collection of drawings, dedicated to the spirit of Scheerbart, of *Der Weltbaumeister* (1920). Through successive operations of *separatio* and *coniunctio*, the perfect crystal for a house gleams in the light of the summer sun and to the singing of children, *das leuchtende Kristalhaus* [the glowing house of crystal]. The stone reveals its wonders. Here the principle of glass, far from being treated (as Benjamin believed) completely without illusions, presumes to disclose the quintessence of an interior. But the glass does not possess an interior to exhibit and therefore has none to negate in the absolute command of language. The interior that its word seems to magically produce is nothing but, again, "*blitzendes Glas*": the glass that reproduces its own sterile image. It reflects its own reflection. Lost experience is replaced with every wretched pan-cosmic *cupio dissolvi* of the individual and finite form. This is nothing but a road traveled in order to reach the point of departure: a chain of glass.

It must be added that glass has a totally different value in Mies van der Rohe, and that Benjamin should have turned to Mies, not to Scheerbart. Mies's transparence is total because it is born from the exact and truly desperate awareness that there is nothing left to "collect" and, therefore, nothing to make manifest. Glass no longer violates the interior, but appears, now, as a ghost of itself. Its function has become as "archaic" as the very thing it helped to destroy. Is this decree, which finally finds an exact definition in Mies, also applicable to the problem that captivates Loos? Where glass plays a fundamentally structural role, as in the American Bar for example, it reflects and multiplies an interior. It doesn't disclose an interior. It is as un-transparent as a smooth and precious plate of marble. Loos's tireless efforts to find ever more delicate and subtle marble plate clearly demonstrate how he was inclined to replace the principle of glass. The glass interior of the American Bar does not say that experience takes place there, and it does not emphasize the surrounding space as if it were a rediscovered treasure chest. Nor does it produce it in language—although it holds back its possible development. Glass dilates the interior into a long pause, into an enduring delay. In this delay the interior reflects itself in its *otherness* and reflects upon a possible zone for experience in a possible not-yet. It is indecent to pursue in reverse the no-more of experience, but it is just as indecent to declare that everything is just glass and steel. The possible does not advertise itself, does not shout, does not even leak a rumor. But perhaps it gives a meaning to silence and collection while waiting.

Invalid des Todes

Joseph Roth hated *Glaskultur* and understood the current poverty of experience. The complete uprooting of the very possibility of a zone of experience is Roth's great theme.

Roth's *Heimat* [native land] is a vast interior, an unconfined zone of experience, where the Hapsburg Viennese interior extends without breaking continuity through the line of Czechs, Slovenians, and Poles, to find its alter-ego in the shtetl of *Ostjudentum* [East European Jewish culture]. *Heimat* is feminine, as is interior. Its surrender (Claudio Magris insists on this "category")[48] is, basically, a surrender of any possible return (*Heimkehr*) to conditions of experience.

This zone of experience is not German. German experience is *Glaskultur* and avant-garde. "Only our Germans, the ethnic majority, betrayed Alpine dolts and Sudeten Bohemians and Nibelungen cretins," exclaimed Count Chojnicki in *The Emperor's Tomb*.[49] They razed Sipolje, empire and shtetl, every *Heimat*, to the ground. Austria's soul stayed at the outskirts. Loos believed God is in the details, and that is why there are *no* details. The soul of Austria was "collected" by the Jews in Boryslav caftans, by the horse dealers of Baksha, by the Muslims from Sarajevo, by chestnut vendors from Mostar. It was loud hillbillies from the Alps that sang "Watch on the Rhine." And they won. The empire was an enormous interior with extraordinary detail, an infinite number of people capable of having possessions, bound to the inalienable right to possess their own things. But these things were destroyed forever—and the details, now, are fragments, meaningless shards, neutral material for collage.

Thus fade the Viennese nights, leaving us in cruel play between surrender and unquenchable desire. In the wake of the old capital city comes the essence of metropolis, that "turns the earth into asphalt, walls, and bricks," that "without doubt" raises a province around itself "only to devour it in a day." There are places for passersby and for coins: theater, market, art, commerce, cinema, subway. The world is already consolidated "to the point that even editorial pages could be revolutionary." This is the world where the lost and superfluous end up, as well as everyone who survived the death of experience. The act of holding nostalgia for ransom sometimes tears through Roth. It is precisely this awareness of having survived, inflexible against oneself in speaking nothing about the no-longer and hoping nothing for the not-yet. Franz Tunda goes all over Europe, has meetings, speaks many languages; even Trotta in *The Emperor's Tomb* is full of events; and Mendel Singer is assaulted by the same weakened destiny. None of this is experience, though. It is the negation of experience. Their world is everything that is the case. That these characters take part in it does not change nature. *Flight Without End* is an endless flight from experience, not through experiences but through mere cases that negate the very possibility of experience. Experience takes place before the story begins. The story (or narrative) is singularly the account of the death of experience. It is the account of cases that drag the survivors (that have been judged *unfit unto death*) into experience. Peter Altenberg's "Invalid des Lebens" finds its fundamental sense in the "Invalid des Todes."

Read in this way, the conclusion of *Job* does not appear consolatory in the least. Whoever has been judged unfit to die (together with their interior at their own *Heimat*) is obliged to be swirled through events persecuted by the case and by things (in the indefinite plural). Only by "greatness of miracles" can everything be regained. The conclusion of *Job* is the rigorous negation of all happy endings. Far from home, the shtetl gone, *only by a miracle* can the child conceivably be found. No story, no narration can emerge from this encounter. The story is only about the diaspora and about exile from the very sites of the diaspora. The miracle that connects to experience shows only itself. Seen in the equivocal light of the biggest metropolis, it is unutterable. That is why not even the most painful nostalgia reveals itself in language. Experience is not to be spoken. It was before, and it can come back again, but only by *striking* like a miracle. Certainly it can only come back to overwhelm those who had lived it before. And therefore the disappearance of these inhabitants (which already do not include Tunda or Trotta or Kargan) is the disappearance of the very possibility of miracles.

Chojnicki appears to maintain ties to experience. He is a profoundly good and spiritual figure, like the figure of that friend of Loos and Kraus, Ludwig von Janikowski, who left no written work, but is known through the impressive portrait of him by Oscar Kokoschka. The "young friends" are too fragile in their modernity to recognize the cavernous wealth of these figures. Trotta's mother, too, has certainly passed through experience, but without being able at all to communicate it to her son, except as nostalgia and surrender. "What a great deal this mother must have undergone and read," thinks Trotta. His interior cannot even resist the transparence, and his house is turned into a pension. Among the guests, there is a typical exponent of *Glaskultur*, Elisabeth, Trotta's fortuitous wife. She works in the "applied arts" with a "new" woman whose name Trotta's mother cannot pronounce (her name is "inhuman," like those of Scheerbart's heroes). The art of *Modernität*, of the original and functional, of simplicity opposed to Wittgenstein's *Klarheit*, inexorably occupies every interior. Both Loos and Roth are too far from Mendel Singer to be able to wait for miracles.

Roth's characters are incapable of experience and incapable of sharing death. They fruitlessly reflect on their demise or search in vain to exceed it by mistaken or interrupted pathways (like Kargan). Does this circle enclose them in a "perfect" way? Or can survival itself, in its apparent superfluousness, preserve the possible, collect a meaning? Can one listen to an unpossessed silence that is not experience but that is open to the possibility of experience, by living with its death? Can this be done without betraying it into ornaments and images and by repeating the radical difference between interior and exterior? Can this be done by forbidding the exterior from assuming the value of a unique Logos, by going into exile without wanting to "co-exist" in the various countries and languages? The souls of those whose throats were slit in the name of the Gospel are dressed in white and are told to wait "for the quota of their families and comrades who must be put to death with them." It is an unpossessed silence that is not experience, but a condition, today, of an extreme possibility of experience. The last pages of Musil's novel are alive to this concern. So, perhaps, are the last pages of the *Tractatus*, sober as they are on the surface.

Figure 1 The Church of St. Leopold at Steinhof, Vienna.

Figure 2 Alfred Kubin, *Unglücks Vögel* [Birds of bad luck].

Figure 3 Alfred Kubin, *Madame Mors.*

Figure 4 Alfred Kubin, *Sumpfpflanzen* [Swamp flowers].

Figure 5 Alfred Kubin, *Rübezahl II.*

Figure 6 Max Klinger, *Centaur mit Wäscherinnen*
[Centaur with launderers].

Figure 7 Max Klinger, *Verfolgter Centaur*
[Centaur pursued].

Figure 9 Max Klinger, *Gesandschaft* [The ambassador].

Figure 8 (left) Max Klinger, *Bär und Elfe* [Bear and fairy].

Figure 10 Arnold Böcklin, *Melancholia.*

Figure 11 Alfred Kubin, *Die Haarschleppe* [The train of hair].

Figure 12 Alfred Kubin, *Das Gezücht* [The brood].

Figure 13 Alfred Kubin, *Die Spinne* [The spider].

Figure 14 Max Klinger, *Tote Mutter* [Dead mother].

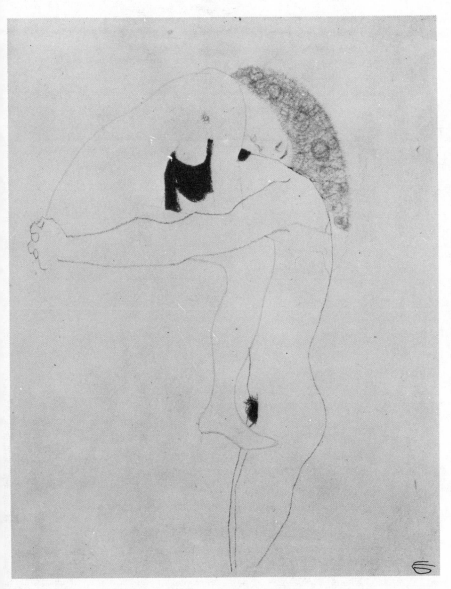

Figure 15 Egon Schiele, *Liebespaar* [Loving couple].

Figure 16 Egon Schiele, *Häuser und Föhren* [Houses and pines].

On the Mystical
Again

Giorgio Agamben writes, "Experience is this: people are born without speech. They were once and are ever in-fants (from Latin, 'without speech')." Infancy is the arch-limit of language. Its expropriation by language is never complete and must be repeated constantly. For Agamben, the mystical in Wittgenstein would be such an arch-limit, permitting a correct definition of language. For others, though (such as for Gianni Baget-Bozzo, who confronts the problem in the strictly theological frame of the speech or silence of God), the ineffable in Wittgenstein would itself be seen as an effect of language, defined as a cardinal function of a decree that, developed, might sound like this: "I say: I (here) am silent."[50] The possibility of transgression is in the very essence of the decree. How might the possibility of transgression be conceived?

Let us look again at the final propositions of the *Tractatus*. Nothing can be spoken but *Sätze der Naturwissenschaft*, "propositions of natural science—that is, something that has nothing to do with philosophy" (*Tractatus* 6.53). The "true method" of philosophy would consist in making it vanish, just as the problem of life is resolved when it vanishes (when one understands that formulating it is impossible, that it is not a question). Yet we feel (*wir fühlen*), even when every possible question has an answer, that the problems of life remain untouched. The ineffable belongs to this dimension, where the problem cannot be articulated in the linguistic domain of the question. Baget-Bozzo calls this concept of the ineffable "ingenuous." Agamben, however, calls it an image of infant speechlessness that transcendentally accompanies language (because of which humans cannot be reduced to a glass chain of questions and answers). One sees in the ineffable the simple negative of language; the other sees its transcendental origin. In both cases, Wittgenstein's last propositions would become perfectly clear, and the problem gripping us would vanish.

Wittgenstein's text confirms without a doubt that: (1) since there can be in language only what there is in the world, the limits of language are not an enigma; (2) the true method of philosophy consists in demonstrating how certain meanings correspond to certain sounds and in making the rest vanish (that is, "the problems of life"); (3) all that can be spoken are "propositions of natural science"—but it establishes that, at the same time, (4) none of this takes an Enlightenment form of progress capable of slowly abolishing the ineffable. The ineffable *remains*. "Es gibt allerdings Unaussprechlices." The "allerdings" presupposes an adversative that must be made clear in the translation: "There are, *indeed*, things that cannot be put into words." The ineffable cannot be said, cannot be shown (which is perfectly obvious); the form of its expression cannot be linguistic—and yet there it is. It happens. The mystical is the form of its being there. Put more precisely, ineffable things appear: "They make themselves manifest." The accent falls here, and not on the "trivial" fact that the unutterable cannot be spoken or that there is a dimension of human existence that cannot be reached or penetrated by the language of equivalent propositions. Wittgenstein does not characterize the ineffable as negative—not at all. He says that things that cannot be put into words make themselves manifest. Theirs is the plane of epiphany, which is the mystical.

Epiphany is recognizable. To understand it requires a true "intensity of recognition" that Baget-Bozzo and Benvenuto find in Saint Augustine. (Not by chance is Augustine a primary influence on Wittgenstein.) This recognition cannot be communicated or demonstrated in language. It can, however, be shown. Wittgenstein does not deny that after a long period of doubt, "the sense of life" may become clear. He, like Roth, does not proclaim miracles to be impossible. He limits himself, rather, to asserting that there is no way to say it. For Augustine, too, the ineffable is that which cannot be expressed or said, but of which one must nevertheless forever speak. Wittgenstein glosses Augustine listening to silence: the only possible way to unsilence the ineffable is to recognize its manifestation. This is the *implicit* "transgression" in Wittgenstein's declaration (apparently contained in the final proposition) that gives him complete mastery over his limits.

There is no room in Wittgenstein for an ingenuous and all-encompassing idea of what can be spoken. But neither does Wittgenstein balance what can be spoken against silence "for the sake of symmetry and negation" (Baget-Bozzo and Benvenuto). The ineffable cannot be understood simply as the silence that accompanies and transcendentally limits every proposition, the silence that binds speechlessness, truth, and language in a "founding relationship" (Agamben). This reading, if it cancels all "mysticism," does not capture the *autonomy* of Wittgenstein's dimension of the ineffable or the problematic possibility that it can exceed the limits of that relationship. A linear connection between the dimension of the mystical and the questions that we feel we cannot "sensibly" ask, the doubts that persist even where there are no questions, the enigma "*outside* space and time," is far from evident. The mystical is the dimension of self-manifestation and of the "intensity of recognition" that invests it.

So the mystical is not understood as an otherworldly dimension, above the plane of the utterable and its propositions. Having thrown out the scale we used to measure the "correct method in philosophy" (in Wittgenstein's paradoxical philosophy), a new Kingdom of the Mystical does not appear. Had it been so, we would still understand the mystical in terms of the ex-static, the sublime, as the way over the poverty of experience. Agamben is right. The mystical inexorably accompanies the utterable. But it does so in a dimension other than that of the utterable itself, in contrast with it: as manifestation. That which manifests itself is not spoken, is not produced by saying. It is the premise of speech. As speakers, we are ever mere in-fants. We exist prior to the dimension of manifestation, before that which manifests itself, before the premise, the presupposed. The premise is not the "sublime." It means: that the world exists, and the world is a defined, limited whole.

The mystical in Wittgenstein cannot be understood in a generally esoteric or gnostic sense. It does not indicate a plane of occult knowledge—as if most of the *Tractatus* had addressed the profane and it now alluded to the initiate's silence. The mystical manifests itself. Therefore, it is not obscure. The ineffable is a presence, and it is the premise of speech. It is an open area: it manifests itself. We cannot indicate any hidden parts: it manifests itself simply and entirely. Not by accident does this self-manifestation remind us so much of *aletheia* [unconcealment]. The language of equivalence radically obscures the problem of *aletheia*, since it essentially pursues the cancellation of the premise. Wittgenstein reactivates the problem with a gesture of classical *Klarheit* destined to leave its mark on every new, authentic thought. He defines the metaphysical limits and essential historicity of the language of equivalence. On the one hand, there are equivalent propositions, where *aletheia* is not a factor; on the other hand, there is self-manifestation as an area of unconcealing, not reducible to speech. It is an area that is not "beyond" the utterable, nor is it an object of all-knowing awareness or a negative of language or its mere transcendental arch-limit. It is an area about which there can be no declaration at all, about which it is necessary to be silent—yet its existence is certain because it manifests itself. It manifests itself; it does *not* declare itself. The utterable cannot reach any premise or unconcealedness, because the utterable is merely productive. It cannot negate the premise and its unconcealedness, because, if it could, these things would become fully utterable, since negation is nothing other than a form of the utterable. Therefore the mystical holds out as absolute difference along with language. It is as powerless to exhaust or go beyond language as language is able to declare its absence.

If the dimension of the mystical as self-manifestation resembles the problem of *aletheia*, then it recalls Franz Rosenzweig's *Offenbarung*.[51] Self-manifestation, as a premise, is revelation—becoming clear and open. There is what is shown, what shows itself. Philosophy's mission and destiny is to eliminate this premise, *das Gesetz*. To represent the problem of *aletheia* means to take account of philosophy's entire mission and destiny as the problem: to define its metaphysical limits. Yet it is absurd to wait for the philosophical logos to "naturally" encounter the "problem" par excellence, which is the manifestation of the prelinguistic premise—because it exceeds the limits of productivity of the logos. It would no longer be a manifestation if it were to derive dialectically from the rungs of philosophy or if it were to wait for its culmination. The manifestation can come as a surprise anywhere, because the problem (*aletheia*, the prelinguistic premise) can return anywhere, in spite of any prior declaration and any *Selbstüberschätzung* of language. Language that sustains such *faith* in itself as to make believe it has resolved every premise is intrinsically contradictory. It turns its own equivalence into a value: idolatry.

Is there a possibility of experience in the labyrinth of these relationships? In the pauses, perhaps, that divide and interconnect the crossing of the philosophical ladder with the manifestation of the unutterable; in language radically critiqued in all the instances declaring the speechlessness that accompanies language, yet open to the problem of the prelinguistic premise, *Offenbarung*'s "surprise" of the premise. In this circle there is perhaps the word that "exceeds" the chain of glass, the place where the possibility of experience has withdrawn. Neither the when nor the how of the not-yet can ever be spoken. But in the manifestation of the mystical there lives the near-memory of the premise, and the intensity of its recognition for a moment seems truly to interrupt the nihilism of the logos.

Abendland

The intersection of the lines of Rosenzweig and Heidegger at their point of origin, in Wittgenstein, leads to that area of Georg Trakl's poetry about which Heidegger wrote a definitive essay.[52]

In his Opus 22, Schoenberg resumes a dialogue with Rilke that he had begun with Stefan George. But he never met Trakl, who instead became Webern's favorite poet. The territory where the manifestation of the unutterable is already a first step toward the not-yet-said, where the thought of the crisis attains complete *Klarheit*, seeking new possible orders of language not only internally but also in the very speechlessness of language and the words that surpass it—this is Trakl's territory and the zone of Heidegger's *Erörterung* [discussion] of Wittgenstein's "too deep" and distant friend.

Heidegger's essay is definitive because the "site" that it indicates for Trakl's poetry is the same for the problem of the general condition of contemporary humanity. It casts a direct light on the entire Heideggerian interpretation of contemporary fate. The discussion focuses on the poem "Frühling der Seele." The soul is called *ein Fremdes* on the earth: a stranger. But being strange implies being a stranger in transit, passing through on the way to somewhere else. The word has the same etymological derivation as the English "pilgrim": one who journeys in foreign lands. Being a stranger means to seek one's own place, a homeland. It means going to a calm, secure home. "The soul seeks the earth, it does not flee it." The soul wants to spend time on earth, to save the earth as earth. In Rilke the journeying soul, the stranger, describes things by name; in Trakl it describes the continuous metamorphoses of nature, the play of its colors, and the sounds that surprise us and take hold of us—the foundational Being, independent of our "measures," of the premise. To feel the thing itself anew in the name as foundational Being, to free it from its common dailiness, to rediscover in it the magic relationship with the world—this is the poetry of the soul, *ein Fremdes* on earth.

The soul shows its own going, its own state of being away from home, to the "rational animal," to the human who is not yet "fixed" in the security of true being, to the "blue wild game" of the last stanza of Trakl's poem, "Summer's End." The "blue wild game" can become aware of being away from home only by listening to the voice of the estranged soul. Then, the very person becomes *ein Fremdes, ein Einsames,* a solitary loner who abandons his own already decomposed form and is changed into the form of the departed (*der Abgeschiedene*). The blue game animal who is open to listening reaches the place of departure, and this site signals the unity, for Heidegger, of Trakl's poem. But where is it departing to? The soul calls out to abandon its earlier form, calls out to death that divides it off but does not signify the end. "The dead one lives in his grave": "The end—being the end of the decaying kind—precedes the beginning of the unborn kind." Heraclitus assumes the departure is all spirit and fire, "burning flame of the spirit," which leaps off the stump consumed in fire. In Nietzsche's eternal return, the "dark wandering of the soul" takes mortals back to their origin, to that which has been, to the "primordial dawn of day." Thus Heidegger interprets the death of Elis as preparing the "future awakening," "der sanfte Gesang des Bruders am Abendhügel" ("the gentle song of the brother by the evening hill"),

> die kühle Blaue und die leuchtende Neige des Herbstes,
> das stille Haus und die Sagen des Waldes,

Mass und Gesetz und die mondenen Pfade der
  Abgeschiedenen

the frozen blue and the shining descent of autumn
the motionless house and the legends of the woods,
Measure and Law and the lunar paths of the departed

that revolve around the "patience" at the end of the "Song of the Departed." The death of Elis, the blue wild game kept apart and departed, connects to the speechless measure of the prelinguistic premise, of *Gesetz.*

The one who tends-toward, who sets oneself apart and gathers all the pain aroused by the spirit-flame leaping to its death off the stock ("'flaming' pain tears away"), is a *Wahnsinnige,* a madman. He listens to the soul, the stranger, and feeds on "a mighty agony, the grandsons yet unborn" ("Grodek"). Through his own death, his own departure, the madman passes to the dawning of the origin and invites his brother to follow him. This motif of Heidegger's *Erörterung* harks back to Wagner's *Parsifal.* That hero's name, Parsi-fal, also signifies *pure madness,* and he inhabits a realm of apartness. From his very first appearance, he has no shared memories. He comes from "caverns of silence." He is the unborn. More than abstention (the plane of Parsifal in the mystifying interpretations à la Bayreuth is not apartness, but abstention), his is the realm of strangeness. Parsifal is *ein Fremdes auf Erde.* The way of the unborn does not pass *through* "gloomy towns, . . . lonely summers" ("Stundenlied"), but only *past* them. And like Trakl's soul, Parsifal also calls mortals to follow him, and he carries them, upon "the sweet wings" of his madness, to the fatherland, to the "home" that Wagner intends in the sense of "sublime" redemption, of an inside knowledge. Heidegger, in the style of Nietzsche, intends "home" in the sense of the earth and of the redemption of the earth—of the foundational ground, the earth of Heraclitus, that perhaps breaks through in the finale of Mahler's Second Symphony.

Heidegger names this earth *Abendland* (the land of twilight, the west), this earth that "consents to be lived in," to which the soul calls, to which madness holds us, this earth that the death of Elis keeps for the unborn. It is an older western world, "which is to say, earlier and therefore more promising than the Platonic-Christian land, or indeed than a land conceived in terms of the European West. . . . The land of descent is the transition into the beginning of the dawn concealed within it": going toward the twilight of the soul is not therefore a simple self-dissolving, but a return to the yet unrevealed land, not simple decline or ruin (*Decline of the West!*), but "der süsse Gesang der Auferstandenen" ("Abendländisches Lied"), "the gentle song of the revived." Only in the twilight (on earth, which is the land of twilight) is the possible still unrevealed, that is, the possible revelation, its manifestation, which is now unrevealed. That is why the madman heads toward twilight. He seems mad because he tears away toward death. But only where the sun shines can there be a way through to the sweet song of the dawning day, of the revived. Through the silence of Parsifal's road, in the dark caverns of the more silent people, these lines are composed: "aus harten Metallen das erlösende Haupt," "the captain is called to redemption from strong metals" ("To the Silenced").

Why is Heidegger's *Erörterung* crucial? Because it reinterprets the entire course of Trakl's lyrics as the destiny of contemporary lyric poetry. Lyric cannot be understood only in Benjamin's terms of urban dilation of intellect, much less as thinking of decline and ruin, but rather as the plane in which the road through a radical poverty of experience intersects thinking on the eternal return. This interpretation unhinges the traditional "pessimistic" visions of contemporary lyric and captures the epochal meaning of its "hermetic" spirituality. This interpretation is also crucial because it locates the home of the *Wahnsinnige* in thinking about the *Abendland*. Here the madman can speak to the angel again, be surprised at it and at peace with it. Contemporary lyric takes the form, therefore, of language on humanity's *historical* condition (*Geschichte*, not *Historie*). It takes the form of language on a time that does not know the future as a "simple extension of the present," the only future, in fact, that Europe knows (Europe, not *Abendland*). Trakl's lyrics would be the place for a reversal of West-

ern metaphysics, or better, for its going mad, a reversal that could
create the void in us for hearing "the gentle song of the revived."

Is Trakl the only one to say this? Heidegger's Trakl is articulate
under the sign of Heidegger's reading of the rapport between Heraclitus and Nietzsche, which assumes here the appearance of a Parsifal revisited and even, as we shall see, of Otto Weininger. Heidegger re-systematizes Trakl; he turns him into discourse. Trakl's
deep and fundamental enigma passes through Heidegger's interpretive net. Heidegger takes on what the lyrics *say* as a problem,
not the relationship between this "what" and the song itself, the
"who" of the song.

The song is not, indeed, the song of the soul, of the stranger,
nor is it the song of the *Wahnsinnige* dying to follow it. It is the
song of the soul's brother, of its friend. The soul takes its leave, as
in Mahler's *Der Abschied*, but it creates silence in this leave-taking.
The music that is still heard is the song of those who are left behind. The brother and friend of the stranger are left behind. They
do not know how to detach themselves. This is Trakl's tragic apo-
ria, as it is Rilke's, and it seems to have escaped Heidegger's notice:
the poem or song is not the word of the departed, the word that
names foundational Being, that intuits its return, that saves the
earth. The language of the Heraclitean poem is impossible for
Trakl. Its singer is none other than the friend. But the friend is precisely the plane from which *ein Fremdes* takes leave and departs.
The friend sings of this departure, but can only be its witness. The
friend knows that departure, this twilight, is neither ruin nor pessimistic decadence, but a going-toward, a seeking. Yet, what is
sought cannot be intuited through song. Poetry will never be in
its presence, because poetry flows from the friend who remains behind, not from the stranger who tends-toward. The poet hears and
re-states "the spirit's euphoria in departure." The poet participates
in departure, but can only hear it and translate it, nothing more.
He "translates" the stranger's steps, he does not create them. The
departure does not speak poetically, nor does the departed. The
soul does not sing. We have, perhaps, a record of its song, the
words on record. So how is it possible to say what the soul sees

and, even before that, how the soul sings this song? We have "translations" only. Never direct intuitions, unconcealment of Being—never again will this poetry be *poesis*.

The great utopia of Heideggerian thinking about art, as it appears in the essays on Trakl and Rilke, is rooted in the idea of poetry as *Wahnsinnigkeit* [the stuff of madness] that seeks unconcealment, *aletheia*, in the place of foundational *Abendland*. This "system" is a bit narrow for both Trakl and Rilke. The tragedy of their lyric poetry consists in the full awareness of the impossibility of speaking the utopia's name. The utopia is neither absent nor overlooked. Lyric intersects its territory, but it is not where lyric lands. Lyric lands at the recognition of the soul's silence, at the silent farewell of the stranger, and at the song's being merely the song of the friend left behind, a broken symbol. The intuition of departure is retraced in this song. The meaning of departure is kept in the interior of whoever is powerless in the face of separation, in the mortal disease of everything that exists.

The stranger in the dying crowd is *sprachlos* [speechless] and nationless among broken families, "falling stars" that live in "great cities built of stone on the plains" ("Abendland"). The madman is dead, "the stranger is in his grave" ("Psalm," second version). This death and burial are not "images." The one who is buried begins his cycle, is *sprachlos*, "exceeds" all possible language. He can hear his poet-friend only at the first step of his quest. He does not, however, possess the name of resurrection or return. At the end of "Helian," after the description (and language is enough for this) of the "horrifying twilight" of the ancient stock, there begins an interminable pause. A song commemorates the boy's madness. A song recalls his departure. But faced with thinking about return, poetry is silent: "our silence is a black cavern." Song retraces and sustains only this: "lasset das Lied auch des Knaben gedenken, / Seines Wahnsinns, und weisser Brauen und seines Hingangs . . .": "Let the song recall the child, too, / His madness, his white eyelashes and his departure . . . " The poet who must remain behind remembers the exact time and place of separation. The site of separation is not the same as that of unconcealment.

O, wie lange bist, Elis, du verstorben.
Dein Leib ist eine Hyazinthe,
In die ein Mönch die wächsernen Finger taucht.
Eine schwarze Höhle ist unser Schweigen,

Daraus bisweilen ein sanftes Tier tritt
Und langsam die schweren Lider senkt.
Auf deine Schläfen tropft schwarzer Tau,
Das letzte Gold verfallener Sterne.
("An den Knaben Elis")

Oh, Elis, how long have you been dead.
Your body is a hyacinth,
In which a monk digs his wax finger.
Our silence is a black cavern,

where a gentle creature comes out
and slowly lowers its heavy lids.
A black dew lies on your temples,
the last gold of the fallen stars.

And in "Rondel": "Verflossen ist das Gold der Tage . . . Des Hirten sanfte Flöten starben": "Flown the gold of day . . . the gentle shepherd's flute is dead."

On Cliffs
and Swamps

Alfred Kubin was obsessed with picturing the land of decaying tree trunks and fallen stars, where the soul, *ein Fremdes*, climbed over the horizon. Ernst Jünger saved detailed maps of Kubin's woods, where "splendor and rot, proud wickedness and nauseating putrefaction, the cult of sublime and unfocused pain" manifest "universal life operating so mysteriously in humanity, in animals, in plants, in every rock."[53] The old sage of Zwickledt, Jünger says in *Strahlungen*,[54] belonged to that troubling "pack of Eastern authors" who knew how to describe our decadence more profoundly. Kafka calls out its demons, Trakl gets its putrefaction (and only by way of putrefaction did he arrive at the *Abendland*). Kubin *sees* its dust and mold, and like Horst Lange, whose work he illustrated, he sees the expanding swamps, the unstoppable spread of brush and swamp. Our world has gotten old. Kubin documents its catastrophe. His images, pulled out of the rubble, translate no words but see this world as *Todessymbolik*, a grand astral theater where the powerful breath of Saturn expresses the hieroglyphs of death.[55] Universal life is described here at the end of its cycle. When a cycle nears its end and comes to its questionable *Abendland*, in the gray color of the swamp, the realms are confused. The line does not contain forms in flight, but it splits them open, it chops them up and mixes the pieces together. Girls fly like birds over the swamp. Fish-men and toad-men hunt weird beasts together. A death arrow hits a farmer from a tree, or the bird of evil omen crashes into his house from a leaden sky (*Unglücks Vögel*; see Figure 2). The sun remains ever hidden behind thick clouds that rise up from a sour earth. Universal life is expressed here decomposing the forms of its old cycle. But decomposition is also *irony*. Irony is a powerful caustic philter, the subtle work of the diabolical smile, resulting in a deliberate confusion of realms, not an unforeseen catastrophe. Irony produces an unceasing exchange between forms—testimony to their tremendously illusory nature. That is why universal life is ironic whenever it produces a catastrophe. Its smile disperses the apparent gathering of forms, their specificity and distinction. It "dissolves" them.

Irony and the disintegration that it produces are *hybrid*, like the demiurge of Pearl, the capital of Kubin's fantasy novel, *The Other Side*.[56] Disintegration leads to pure possibility: future realms and future forms are given as purely possible. The swamp festers with germs. Its most troubling aspect is not the decaying of what has already been, but its exhibiting this decay as an unexpected, unpredictable growth. New forms and new orders will be born, slowly, from this lacustrine realm of the indistinct and uncomposed, but we cannot foresee their outline. The irony is twofold: on the one hand, it demonstrates the illusory nature of the idea of a universal life peacefully progressing from form to form, through continuous improvements canceling out every archetypal swamp; and on the other hand, it smiles over the absolute image of death produced by catastrophe. The face of death jumps out from the thicket of reeds wearing a student's cap and points a finger adorned with a fake grasshopper. In another apparition, Madame Mors dances among the tombs like a skeletal courtesan. She tries in vain to hide her decadence behind a mask and a blond wig (*Madame Mors*; see Figure 3). The swamp's disintegration is a kind of decadence. Madame Mors is one of the many apparitions that flash among the will-o'-the-wisps of disintegration. Disintegration is represented as a hybrid of decomposition and germination. In a 1905 drawing, fantastic swamp-born flowers blossom out of the corpse of Ophelia (*Sumpfpflanzen*; see Figure 4). The perennial endurance of life, in the metamorphosis of its realms, plays dead.

The swamp is a "disintegrated" realm of play, where not even death is sacred. Sometimes there is a Shakespearean Fool to describe it (as in some of Kubin's drawings of the *böhmisches Land* [Bohemia]), and sometimes there are the genies of the hills, whose figures are made of crazed roots. The light of the woods is lunar, or rather, it comes from the diamond that Rübezahl brought out of the earth (*Rübezahl II*; see Figure 5). An illusory brightness emanates from the moon. "It is—how shall I say—a slow convergence that, like a magic lantern, reverses the action of that damned arrogant sun's creative life-giving rays. It bewitches the human mind, projecting every kind of concrete form into a seeming reality, and causes the poisonous liquid of death and putrefaction to spread and breathe under the most diverse forms and shapes." Gustav Meyrink, whom Jünger forgot in his "pack of Eastern authors," seems to have presented the precise image of the Old Magician of Zwickledt in *The Four Brothers of the Moon* [*Die vier Mondbrüder*]. For these brothers, forms are simply dreams, and bodies "convulsions of ether." Kubin, unlike Meyrink's lunar brothers, does not declare "I am, I remain" when the entire universe goes to pieces. Nor is his house what Meyrink imagines—"then, to distract myself, I lean my curious ears toward the wild howling that reaches me across the surrounding silence from a nearby castle of bandits, in which the wild painter Kubin now lives, who celebrates decadent orgies in the circle of his seven children until the first light of dawn." Nothing can last, nothing can remain entire until the return of *Urschlamm*, the primeval swamp, and the decadent orgy that takes hold of things, plants and animals, takes hold of the ego and its very death. Only possibility, the infinite swarm of possibilities, can fill this halfway world, this equivocal plane, this *Zwischenwelt*. Irony itself belongs to the halfway world, suspended between putrefaction and possibility, where only possibility is real. Infinite worlds carry this swamp within, and, as Kubin's friend Paul Klee recognized, very few figures emerge from it. (Klee's illustrations for *Candide* fully reveal his "exchange" with Kubin.)[57] The swamp, then, is not only the putrefaction of the has-been, but also the death of many possibilities. The tragic peak of irony does not consist in simply dissolving the illusory nature of given forms, but in shadowing the work of death upon possibility itself, in allowing for a notion of the disintegration of infinite, invisible possibilities.

In Kubin's novel, Pearl lies beyond deserted swamplands. Vast reaches of forest and swamp stop the sun from shining. An opaque olive green, a greenish gray, wipes out even the memory of the "damned arrogant sun." The entire disintegration of forms ripens in the melancholic hue of Pearl, in the shadow of bureaucratic practices collected from all over the world "to promote a special kind of homo sapiens." A mountain made completely of iron rises up in the center of the realm (Trakl's fallen stars!) protected by powerful magnetic charges from the wanderers and vagabonds who want to visit it. The swamp with its demons laps the edges of the sidereal iron. Its discharges of electricity pervade the realm of Pearl, saturating its atmosphere and producing continuous metamorphoses. Kubin's style, fragmented, contorted, multiplying itself in every direction, expresses this impalpable, fecund, and disintegrating *energheia*.

Like the damp folds of the land, Patera encloses infinite faces. Its sovereign is Proteus, seen the way another authentic citizen of Prague, Arcimboldo, had portrayed him.[58] Quick as a lightning bolt he is a young woman, a child, an old man, fat, skinny, kind, wicked. A theatrical magic incessantly transforms his appearance: his and that of all men together, and all animals, jackal and stallion, serpent and bird. Kubin remembered the revelation of the "sovereign form" of Krishna on the field of battle at Arjuna in his description of the metamorphosis of Patera: "I see you with multiple arms, multiple bodies, and your faces, and your eyes, with your shape everywhere unlimited" (*Bhagavad Gita* XI) that, later, Hesse recalled in the transfiguration of Siddhartha in the eyes of Govinda. But while Krishna is time that makes the world waste away and then absorbs it again into himself, into his completely developed perfection, and Siddhartha appears as a unity of Nirvana and Samsara, Patera participates in the confusion of elements. Not only did he produce the swamp where the corrupt elements reciprocally dissolve themselves, but he participates in their degeneration. From the wild regions that surround Pearl and that were considered sacred, numberless animals come and finish the work of decay. "A morbid and irresistible dream" annuls the endurance of the ancient cycle. But to that cycle, apparently, belongs also that ancient citizen of Prague, Patera.

The finale of *The Other Side* is not a cosmogonic sacrifice. Doubt and equivocation form "the sun, the great sun" that, "like the brilliant sound of a fanfare," dissolves the clouds of the realm of dreams, appearing from behind the snow clouds at the conclusion of the grandiose *polemos* between Patera and his double, his Lucifer, the American. Patera was tired and probably "weaker than everyone else." "Perhaps the true sovereigns were the blue-eyed men that galvanize an inanimate puppet with their magic powers." Perhaps Patera is none other than Meyrink's golem that wants the brothers of the moon, and the great sun is not enough to close the abyss of dreams "where I sank." In the days following the apparent triumph of the sun, or rather, "in the nights following, full of moonlight, . . . I thought about my death as a great, heavenly joy, as the beginning of an eternal wedding night." The "dissolute" realm of play has no end here. The work has no conclusion. His teachers ignore the *I Am* and live in that perennial *Zwischenwelt*, a chiaroscuro where "the most sublime moments are subject to the ridiculous, to mocking, to irony," and where General Rudinoff's operetta-style occupation succeeds the great myth that narrates the collapse of the realm of dreams. The teacher is too tired. Subject to the rituals of the wild regions, he knows the formulas of metamorphosis and degeneration, but is powerless to produce the forms that will survive Madame Mors's barbarian toss of dice. The secret of possibility is perhaps in the hands of bizarre elves, swamp demons, or impenetrable blue-eyed figures that impassively assist the workings of the realm of dreams. For us, "the demiurge is a hybrid."

A closely woven net of affinities, reflections, and allusions binds works apparently so far apart as Jünger's *The Other Side* and his *On the Marble Cliffs*.[59] The Chief Ranger can see from the dark swamps that border the Campagna all the way to the forest that extends its wooded arms into the grazing meadows. "In the deep recesses of the forest" lives a gang of wild bandits from Poland and the lower Rhine, "in Nibelungen caves," beyond any law, outcasts from heretical sects, wizards and witches. "A river of foul blood wound its way from here through the veins of the world." This oppressive atmosphere of horror, made of swamp and unpassable forest, of animated desolation and bubbling clouds, is a vision straight out of Kubin. The Chief Ranger is this realm's master: a sinister magician who is regarded with repugnance and terror by legitimate alchemists. The pure alchemists of the Marina seek "the immutable element encased in a box of appearances," and they seek it according to the ancient spiritual orders, beginning with "breathing exercises and a strict diet." The end of this work consists in the salvation of whoever practices it, in a capacity to command, "like holding the reins of a charger," the powers of life that the Chief Ranger would rather savagely liberate. The severe logic of forms answers whatever is "solved" and perfect in itself, "Olivierian," understood only by the profane power of the Chief Ranger. The severe logic of forms neither ignores nor scorns appearances (a box), but helps them to manifest the gold of the spirit.

Here too, as in Kubin, disintegration comes from the slow but unstoppable penetration of the swamp demons into the cultivated Campagna and into the Great Marina's culture. The opposite principle—at its moment of twilight—also appears in Jünger: the magic that preserves elements from destruction. In the scope of this magic, disintegration, like fog, is only "at the surface of things." Magic preserves things by naming them according to their true essence. Kubin's visions come after the sack of the Marina: *On the Marble Cliffs* constitutes a kind of secret prologue to it. Brother Otho and the Narrator live in the last days of the Marina with desperate awareness. Unspeakable melancholy is their lot. They are intent upon distilling things in the eternal, as they learned from the aged master Nigromontanus. Whatever burns in the magic mirror turns invisible and is preserved there "as if it had been closed and hidden behind armored gates." To spare themselves the

[margin note:] and Machen and Grimm

hour of their annihilation, they can only take refuge in the security of nothingness. The beautiful coastal landscape, their fine erudition, cannot endure and be saved except in the invisible, and in absence.

The Marina's landscape pertains to absence, and that is the root of its fascination. The mirror of Nigromontanus purified it in the Rilkean invisible. The symbolic shining of its details resembles the vision of a memory that still observes the most minute details of the past, while desperately aware of it being past. The image of *dichterisch wohnen*, of dwelling poetically, is perfect, therefore, in every sense, where the providential gods of wine and bread are venerated, where the dead "gather invisibly around us," where mythic correspondences unite vine, human, and animal, the cultivator of the field with the cultivator of the word. The Chief Ranger profanes the ancient meters, since he scorns the cultivation of vineyards and grain fields. His hunters "crossed the rich earth as if it were desert, barren and unused," and his blind guitarists return "to the vulgar iambs of hatred and revenge, hissing in the mud." A wild Diana gleams monstrously between the magician's forest and the swamp, while the divine in the Marina is none other than the perfect consonance between various works and various steps of existence. Heideggerian *Geviert* [square] is divine in the Marina, the harmony of *dichterisch wohnen* with earth, sky, god, and mortal. In the woods, however, the dissonance of idols prevails, announced by the deities of the shepherds, "roughly shaped in stone or ancient oak," at the crossroads in the Campagna. At the Marina and in the Rue-Garden Hermitage observance is expressed in working. Work does not transform nature except to liberate its name, its essence. For the Chief Ranger this is oppression, violence, a change for the sake of control. The sense of this work is manifested in the wild charge of his bloodhounds, led by Chiffon Rouge. The beasts and idols of the swamp and the woods, as imagined by Kubin, even hurl themselves against the mirror of Nigromontanus. Here the serpents of Erius—of the hermit child, son of work—destroy "the entire forest crew." The idol cannot touch the eternal. By now, anyway, eternity belongs only to memory.

The Marina's dwelling poetically carries the seed of its own demise. It rotates powerlessly toward the death of its cycle, as if its decline carried down the Chief Ranger. (The desert that he imposes participates in the present good times.) *On the Marble Cliffs* cannot be reduced to the fatal contrast between culture and an anarchic will to power. Any interpretation of the kind would lose the extraordinary wealth of relationships, details, and variations that make up the work. At its center is the bloodless fragility of the dwelling place, the inner wavering of the ancient meter, and weariness even with living happily. The reasons for the Marina's slow weakening flow out of Jünger's writings almost without notice, since memory tends to remove them. The Marina itself is a *hybrid*. The saturation of its colors and the metaphysical wholeness of its landscape can only hide that fact with great effort. Even Marina, its symbol, is full of vacillating contradiction: her certainty that destruction is not real, that it is an illusion and not happening, seems too weak to the eyes of Braquemart's "definitive nihilism" as well as to the Chief Ranger's "wild anarchy." What Brother Otho and the Narrator think—that the crown of gardens shines more brightly from the Rue-Garden Hermitage "before the sun goes down past the horizon"—has traces all through the Marina's life and in its very *humanitas*. The evening light of sundown is necessary to see the Marina—because the Marina is *Abendland*, its *hybrid*.

The *consonantiae* of the Marina are in reality composed of elements that tend to disintegrate into each other and dissolve. The work that brings out their accord and the harmony that makes them resonate in the here and now are ephemeral. Work and harmony are utopian. The most profound content of this utopia is the perfect symbiosis between pagan and romantic, classic and Christian. Look at the description of the festival at the Marina, in the days of its "wild abundance," when in the autumn the guardians of the vineyards go masked through the fields hunting birds or when in spring "we celebrated like mad." Even the two inhabitants of the Rue-Garden Hermitage participate in the festival ("at the hilltops of the vineyard . . . I found her, exhausted, and I took her trembling in my arms and I lowered my red mask onto her face"). Brother Otho, too, whose discourse on humanity comes out of Pico's *De dignitate*, goes to the Woodpecker group, "which plays its march beating ladles and spoons against a wooden barrel." The game here reveals anew its ancient ritual sense. The "orgy" permits man to participate in the eternal cosmogonic event. It periodically reestablishes the original chaos in order to permit *renovatio*. The festival and its license have symbolic value. That is why Brother Otho and the Narrator take part: the proceedings of the festival "imitate divine gestures or certain episodes of the holy drama of the cosmos" (Eliade). Regeneration can only occur by reconnecting the sphere of play and the sphere of the sacred in this way, and by hearing the "archetypes" that are common to the various religious traditions, tending toward that foundational unity where the ascetic humanists of the Marina fix their gaze.

The figure of Father Lampro, practically the tutelary spirit of the Marina, repeats this nostalgia. The very name of his cloister is a transparent symbol of it: St. Mary of the Moon. The pagan goddess who carries a scythe and the Virgin who is "ruler of all that changes" both inhabit Father Lampro's priesthood. Father Lampro, in fact, "didn't like contradictions." Therefore he liked neither the dialectical struggle nor the decision implicit in Christian metanoia. The "double" of the Mauretanians is equally irresolute, the defined order that the lives of the Marina depend upon. If the exercise of power wants to take form through their doctrine of *semper victrix* and no compassion can adulterate it, then it is inevitable that violence and tyranny will cling to its "definitive nihilism" like a poisonous vine. The mortal struggle between forest and Marina appears, in the double light of the story of the Mauretanians, to be the catastrophe of a single organism, the fruit of its secret disagreements and fissures. Brother Otho and the Narrator understand that Braquemart is powerless to oppose the Chief Ranger, and they also see the bloodless decadence of the prince who goes with him. The severe logic of the Chief Ranger embraces Braquemart's utopia of order's original *intentio* and its *renovatio*. In this light, the image that closes the novel may appear all that much weaker: the amphora containing Braquemart's head, resting on the first stone laid in the foundation of the Marina's great cathedral, the great work's cornerstone. This distant and unreliable promise of *renovatio* is reversible, however. It can mean that "definitive nihilism" lies at the foundation of the Marina's Christian resurrection. The rock that should have been the foundation takes on aspects of diabolical imagery—the "rock of shame." It is not the Marina of *Geviert* that rises; it is not the utopia of a pagan and Christian synthesis that emerges, but the cathedral of Christianity qua "definitive nihilism." The rock on which the Church is built is only the rock of nihilism.

In the "rich life of studious leisure" that takes place in the Rue-Garden Hermitage, "we followed the lofty example of Linnaeus." The order that he confers on things is one of names and language; the immutable standard is the standard of discourse. Even Father Lampro teaches how to name things. Naming expresses dominion of the spirit "over the fields in flower and over the innumerable legions of insects." However, even this dominion appears unfounded in the end. When things capture us in their light and surprise us with it, then words are detached from appearance and will no longer serve in the usual way. The glory of things makes process and destruction seem illusory, but that is exactly what constitutes the ineffable. Our words, Linnaeus's words, name appearances and put them in order. Appearances do not exist except by the light of words. "The dazzling new splendor of things" seems to lead to the edge of silence. The highest authority of the Marina, that of the word, falls short before this splendor, since even such an authority is an unresolvable *hybrid* made of "definitive nihilism" ordering phenomena in the presence of discourse, mixed with "saving" the world, freeing its very essence.

However different the design of Pearl might seem at first glance from that of the Marina, the asphyxia that seizes both landscapes is the sign of an incurable, internal illness. The sun that shines on the Marina is as melancholic as the atmosphere of Pearl. If one looks closely, the greatness of the opening pages of *On the Marble Cliffs* does not depend on colors, but on the contrast of black and white. We stand before an engraving, not a painting. Linnaeus's terms are not adequate to name the sun, no matter how they may try. The art of drawing can do it, as in Kubin—and as in one of his teachers, Max Klinger. Can one think of Patera as a lost Mauretanian? And of the blue-eyed men, who seem to judge him in the end, as the order that can by now only serve in the game of destruction and becoming? History knows nothing but the downward path of disintegration, and the description of the forces that afflict it are identical in Kubin and Jünger. To whatever extent the description in *On the Marble Cliffs* may resemble Kubin, that is how much the initial landscape, from the spreading sea to the orchards and vineyards, from the Campagna to the icy Alta Plana, belongs to Klinger's drawings.

Blanchot's writings about Jünger and De Chirico's about Klinger are—not by accident—interchangeable.[60] The landscape of the Rue-Garden Hermitage is perfectly described, and anyway it's beauty cannot be captured "the way you might capture a land of enigmas" (Blanchot). The festivals of the Marina are enigmatic. The encounters with the primordial genies of the land that animate the festivals are enigmatic. The very images of the Rue-Garden Hermitage, of Brother Otho and Little Erio, lords of snakes, are enigmatic. And yet the things dreamed in thought are expressed here as figures. The admirable cool and cruel dignity (Blanchot) of their language leaves no room for facile evocations of fantasy. Not fantasy, but *imaginatio*. Thus in Klinger the neatness of contour, the perfection of the image, is a gift of distance (the patience of Father Lampro). The landscape opens its own interior only to those who observe it from afar. Only melancholy born of detachment can lend reality to the things dreamed in thought dreaming about itself. Then nothing is abandoned to impression or chance. Thus the centaur that talks with the washerwoman from behind a wall and reaches out to finger the white sheets hung out in the sun is an *image*; the centaur that flees across the field and spins around to shoot an arrow into the throat of his pursuer's horse is an *image* (*Centaur mit Wäscherinnen* and *Verfolgter Centaur*; see Figures 6 and 7). The "realism" of *Eine Mutter, Op. 9*, is found again in the pure dream of the other cycle, *Brahmsphantasie*,

Op. 12. The neoclassical pessimism that assigns "every contemporary work to the glossorist," that holds "that nothing is left for us contemporaries except games of assembly," is here happily and "ingenuously" abandoned for another "method," thanks to which "the ancient myths, in their reappearance, will offer us their enigmas and their exorcisms with an unrecognized face. The fiction of the myths consists in new fatigue and new terrors."[61]

The intellectual art of assembly and the reappearance of myth have rarely been so fully realized as in Klinger's glove cycle, *Paraphrasen über den Fund eines Handschuhs, Op. 6.* The "banal" event of the first two plates is transformed, through the springtime nostalgia of the third, into the dreams and nightmares of those that follow: from the Marina's demons of *Ängste* to the monster bird that steals the glove off the outstretched hands of the dreamer during the night. From the glove that lies "so bourgeois" on the track, to the goddess of love in triumph on the foaming sea, to the glove, finally, on the last table that the winged child observes with an ironic smile—the figure and its sign are identical. As in Jünger, the game of assembly, even carried to the peak of complexity and sophistication, is foreign to all allusivity, to all ornamental likeness. Myths can be fabricated.

Kubin discovered Klinger's glove cycle in Munich at the beginning of the century, and he found it enlightening. "A completely new art was revealed to me here that offered the possibility of expressing in quick suggestive strokes all possible emotions. . . . I was suddenly brimming with a torrent of visions and images in black and white." Kubin's predilection for the glove cycle, like that of Giorgio De Chirico, Max Ernst, and the symbolists, is well understood: it presents a fabricated myth in combination with an airy note of Romantic irony. It is the same element of distance that we saw in regard to the landscape. Irony prevents any possibility of becoming one with the fabrication, with the fiction—and that permits the fiction to reach a perfect, definite *image.* The same intricate game can be noticed in Klinger's other masterpieces: *The Swing, Bear and Fairy (Bär und Elfe;* see Figure 8), the *Titelblatt* of the *Radierte Skizzen.* A vast, luminous Mediterranean gulf provides the background for the fairy's feathery game with the bear. (It is humor's game with the spirit of gravity; Kubin also portrays it frequently.) These are the passages that most recall Jünger (like the high plain in the background of *Akkorde* in the *Brahmsphantasie*). They stand in the splendor of the Mediterranean (De Chirico), like blessed islands. Splendor is, however, a principle of distinction and clarity. The sun appears, but it does not burn. A cloudless light allows things to appear, but at the same time it cancels out their colors. De Chirico notes that Arnold Böcklin's landscape is completely different. The same Mediterranean sea is here swollen with its own deities, sensed through intense chromatic contrasts: a Nordic, continental dramatic force. Klinger's themes are here, too (and everywhere the influence of the painter from Basel—city of Nietzsche, Burckhardt, *and Böcklin*, as Hermann Hesse had to say), but as if tormented "by north winds and Nordic demons." Satyrs and nymphs are mixed in the oceanic element. The very silence of the sea is figured as a siren, a temptress, in the drowned man's monstrous reflex. In *Gesandschaft*, however, where Klinger's graphic genius more fully informs the quality of the painting, the lovely sphinx of silence on a boundless and deserted beach queries the hero-bird who dares to approach her (see Figure 9). No gesture, no dramatization disturbs this moment.

Böcklin and the portrait that Alberto Savinio made of him in *Men, Tell Your Story* and his fabrication of myth all inhabit *On the Marble Cliffs*. The sudden apparition that surprises the Narrator and Brother Otho on the way back from the Rue-Garden Hermitage ("thus images broke into our dark drunkenness then, perhaps one of those goat horns on a long pole that farmers plant down in their gardens, or perhaps. . . . Certainly we remained still as rocks and a sudden fright took hold of our hearts") seems taken from "Pan and the Pastor." Böcklin's chromaticism sometimes breaks into Jünger's Klingerian drawings, and this constitutes the bridge to the Kubinian visionary crescendo that traverses the collapse of the Marina. All of these threads come together under the sign of *Melancholia*. Its season is autumn. Its element is the wetness of the sea, of the shore, of the swamp. Its line is the horizon. In the monumental figure of a woman with a black-veiled mirror in her hand that Böcklin finished in 1900, his last work and the last work of the century, we find the figure of *Herbstgedanken,* she who contemplates the slow-moving currents of the stream under the shadow of autumn branches (*Melancholia;* see Figure 10). She sits in the landscape of *Heiliger Hain.* She is the woman who gazes at the beach in the distance in *Villa am Meer.* She is Iphigeneia forgotten against the background of a classical villa, prey to the encroaching wild. We find the famous, funereal cypress trees of the *Island of the Dead.* We recognize these, in fact, in the mirror's black veil. The vast beaches, the moors, the Campagna (so admired already by the German Romantic painters who lived in Italy or "through" Italy—it would be possible to trace the elements of imaginative continuity from them to Böcklin),[62] furrowed by brooks moving slowly among autumnal trees until they arrive at the swamp, the lacustrine landscape, the silence beneath the woods: all these images, variously accentuated and experienced, are also found in the Jugendstil. As Ernst Bloch was to say,[63] the land of the Jugendstil is *Sumpfmoor* and *Heide,* swamp, marsh, and moor. The landscape is built on the horizon line, horizon by horizon. The tree in its emerging does not indicate anything except the caesurae of this broad meter. The very lines that make up Jugendstil ornaments are derived from "*flacher Sumpfmythos*" (Bloch): complications and "scrambling" of the horizon. Loos does not notice this origin. They are details, fragments of *Melancholia,* bits of mosaic in the fiction of the myth, broken into pieces by now, shards that survived the smashing of the images of death (the images of war and plague, recurring obsessively in Böcklin and Klinger and Kubin). The line is ever the unreachable horizon. In Jugendstil it curves, circles back on itself, seeks new rhythms—but remains the line that indicates the horizon, the impassable limit. And even the colors, however much they may seem to be freed from any descriptive purpose, remain the colors of autumn or of uncertain springs.

Centaurs

In those years, Basel was also the city of Johann Jakob Bachofen. Arnold Böcklin's fabricated myth is directed at mourning, at *threnos*. It is a Lycian rhythm—whose twofold nature was discovered by Bachofen. The required horizon line expresses the idea of repose. *Melancholia* seems to reflect on the motto "that the oracle recalled to the inhabitants of Camarina, in Sicily, as the supreme principle of the sacred," *akineta me kinein*, do not move the unmovable.[64] The way Böcklin's *The Island of the Dead* reproduces a Lycian necropolis has escaped notice, along with the way it describes "a sepulchral and grandiose world, solid as a rock, destined to endure through eternity" (Bachofen), monotonous as the flat sea that surrounds it and the silence that inhabits it. The Lycian cities of the dead command the most beautiful sites, "at the heights of cliffs struck by the first rays of the sun in the morning and lit by the last rays of the sun in the evening." They participate variously in the lives of the living, visible from amphitheaters, halls, and stadiums. The Lycian cult of the dead, Bachofen explains, is associated with the idea of awakening, with the worship of the sun, whose nature is expressed by the very name of the people. This element is completely missing in Böcklin's *Toteninsel*. It shows a desperate Lycia that appears in the figure of Glaucus, when Diomedes encounters him in the tumult of battle: "Men are like leaves shaking at the stem." (The identical comparison appears in the Brahms

123

Requiem.) The solid cliffs of the Toteninsel do not yield the birth of spring (*ver sacrum*). The *ver sacrum* will be nothing, really, but an autumn of broken horizons, fragments of woods and country-side.

The landscape of the Great Marina is perhaps closer to the Lycia imagined by Bachofen. Kore approaches Apollo's rites, and the tellurian presence sits beside the luminous power and shines. (The Marina's hierophants are double, like Böcklin's and Klinger's.) Yet the physical structure itself seems drawn from Bachofen's enthralled description of Lycia: the glance of the traveler "rests now on the snowy fields or on the dark wooded slopes of the high mountains, now on the dark blue mirror of the sea. And in an illusion created by the incomparably limpid sky, the contours of woods and sea frequently join in what seems an unbroken line." The ancient culture of the fertile valleys, the very character of the people who live their lives there without feeling the need to travel to foreign lands, belongs to the myth of the Marina. As the harmony of the Marina is destined to shatter into its various parts, so Bachofen's *Land of Dawn* breaks down into its constituent elements. The fortunate symbiosis between Lycian Apollo and Kore cannot endure. In Lycia and at the Marina, night and day are still united in the light of dawn. But the successive development's destiny will be to "progress to the idea of an unchanging source of light" (Bachofen), uncontaminated by night, *ignis non urens* [unscathed by fire], as the Delphic nature of Apollo.[65] The catastrophe of the Marina seems analogous to that of the impossible Lycian symbiosis. Bachofen's "progressive" idea of evolution rests in Apollo's superiority. Yet the swollen night of hurricanes that approaches Böcklin's necropolis is far more menacing. The horns of the forest that threaten to contaminate Junger's Campagna are far more disturbing. Böcklin's deserted Lycia becomes merely a necropolis, as the dark demons of the Chief Ranger follow the collapse of the "happy case" of the Lycian utopia. Bachofen's Delphic Apollo merely expresses the other side, the symbol, of this collapse.

The Lycian utopia is too complex a game for Otto Weininger's pale, juvenile enthusiasm. Here Apollo reveals the hybrid quality of his light, the equivocal source of his Delphic splendor. Even in

Evola's analysis[66] (which brings out several obstacles in the older Bachofen), the Lycian motif is left in the background, while the foreground looms with mortal, absolute disagreement between all the tellurian forces below and the great Olympian mysteries, between Samsarian existence "conceived as an eternal and meaningless wheel of birth" (Evola) and the "true" Hellas, the Apollonian, Olympic Hellas. Even Weininger (with less erudition but with more inventive force) denies this absolute contrast that confines the "civilization of the Mother" to the pure, dynamic appearance of the Pelasgian figure of Gaia. Weininger tries to adapt Kant in a "paradoxical" sense to this mythic scheme. (Kant delivered the "academic philosophy" of his time.)

The most surprising and disturbing aspect of Lycian experience is the fact that the dominion of light preserves "the pre-eminence of the maternal principle." Furthermore, Apollo remains variously associated with the Pelasgian element and "in perfect correspondence with the ideal of the most ancient Orphism" (Bachofen). The god still appears a child of Leto, the surging genetrix of Aurora. We have seen the positivistic and progressivist schematicism Bachofen uses to resolve the paradox: Lycia would not be "elevated" again to the level of a Delphic religion. Lycia would "never have reached this superior level, the Hellenic idea of the divine." "Progressively," the child of Leto frees himself from earth's lap, *gremium matris terrae*, cancels his Thracian Orphic traces, and pronounces his plain affirmation: the *is* of being. Lycian Apollo would be, finally, incomplete, and his incompleteness would consist in the ambiguity of his actions. "Progress," therefore, is simplicity, good form, "economy."

Weininger is limited to "resolution" of Bachofen's Lycian Utopia (whose polemical groundlessness Giovanni Colli demonstrated in other terms, incorrectly, in Nietzsche):[67] on one hand Apollo and on the other his opposite, the "femininity" of Dionysius. As Bachofen confirmed in *Mutterrecht*, the relationship between Dionysius and Kore passes to a new plane in the relationship between Dionysius and Aphrodite. The Lycian Utopia founders under symbols from the "well-ordered" mother of grain harvests to the Bacchic bunch of grapes and voluptuous fruits, from milk and honey to "wine, bearer of drunkenness and of sensual excitement" (Bachofen), from the lofty symbols of Demeter to the tellurian weight of the swamp with all its creatures and flora. The harmony of bread and wine, which is celebrated in the happy temples of the Marina and Lycia, collapses when the swamp and forest surge. Wine accelerates into drugs (not by chance did Ernst Jünger dedicate one of his best books to drugs),[68] and bread becomes the fruit of *Abgrund*, of the abyss. Jünger, too, still resists the idea of utopian harmony. In Weininger, this idea needs to be struck. The hand that strikes it proclaims itself Olympian. The target, however, is the same one that the Chief Ranger's mute wild woman pursues. We wait for the paradoxical exchange of roles that renders Klinger's centaurs so enigmatic. Who defends the Marina? Who are its inhabitants? Who can gaze upon the splendor of things in the Mediterranean light? Perhaps Klinger's centaur in flight (see Figure 7) is the inhabitant of the Marina that defends its land from the Chief Ranger's hunters. The centaur has a double nature—he preserves in his figure the doubleness that constitutes the Lycian utopia. The men who pitilessly hunt him want to resolve, define, divide him. He cannot rest in peace between divine and human, man and animal, Apollo and Kore. Is he not Chiron, who passes his knowledge on to men, drawing down upon himself the hatred of the new gods? Does he not sing along with Orpheus? And do not the centaurs live "where the banks are rich with cliffs and grottos," in the regions where "the river had to wind before finding its way?" Glossing Pindar, Hölderlin sees the centaur that lives in the in-between time when the earth tries to give its own elements form, when the dry things congeal and the rivers find their direction through "strong rooted trees." The Lycian utopia also exists in this in-between time, whose wisdom still knows how to reconcile opposites. It sings "the true songs of Centaurs, sung with the spirit of the river." But the centaurs embody the earth when the new regime of the hunter breaks out in it: man and horse divided. And the honeyed wine that they experienced for the first time served only to make them lose the way.

Weibliches

Arnold Böcklin's oceanic creatures embody the tradition that ends with ignoring Apollo's Lycian relatives (Nietzsche's Dionysius is in fact very close to them) and with imagining women only in the figure of Io tormented by desire. Bachofen remembers that Io is driven by passion all the way to Cilicia and Panfilia, but she never reaches Lycia. A painting like *Ulysses and Calypso* could illustrate Weininger: Calypso, who holds the harp of seduction, gazes toward the figure of a man, upright on the cliff, sick with unbound nostalgia. The man turns his back to the woman, who wants to hold onto him. He is all longing and strife, *Sehnsucht* and *Streben*, a figure of the transcendent. While the woman is not the Iphigeneia in Taurus of the *Villa am Meer* or *Melancholia*, she is the appearance and enchantment of becoming. This Pelasgian image of woman continues down to Gustav Klimt's streaming goddesses (and Egon Schiele's, following Klimt's example). She evidently operates in Kubin, too. In one of his most beautiful drawings, an immense wave of hair falls from a proud figure shown in profile (*Die Haarschleppe*; see Figure 11). Elsewhere, the myth of Gaia comes up oppressive. Gaia in her tellurian obscurity (*Unser aller Mutter Erde*) or in her animal generation (*Das Gezücht*; see Figure 12), even transforms herself into the incubus of the *Temptation of Saint Anthony* or of *Die Spinne* (see Figure 13). In Klinger the female's belonging to the marine element is taken for granted.

In *Die Quelle* or *Die blaue Stunde* or *Am Strande*, her figure is contemplated as such by whomever must be detached or by those for whom detachment means pain, for whom loss is anguish. In Böcklin, in addition to the Siren, there is Flora, who sows the earth with flowers and the Elysian Fields with the love games of the blessed.

Otto Weininger's exasperated univocality might seem a wretched desperation indeed compared to the complexity and wealth of these motifs, but even the young Viennese knew how to fabricate myths, and these remain crucial for explaining the verses of Trakl, and Schiele, and the Heideggerian *Erörterung*.

The myth of Poros and Penia is found in Plato (*Symposium*, XX). Drunken Poros, failing in his role as the son of Metis, embraces Penia's endless thirst, embraces the non-being of illusory, ephemeral satisfaction, the privation and poverty that follow every apparent satisfaction. Eros is born from this submerging of the power and fullness of Being. Pandora is the fruit of this derailment of Being, the female embodiment of cupidity for whose sake, according to Hesiod, death entered the world. Women are an abyss for *viryâ* (energy), the figure that siphons off the magic virility of Being and determines its fall. Weininger's vision of the embrace is obsessed with this myth. The expression *viryâ* indicates arresting the flow of becoming or stopping the wheel of appearances, the way of high ascesis. Women are made of desire. "She darkens the sun." They are the eternal sorceresses that fascinate, that *seduce* the ascetic. They deflect the ascetic from the straight path onto the path of error. Women, who can give life, bar access or tend to bar access to all that lies beyond life. They reduce man to mere bearer of the phallus.[69] Weininger's war between the sexes cannot be reduced to paradoxically rendering Kant's ethics into absolutes. As in Meyrink, this is born of a great capacity to feel the myth nearby, as part of experience. (Briganti has noted the same intensity in Böcklin.)

In Weininger the ascetic and transcendental traditions of *viryâ* are continuously betrayed in ethical and moral terms. The reason for *viryâ*'s presence, insurmountable although embarrassing, in the

entire Viennese "apocalypse series," lies in its imaginative force, in
the imposing mystical background of Weininger's (evil) "metaphysics of gender." Running through the whole "apocalypse series"
is Weininger's idea of the pure lover, the absolute unfurling of
Eros, placing women in a superior order. He renders women aware
of the void that contradistinguishes their essence, aware of the in-
exhaustibility of their thirst. At the peak of their erotic potential,
women can finally comprehend all their misery and intuit the possibility of and the conditions for achieving a superior existence.
The fact that this argument changes its form in Kraus, for example, does not for one moment alter its inner structure. What is
Olympian for Weininger becomes for Kraus the cross of his condemnation. For both, however, the subject is the same. Kraus falls
into curious "sociologistic" errors whenever he sees in "the struggle
for pleasure" nothing other than a superstitious manifestation of
bourgeois morality. For Kraus, feminine amorality takes an offset
print, uniquely reversing the appearance of Weininger's terms for
feminine *kâminî* (she who is made of desire, Pandora). Kraus sees
women symbolized in Lulu, eternally pursued, confined to the bed
of Procrustes. Such women remain the centripetal force of
Weininger's mythology. Morality wants to crucify Lulu and take
revenge on her (Jack is none other than Lulu's ultimate torturer),
because she flees morality and does not allow herself to be possessed, and remains an elusive virgin. The elusiveness of the "absolute" woman is a central idea in Weininger: as much as men fall
for her and lose themselves over her, they will never succeed in possessing her ideal. Man may not possess if he embraces Penia. This
"reversal" of appearance that Kraus effects is even more evident
when considering his interpretation of Lulu as an "angel" to the
extent that she is delivered from the will to procreate. Weininger's
female lover, the *Typus-Weib*, is free from all reproductive instinct.
She loves without producing and finds desire complete in the act.
This is Penia's true, paradoxical nature. The feminine lover gives
herself eternally. She knows how to lose herself and so she is able to
lose. Kraus's critique of the productive (that is the center of his
Eröterung of the text of Frank Wedekind), however "prophetic" of

crucial moments in contemporary thinking, is substantially expressed by avenging the heroic character. This is the same figure that for Weininger prevents any heroic *Streben* and masculine nostalgia. The critique of aggressive male productivity registered in *Salomé* shares with Weininger an analogous relationship. Lou Andreas-Salomé reflects Weininger in her analysis of the "great presence" of the body in love, of its power to preserve, of its tragedy for the soul.

Weininger's reversed presence in later "immoralism" and in many later examinations of "values" makes him that much more important. Wittgenstein confirmed that Weininger's greatness consisted of his "enormous error," "which on the whole means that if one answers 'no' to his entire work, he is speaking an important truth." And what of Kraus's "no" or of Andreas-Salomé's even weaker "no"? And what of the simple examination of eclectic mixtures of traditional thought and morality? Or is it necessary to conclude, with Freud, that women hold the place of an impenetrable enigma, decipherable only in fragments and pieces? ("If you want to know more about femininity, look into your own experience.") Freud's conclusion turns out to be not very far from Weininger's. Because what is woman if not becoming and flowing, and thus decipherable only in pieces? What expresses her figure if not absolute opposition to the *standing* of law, to which man aspires? And finally, would the truth that Weininger indicates as a very "bourgeois truth" be a "no" were it appended to his entire work? That "no" would necessitate advocating a complete legal parity of genders. (It could just as well happen on the basis of reconfirming a metaphysical difference between them: Weininger is *apertis verbis* for legal parity, and he cares deeply about differentiating himself from the intentions of the "banal" Möbius.) Weininger's truth can emerge only by negating it, not by merely reversing it. No critique carried out in the name of "values" that he repudiates and disowns will ever be able to touch him. Such a critique persists in the fundamental opposition of the two principles: the transparence of the norm on one hand and the way of non-being, of desire and of its constitutive misery, on the other. The transcendental nostalgia of Olympian man is in absolute disagreement with the "exclusive" woman of the hour. Woman embodies man's obligation, straps him down, and keeps him down by the force of her body, blinding him to the idea. The "no" that opposes Weininger can only look upon the refusal to decide in terms of this recurrent discord. (There are infinite secular bastard varieties of this myth.) This discord ignores the "double" of the Lycian Utopia, the Nietzschean game between the masks of Apollo and Dionysius, between redemption from time and ruthless critique of every metaphysics of Being. Its unilateral nature is demonstrated in the very questions to which it yields. On one hand, women receive their own existence from the sexualization of men, from men's guilt and fall, and therefore women are not a true entity. (Women exist uniquely as an expression of Don Juan.) On the other hand, one wants to find out how to abandon this specter, to become the active force that helps men to realize themselves according to their supposed being. Women are the ones capable of disturbing the seers sent by the king to *seduce* the boy "born to Enlightenment," born to study the ascetic and to save the Buddha! Gender and character seem to end in this invocation that finds new accents in Lou Andreas-Salomé (the abandonment of women to productivity, her custody of a self-enclosed "happiness," complete and pure in the sexual impulse).

Andreas-Salomé is just the right figure to help us make a final pass at discovering Weininger's "truth." Her abandonment is a nostalgia for the idea. She wants to provide a form, in and of itself, to Weininger's idea. In wanting to assume man's nostalgia for herself, she reveals the basis of her desperation: an authentic *desperatio de viro*. Man is by now, in reality, driven into an indistinguishable chiaroscuro of Poros and Penia. A pale memory of the Olympian can live only in women, since only women suffer its absence. Whether women attempt to express Weininger's idea in and of itself or whether they rise up against it (thus regenerating it continually, denouncing it as law, as the norm, as moral suffocation of desire), they do not succeed in naturalizing themselves in its absence, in the void that its absence leaves. Either women try to substitute themselves there, or they reproduce the specter incessantly, in order to hurl themselves against it.

All this indicates Weininger's "truth": the man of his myth does not exist. The hero immersed in gardens of Kundry must go back, across abandonment, to the heavens of logic, of values, of law. The hero that goes beyond any *doxa* (even Lukács in those years delineated his tragic solitude) is the specter of a tradition interrupted forever, a hallucination that Weininger forces himself to grasp in vain. Man exists only in becoming and in desire, against which his idea should struggle encompassing intelligence, wandering, and metropolitan prose. Nostalgia for his idea belongs to women. The downfall of the idea provokes in woman an insufferable delusion. The *viryâ* remains as a specter of women, and never so clearly as when women hurl themselves against a nonexistent *viryâ*. Man forces himself to adopt the illusion for himself (as in *Lulu*, for instance), but he only becomes more foolish and strained in that role. As man disappears little by little, as his cycle declines, the more forcefully must he produce a nostalgia for woman, and so the more violent is his assault on the idea. Feminism is the supreme act in which women seek to embody the declining myth of man. "Marfisa is a feminist. Bradamante is a feminist. All the women warriors are feminists who shudder with anger and shame at the very notion of being beaten by a knight. Hedda Gabler enacts a superior feminism when she compensates for the lack of pride, dignity, and courage in the man she loves."[70]

It is clear why Weininger cannot understand Nietzsche. "Human, All Too Human" is already an act of reciprocal nonexistence, so to speak, between man and woman and points to something beyond their metaphysical disagreement. And here Nietzsche finds himself in agreement with Trakl and Schiele, in radical negation not only of Weininger, but of his very "reversals." In Trakl, men and women are a unified family stock. The ancient family, cloven and exiled, embraces both. They form a unified family stock of their own even through discord—since discord is precisely the family's destiny. This curse cannot be surmounted through an ascetic stance toward the world of things and senses. Wagner's Parsifal (even Nietzsche refused to find charm in its libretto) does not have at its core the destruction of the idea of "redemption by means of love," as Weininger resolves in *On Supreme Things*. Instead, Parsifal stands for *parting* from this idea, in the sense of Trakl's Heideggerian *Erörterung*: in favor of seeking the earth, the possibility of which is established in the singing.

Men and women are a *unified* family stock, consigned by destiny to discord, but also open to *parting*, to splitting apart. In its fundamental sense, this means abandoning metaphysical discourse, for which every "doubling," every otherness, seems wrong. The place from which men and women, a unified family stock, become estranged in their ruined cycle is not the unity of Being of metaphysics, but peaceful otherness, otherness that happens on earth and under the heavens, that declares itself as discordant harmony rather than transgression. The parting can be reached only after demolishing Weininger's myth. Colette Peignot, Georges Bataille's Laura, makes a partial attempt when she says, "To declare yourself free you have to imagine the chain that I would be. Then you have something to break, a fixed order to transgress. I, a girl, treating you the way my mother treats me. I must deny what you want because you want it times ten."[71] Vasilii Rozanov also assists this demolition by uncovering Weininger's preference for the "strong sex," the "feminine eye," "his envy of women."[72] But in this Weininger only evokes the specter of man reproduced by woman. Men must "transgress" women and women men. Each becomes the other's norm. Two poles, each fantasizing the other as an obstacle or chain. Each continues to live with the dead myth of the other. And when the vision of this nonexistence can no longer be held back, then hopeless discord breaks out, where "the lacerating discord of the sexes" (Heidegger) seems complete or close to it. What is completed here is, once again, the structure of "appropriation" at the basis of eroticism's will to power. This motif shows up continually in Nietzsche: love between the sexes as an impulse to ownership (*Eigentum*), as an appropriative instinct, as greed. This powerful impulse is based on otherness—on the otherness felt as a contradiction to be removed, to be surmounted, or to be liquidated. Therefore, it is based on man and woman each being a reciprocal norm to the other, a norm that is transgressed in order to obtain unity. Weininger is completely subject to this pattern, and so are *all* of his possible "reversals." The disabling of the terms of rapport is the first step toward the negation of Weininger, already discernible in Nietzsche. This negation strips away the old possessions, disabling them completely. The breaking open of the *Grund* [ground] leads immediately to the mere *Ab-grund* [abyss], whose first images cannot but seem specters of Schiele. They still belong to the appearance of the war between the sexes, of its completed cycle. Yet in this war they are no longer capable of any settled ownership. A hopeless stupor signifies relationships that stifle and are confused, and to these belong a body still capable of suffering.

Beyond this curse, where men and women desire to be overwhelmed and are reflected in reciprocal discord, is there a departure for the *Abendland* of discordant harmony and a rest at home in otherness?

The Eternal Child

Is such a harmony thinkable, if the singing belongs only to the friend who remains, if the singing does not come from parting, but from that "lacerating discord" where men and women have fallen and where they are *nothing* to each other? All the Traklian tones of undoing are present in Schiele. The road of the departed, that which lives in the tomb of the *Wahnsinnige* [the madman] remains rigorously unutterable. Surmounting the curse of otherness, for those who remain alive, is unutterable. The state of otherness disintegrates, exposing its sinews, betraying its ephemeral nature. But, for men and women, it is possible to reach nothing more than the common recognition of the damnation of that state. There is no embrace then, but rather men and women gripping each other, as in Schiele's great canvass of 1917, embracing separation, a death (the monk with his eyes wide open, that shows up frequently in Schiele: for example, in *Death and the Maiden*, 1915). And when the embrace gets tired, because it takes place in disintegration, they remain absent organisms, coupled in a single misery (*The Family*, 1918).

It is the world that Trakl describes thus in "Allerseelen":

> Das Seufzen Liebender haucht in Gezweigen
> Und dort verwest die Mutter mit dem Kind.
> Unwirklich scheinet der Lebendigen Reigen
> Und wunderlich zerstreut im Abendwind.

A cry of lovers trembles in the branches
and there the mother and child spoil.
The dance of the living seems unreal,
strangely scattered in the evening wind.

Bodily flesh cannot be redeemed in the sense of ethics or
Weininger's myth or (although palpitating elsewhere in Trakl) in
the sense of the "lunar voice" of the "sister" across the "spiritual
night" (*Spiritual Sunset*, second version), of an extreme *Geschwisterliebe*. Schiele's bodily flesh is already marked in the gaze of children. It weighs like an insurmountable obstacle on solitary figures,
in spite of their solitude. (Even in extreme solitude one is alone
with one's own sex.) Death here seems to ignore the tone that Heidegger finds in Trakl, almost a preservation of the not-born in order to announce the *Abendland*.

The not-born is already wrapped in the black mantle of death.
In fact, he lives in a dead mother, powerless to give birth to
him (*Tote Mutter*, 1910, see Figure 14; the motif was present in
Klinger). "Alles ist lebend tot," writes Schiele that same year:
everything living is seen in its ruin, the pregnant woman stands
next to death (*Schwangere und Tod*, 1911) and the very lymph that
carries things into presence decrees their undoing. "Where are the
living?" cries the "eternal child" (*ich ewiges Kind*) to Arthur
Roessler. "To live means to cast seed, sow seed, to be prodigal."
But for whom? For eternal scholars? For the dead who masquerade as the living? For the eternal states where life is money? The
child who counts only gifts, who despises school and money, who
opposes his own radical recklessness to productivity, does not
know where to find the living so he can disseminate himself
among them. He is "chosen." (That is why there is no new art,
only new artists. Art is singular, and basically ever the same, the
art that the "chosen" know how to express.)[73] But art has no one
to choose.

In man's vision there is no peace. The same line that in Klimt
indicated the fleeting nature of form is reversed here into a pitiless
analysis of the sinews that hold a body up. The living is already

dead, and the drawing reveals the masquerade. The autumn and winter trees, Schiele's landscapes, resemble the body (*Winterbaüme* and *Herbstbaum in bewegter Luft*, 1912). Even the houses show an affinity to it. Foreign to any idea of dwelling, they seem to be awful refuges (*Tote Stadt*, 1911), blank windows opened wide, like the eyes of *The Blind Mother* (1914). Houses and windows cling to each other, dominated by high, silent bell towers (*Stein's Views over the Danube*, 1913). Even the flowers, like people and trees, are stripped down to the sinews.[74] The stupendous sunflower of 1909–10 is at once straight and withered, "*und lacht und weint*"—it laughs and it cries, like the figures in the self portraits.

Trakl provides words to Schiele's landscapes:

> Häuser dräu'n aus stummen Nähen;
> Helle im Theatersaal.
>
> Kirchen, Brücken und Spital
> Grauenvoll im Zwielicht stehen.
> Blutbefleckte Linnen blähen
> Segel sich auf dem Kanal.
> ("Winterdämmerung")
>
> Menacing houses, huddled close in silence;
> Light in the theater.
>
> Churches, bridges, hospitals
> loom horribly in the dark.
> Swollen sheets, red with blood,
> are the sails on the canal

But "the lunar pathways of the departed" cannot reach in Schiele "das stille Haus und die Sagen des Waldes, / Mass und Gesetz." This image is prohibited to him. (In Franz Marc the woodland animals take charge in their wisdom.) The extent to which it was left an unresolved problem in Trakl was discussed in Heidegger's *Erörterung*. This is unutterable.

The unutterable, nevertheless, manifests itself. The image has weight. The soul that is a stranger on earth carries it along. It constitutes the "too deep" that Wittgenstein suffered in Trakl. Schiele, too, in a poem published in *Die Aktion* in 1916, exhibits it as the *Abendland*:

> Ich roch die Sonne.
> Jetzt war der blaue Abend da,
> sang und zeigte mir erst die Felder.
> Einen blauen Berg umfloss noch roter Schein.
> Ich war von all dem Vielduftigen umträumt.
> ("Abendland")
> I sensed the aroma of the sun.
> The blue hour of twilight now sang
> and first showed me the fields.
> A red glow embraced a blue mountain,
> and all the perfumes dreamed around me.

In "Empfindung," published in *Die Aktion* the previous year, the wanderer travels the earth, without ever noticing the weight of his body, he had become so light. The wanderer travels toward the horizon that shows up in Schiele's *Vier Bäume* of 1917. Also through the harmonic articulation of space, recalling Hodler, the landscape transfigures any naturalistic tonality. The reality that opens up, through the curtain of the four trees, before the eyes of the wanderer or whoever begins to wander over the grounds of separation, is the spiritual *Abendland*. Colors are suspended between dawn and dusk. The sky has the sunrise colors that Heidegger speaks of when he says, "*Dämmerung* is also the rising." The blue takes on qualities of brown and red. In the background appear the blue mountains, again mantled in red splendor. Hidden in darkness, they now call out and choose. An earth calls out near the pale red sun. They are the colors of an ultimate summer, lasting not even long enough to be seen, which is why memory fails to capture them on canvas. It is a screaming self-portrait like Klinger's last work, *Enfant perdu*. The "chosen" is the departed, the *Wahnsinnige*, "I, the eternal child." Trakl says, "Thus, spiritually, the oaks on the forgotten path of the dead turn green, the clouds turn gold, suspended over the lake" ("In Hellbrunn"). And it happens, then, as if the disease that seems to take hold of everything that exists, the non-living of life, revealed by Trakl, were transfigured by the voice of the Angel of the *Duino Elegies*: "But to have been one time, even only one time, to have been on the earth, seems irrevocable."

What couple on this earth rises up, almost imperceptibly? Perhaps the *Liebespaar* (see Figure 15), a pastel of 1909. Their arms are interwoven in a prayer-like dream. In perfect reciprocal trust, their lines present mysterious memories of the foundational discordant harmony.

Songs of the Departed

Closely related to the idea of departing is the idea of hiking or wandering. In Robert Walser's prose, wandering is to departing what, in Mahler, the Lied is to the symphony. The poet gets a "sacred, golden education"[75] from living outdoors. The idea of wandering is "high and noble." Benjamin was the first to fully understand how "difficult" wandering might be and how resistant to Romantic idling. The idea comes "out of night at its darkest, out of the Venetian night." Let us remember Simon's nighttime journey to visit his brother in the provincial town where they "were supposed to decorate a ballroom." And the other, even more enigmatic and labyrinthine ramble to the place where his sister Hedwig was a teacher, marked by the meeting with the poet Sebastian, who had frozen to death. The force that makes this meeting an occasion for joy goes unnoticed: "'Your death under the open sky is beautiful. I shall not be able to forget it for a long time. . . . ' He should have been able to scream for joy in the freezing night pierced with stars." Only a "sacred, golden education" could render its faithful capable of finding in this death no less than "an exhortation to life." "He felt a profound joy for having seen once more, for having met in such a mysterious way, that poor unhappy being." Whence springs this "flame of life" that sweeps away images of death, that transforms the rigid body of the poet lying in the snow into "splendid repose," that embroiders marvelous flowers

140

over the coldest winter night? An irresistible, disturbing force of "yes" emerges from Walser's hike. Wandering is a way of saying "yes" to every image of life and death, of opening oneself completely to the infinite possibility of meeting.

Wandering reveals the facts of the world. It bears silent witness that the world is all that is the case. Wandering brims over with directions, situations, meetings, and impressions. It is beyond any possibility of discourse. Cases that constitute experience make up the whole world. No superior wisdom can redeem manifold coincidence from it. Agony comes of such experience, which stops a Romantic idler such as Knut Hamsun's nomad. In Walser, an absolute sense of decency about language does not let agony express itself. The reality is made manifest, the *fact* of agony, not agony. It is necessary to speak of things, not of words. Marvelously, everything that is utterable is said whenever one simply states the case. Wittgenstein should have spoken about Walser, not about Johann Ludwig Uhland. But to reach such a simplicity constitutes the culmination of the "sacred, golden teaching" that Walser "initiates."

This simplicity cannot be reduced to the opening passages of the *Tractatus* (to the case, the way it appears there) or to knowing how to demonstrate agony with silence. It is even further from "definitive understanding of the provisional and dissonant nature of life."[76] In Walser, the intent of the compact grandiosity of the ego is self-evident. The intent of the Romantic ego as wanderer is likewise self-evident. (Nothing is more "grandiose" than Caspar David Friedrich's pilgrim on the misty sea.) The miracle is that the sort of agony that comes from such an intention is not the essence of the work, nor does a sense of decency (the authentic *aidos*) cause us to remain silent about it. The case is not seen as mere dissolution of the ego, as absolute and definitive dissonance. That the world is the totality of facts does not suggest a radical devaluation. No philosophy of value, no idea about the measure of the world can shed light on Walser's facts—and yet these facts shine with unnoticed energy. They are like miracles.

An unforseeable abyss seems to crack open the surface of the most radical nihilism. There is no value, since there can be no val-

ues among the facts of the world. There are only equivalent propositions, only the utterable. And even this does not mean a desperate glimpse of caducity. Walser ignores the assumed virility of such
a glimpse. He gives up all hope of value, but then the very form of
his despair is seductive and enchanting. His necessary acceptance
of the propositions of nihilism opens miraculously onto enchantment and onto the splendor of the case, a mysterious joy in the
apparently provisional and fleeting nature of the world. This
world, a world without values, shines with its own new light. It is
no longer the light emanating from judgment, whether it be the
wanderer's Romantic agony or the "virile" judgment of a rational
disavowal of a home or dwelling. Wandering does not simply consume the *Entwertung* (devaluation) of the world; it celebrates the
transformation of fact into miracle. It is a miracle that the thing
shines precisely as a fact. It is a miracle that there are facts that surprise us, that impress us, that stand and remain as fleeting and
ephemeral, in a divine fullness, autonomous, ignorant of our reflecting and judging. A moment of grace, inexpressible in itself,
takes place when the same, direct, "simple" description of the fact
demonstrates its divine fullness. Thus in Walser the ineffable manifests itself continually.

A fact is unique. Its singularity makes it solitary, extraordinary,
and not capable of being repeated. "And they want you to exalt
these things that live among the fallen. Fleeting, they throw an an-
chor to us, the most fleeting." Martin Buber says, "Not to repeat
oneself is an eternity of the single."[77] The same applies to Walser's
pursuit of the wanderer: the light of the event that captures it is
that of its singularity. The wanderer is capable of aspiring to the
extraordinary singularity of every fact: the rustle of the woods, the
welcoming inn, the local artist's song. The "flood of gratitude that
breaks forth from a contented soul" that impresses him in these
encounters turns out to be incommunicable to others: it is his relationship with the fact as an autonomous and unique existence
that others find incomprehensible. They don't know how to see
with the eyes of a wanderer. Each case, for them, emerges in sudden apparent caducity. They do not know how to submit to

Walser's song sung before every fact in the world, before pure events: "Eternity, I love you." However, the wanderer teaches them nothing. He only sees that "here it ought to be divinely beautiful to love, to kiss," and to lie "discreetly buried in the fresh woodland ground, . . . to have a tomb in the forest." In this glimpse he meets the gaze of things. ("Es käme jetzt zur Geltung und träte hervor ein reizendes, feines Wirtshaus"—the house where we joyously meet is released from the realm of infinite possibility.)

Walser's journey takes place over the scabrous terrain of Nietzsche's most secret subjects. Only by remaining on their surface is it possible to plumb their depths. Appearance is deep: the eternal singularity of the fact within its eternal self-repetition. There is nothing beyond the "bona fide earth." Everything is here and "I'll have nothing anywhere else." Walser loves this destiny of belonging to earth and to the cases that flourish here. The "sacred, golden teaching" of wandering is a gay science. This is also the source of Walser's special ironic tonality that Roberto Calasso isolated,[78] so different from the Romantic assertion of laughter over the equivalence of the world, not a diabolical irony, but a cheerful one. Irony dissociates an event from the discursive and metaphysical forms that had made it logical. Cheerfulness demonstrates its intrinsic depth and gratefully accepts its eternal singularity. There can be no cheerfulness without irony. There can always be, however, malicious irony.

What makes up this gay science? Certainly it is not a critique of repetition alone (a critique of Kierkegaard's subtle ascendancy—yet another connection between Walser and Kafka). It is not even a Nietzschean critique of the *Grund*, of the study of origins and foundations that the wheel of appearances would celebrate and that would touch the sage through asceticism's methods of self-denial. The true problem of the gay science lies in the relationship between the "yes" and "amen" to life and time, and redeeming time. The profound melancholy that comes from "so it was" confuses the glimpse that takes in the miracle of an event. Is this fortunate fact destined to pass away? Does its singularity equal an eternal absence? Does saying it is never repeated mean it will be

lost forever? At the end of the journey, Walser's wanderer has certainly collected many colorful flowers, but now he must ask himself if they should be strewn over his own sorrow. He is occupied
"by a disturbing and irrepressible thought. . . . Life is so florid,
with all the delightful colors and the joy of living . . . , and one
day you disappear and die." The facts that flourish for him along
his walk seem to recede definitively into the dark night, to abandon him. Was that divine nature that they expressed, then, a fantastic illusion? In Simon's final enigmatic words, the unresolved
Nietzschean connection reappears between becoming (vanishing
while becoming) and the idea of the eternal return (as opposed to
mere repetition). He speaks of the marvelous face of the earth, saying he is in love with it but that it is offended and requires expiation. Simon must repay "all that I neglected, all that I lost playing
and dreaming, all that I left out and all that I got away with." Why
is earth offended and why does it require expiation? Weren't they
earth's facts that summoned him to play and to dream? Isn't knowing how to see life as a game, free of foundations, chains, and *religio*, the greatest praise it can be given? Earth did not require a de-
nial of the game, but rather that the game should not have passed
from nothing to nothing. In the end, earth does not want the
flowers picked on a journey that proceeds from departure to be
strewn over the unhappiness and melancholy of "so it was." Earth
asks the paradoxical redemption from time, *in* time of nihilism. It
asks for a quest for which there is no name. In the time of nihilism, the "glory" of things is nothing but unstoppable lightning
that for an instant rends the course of time. Earth wants expiation
for our powerlessness to halt the quest and to name it. Simon becomes, then, the tragic hero who recognizes this fault and assumes
it radically upon himself. That is why "he will not be lost."

The musical *Stimmung* of Walser's wandering is purely from
Schubert. It belongs to a tradition that concludes "with implacable
exactness" in Webern's ceremonial "syllabification, in his Lied that
shuns the impulse to salvation in order to listen to the truth of the
sound-symbol, in the silence of the internal man" (Bortolotto).

Such a tradition is founded on the "endless attempt to silence agony" that Elias Canetti recognizes in Walser. "The great meditation on the foreigner, wanderer, or derelict" that is "the compulsory gate into Schubertian liederism" and that continues to Wolf and Mahler (Bortolotto) is dominated by the problem of silencing agony. Manifest in the agony of the departed are frugality, moderation, avoidance of frenzy, avoidance of novelty, attraction to the traditional elements, regret over *Modernität*, simplicity that stems from the most ardent engagements, and a decency about language. An inexorable connection unites, in the Webern of Op. 14 and in Trakl's verse, the conditions of being *heimatlos* and *sprachlos* (homeless and speechless). If one lacks a dwelling, one's speech betrays it. Words belong to the experience of dwelling, in the Heideggerian sense. This is clear in the silent splendor of the lovers in Webern's Op. 8, after Rilke.

Nothing is conceded to the *trauriges Lied* (sad song) from the pressing, repeated condemnation of the fugitive in "In der Ferne," from the "I'm not sorry" that the fugitive intones in "Abschied" and from the symbolic journey in "Winterreise." Irony and pleasure jealously guard the secret of composition: a place to linger, the "muss ich vorbei," resounds in the clarity of the deed, in the actuality of going. These same principles are carried by Wolf to their radical consequences. He rediscovers "musically the Pythagorean formula that regulates the rhythms of the world: the march, the serenade, and the dance" (Bortolotto). He is the first to rediscover Walser's rhythm of the step that treads the roads, that cuts furrows in the brow of Mother Earth. The step takes pleasure in friction, resistance, and resonance. In a cardinal passage, Bortolotto explains the characteristics of the music that Nietzsche could not hear, music of deep appearance or, as noted, of the eternal singularity of the case. In a few texts like Eduard Mörike's "Fussreise" or "Auf eine Wanderung," the soul that is a stranger on the earth is very near to a morningtide *renovatio* and to the *Liebeshauch* [breath of love] that blows from the woods at the first light of sunrise. The song has flowers waving in the breeze (the very life in the air). It is sung with extraordinary freedom and invention, and without anything to concede to "the florid goddesses of love" (Bortolotto). It is the happy moment, the *kairos* [crisis], when the soul of the world opens up, when "the marvelous tableau of the present moment" becomes the only sensation: "the days of the future became dim, the past vanished. I, too, was burning in the blaze of that moment." The climactic experience of Walser's wandering already appears in Wolf's "madness," when in every direction there stands out "everything that is great and good, luminous, in shining gesture of blessing." The moment is "divinely beautiful" in its accidental quality. There is no ecstasy, no dream of transcendence. The same "little things" cited in the opening Lied of the *Italienisches Liederbuch* appear renewed, and with them the glimpse of the world appears renewed. "Madness" is the wanderer's intuition of the divine oneness of the case. The wanderer's detachment does not reach beyond the world. It stops at this worldly light, this worldly eternal lighting of the "smallest things." Walser says, "I looked around attentively at how many of the smallest, most modest things there were, while the sky seemed to arch high above and plunge into the deep. The earth was a dream. I myself had become an interiority and I went along as if I were inside the interior. Every exterior form dissolved, comprehended before but now incomprehensible." There is a profound and ineffable encounter in the midst of the extra-ordinary ordinary: that the world exists and is not nothing, and that it resists nothingness.

The departed, the "madman," knows neither *trauriges Lied* nor *klagendes Lied*: he neither complains nor accuses. He has learned calm and silence from the forest. The forest is quiet, and yet its color and motion reveal its secret suffering. "Whoever suffers can learn from the madman how unpleasant it is to prematurely embitter the lives of others with one's own sullen and complaining presence." In Walser's woods the genre of happiness coincides with that of sorrow, just as it does in the Schubert song, and in Wolf and Mahler. "Happiness and sorrow are intimate friends." This woods is not simply the opposite of Kubin's forest, since it also suffers profoundly; it also is a damp, running, overwhelming wave that dissolves forms, a "tumult" of colors that "awakens in humanity only sentiment, not reason." It also, ultimately, is sublime. The gaze that passes through it is renewed. The gaze that takes in Sebastian dead and frozen is renewed, a gaze fascinated by the present that belongs to one who knows how to listen. Simon says (with accents that seem reborn from the spirit of Sigismund), "I am nothing if not one who listens and waits, and in this I am perfect, because I have learned to dream while I wait." Whoever is perfect in listening and waiting cannot fear the demons of Kubin's forest. Agony and delight marry each other there while passing through. Agony is not sorrow. Sorrow is enduring melancholy, self-absorbed, trapped, and enclosed. *Melancholia* can never be the figure of the departed. Rather, agony is the ancient *penthos* [grief] of the earliest hermits, a repentance for their own sins that coincides with a renewed attraction to serve God by force of pleasure: *servite Domino in laetitia.*

Another "perfected being" loved the woods and wandered in them fearlessly, heedless of the monster that lived there. Martin Buber tells how the young Israel ben Eliezer, the future Baal Shem Tov, went to school every day leading the other Jewish children of his muddy village, "taking a wide detour through meadow and forest." The children were happy, picking flowers and green boughs to carry along the way. In the forest there lived a charcoal maker who turned into a monster at night, a werewolf who attacked animals and terrified people there (but who never harmed a human being). One day the Adversary took the charcoal maker by the throat, tore out his heart, and replaced it with his own, a heart out of the heart of darkness. At dawn, the monster, livid and terrible, attacked the children of Israel and terrified them with his mouth foaming. But Israel knew how to listen and wait. He implored the parents to trust him with their children once again, so he could confront the monster in the forest. He led the children to the place by the forest. The werewolf appeared and grew huge before their eyes. Israel penetrated the monster's chest and grasped the heart, dripping with "the infinite suffering that was within it from the beginning." The monster is sorrow imprisoned in the realm of Melancholia. Israel is the power of prayer and of the cheerfulness that goes with it. Israel is called upon to demonstrate this, even if the children soon forget and end up like "grown-ups," going through the countryside with their heads bowed, seeing nothing. Only "perfected" beings know how to wander.

Those who listen and wait do not judge. The very essence of the "sacred, golden teaching" of the wanderer, of Simon, of the helper, consists in not judging. Wittgenstein's theories and Hassidic *pietas* and *humilitas* seem based in this commandment. If judgment is value, it is outside of the world, outside of the case; in the world judgment is impossible. If we judge, our judgment is intrinsically groundless, because if one were to make a grounded judgment, it would be according to Truth, it would have Value, that is, it would exist outside of the world. Therefore, it would not exist. The abandonment of *Grund* (and of the "*religio*" of *Grund*, as Magris and Calasso have explained) carries with it the abandonment of judgment. This abandonment, in Walser, is a source of new affection and not simple "virile" despair. It is a *metanoia* that unexpectedly impresses, that takes hold in the happiest moments, beyond any possible method. Walser's labyrinthine chatter (Calasso) intends to rescind every connection between the discursive nature of method and the way of awakening, the way that mysteriously leads to the "divine beauty" of the case. Not judging is, then, an exaltation of the creation and sanctification of living things, a self-emptying in order to yield to the fullness of what is manifest. What is manifest is certainly not, for Walser, God *signified* by the world or, as in Hassidic tradition, the world as the evidence of God.[79] In Walser, irony itself assumes the function of insuring that his "cheerful" abandonment to things does not seem a yielding to the fullness of the divine. Irony here shows that being a wanderer is a fundamental condition. Since being a wanderer means that one listens and waits, the condition is open also to the possibility of an inscrutable offering, like the existence of Mendel Singer. Walser's idiot declares himself unworthy of this miracle: whoever has no home now can never live in one. But his "madness" has separated him already from the old building. Already this is a cheerful fact, a fact that is praised through the entire scale in the gay science of Wolf's Lieder.

Walser's idiot, like the Hassidic fool, shuns confrontation and avoids any dialectical contest. ("He who weighs and measures becomes empty and unreal like weights and measures.") His ancient wisdom urges him not to condemn and never to think of himself as other than a sinner. (Walser ignores the real meaning of the word.) He is urged to live in peace and to sustain love in spite of the long distances (the relationship between Klara, Simon, and Kaspar seems to be a memory of an earlier life, of a joyful closeness past, that the labyrinths of exile have not been able to erase). Even Simon can confirm that, for him, no one is "the other," that there is nothing in the world that is not touched with life. (Every creature knows it, in unknowing omniscience.) The humble Hassid, however, "ends up on the edge of the cliffs of solitude, perfecting an alliance with the infinite" (Buber). His affinity with terrestrial things and his sympathy for animals are nothing other than the symbol of his alliance with the infinite. They prepare it and they announce it. The kind of wandering that Walser proposes changes its mood like the sky, according the line in a key poem from *Kleine Dichtungen* (1914).[80] His style of wandering does not know the mystery of the soul straining for *the* end (the only thing that never lies and never gets lost). The soul stretches to the point of identifying with the end and living for it. The Hassidim call this intention *kavanah*. This intention is missing in Walser, because the idea of redemption is missing, the idea of returning from exile into *shekinah* [presence], of participating in the divine glory of the Creator. In Walser, the countless sparks of souls fallen and strewn among creation make no pilgrimage to their source. Instead, they end up contradicting themselves in their joy and suffering, in their guilt and innocence. Walser does not discuss simple absence of faith, but rather an infallible instinct directed against any possible form of dualism. Walser has never been able to say, like the zaddik introduced by Buber, that he awaits redemption as he opens the window, and looks about, and declares, "There is no renewal." Walser's waiting corresponds to the continuous renewal of the landscape and sky. In his eyes the world has no need of redemption, but his eyes need to recover from loving the world's singularity that eternally renews itself. How is it possible to think about redemption and not see, at the same time, the world as shell or mere appearance, or as an obstacle to the divine? How is it possible, through this faith, to surmount dualism?

The dialogue between Klara and Simon in *The Tanners* is unforgettable. As for the young Baal Shem, nowhere is more pleasing to his God than the woods. ("God seems to have created the woods to pray there as in a holy temple.") Like a zaddik, God remains in ecstasy whenever he is thanked, "even just a little, even superficially." God is *grateful*. He is "happy if his creatures remember him somewhat." He is *humble*. He confines himself in a realm of silence, of soft modesty, of apparent "indolence." He is *otiosus*, idle, but not because humanity forgets him or replaces him with other names, but rather because "he doesn't insist on anything, doesn't want anything, doesn't need anything." Perhaps he has "forgotten" his creation. When humanity adores him, "they pray in the woods without meaning to." It is as if God had remembered for an instant and were content with that memory, even though it is nothing to him. The absence of God has never been explained in more mysteriously simple terms. God is silence, but a secret current of affection binds this silence to the prayers of the heart that prays to him (and praying is the same as "becoming lost in thought"). The exile of God from the world is interrupted, at times, along the sudden arch of this memory. The painful awareness of this exile and of that silence can yield up cases of happiness. God does not want "people to be believe too much in him." God "wants to be forgotten," wants to be *otiosus*. He does not intervene, does not enlighten, and does not guide. He is the opposite of infinite production that characterizes his "official" image. He does not want to be called back from exile and oblivion—which is what the Hassidim seek in their excessive faith through unceasing prayer. The blind pride of man believed God's idleness was the result of his gaze and judgment! He, amenable, retreated, "delighted," before the injuries that would batter him and declare him dead. He "permits all thoughts." Where does his extraordinary richness reside? It resides only in the "lower regions"[81] of the profane, of the quotidian, of babble, only in the regions rejected by the arrogant pride of producing, only in the particular and in the humble sympathy for things and their events, only where faith is "little" and silent. Only there can a new and secret connection light up, forgotten, between creation and an "incautious" God. The greatness and goodness of the image of God rests in his desire to be forgotten and in his pliancy. The truth about God in this world lies in his not appearing here and his not producing here.

Klara feels herself beautiful when she says, "Whoever I caress with my hands can be happy." The perfect statement about listening and waiting is hers, however much suffering and "madness" it requires. It is madness in the manner of Hölderlin, according to a likeness that Walser perceived exactly, and it casts new light upon his entire doctrine of wandering. Hölderlin is "the hero in chains," a "royal Greek" obliged to move about within the narrow, horribly papered walls of a bourgeois room.[82] Hölderlin is a spirit who is capable only of living free. Freedom, however, is now a dying dream, and his song uncovers the empty squalor of life. "The hands that hold destiny pull it out of this world." They free it in madness, in the noble, good, and luminous abyss of *Wahnsinn*. For him, everything becomes "an abyss, an unbounded," free and open space. This is the madness of the solitary wanderer, of Simon, hardly masked by Klara's words. For Walser, the wanderer is the extreme figure of Hölderlin's kind of madness.

Hölderlin intones his highest and most regal song at the waning of the dream of being free in the world, of being here and now in the world in the light of the infinite. His tragic *threnos* accuses the world of the absence of God. In Walser, the tragic word is absent. Rather, continuous vigilance obstinately impedes any minimal hint of it. It is not simply modesty, not simply a sign of our poverty; it is the quest for a new way of looking at the time of the no-more and the not-yet. It is the attempt to see this time with love. Its desert is the only place where our destinies may cross, where one may listen and wait. Its singularity is loved and served. The desert of crossed destinies provides a foundation to our going—and journeys can have secret destinations that not even travelers know. Poverty is bitter, and the desert also means preserving, caring for this secret possibility. Its image is reached through tragedy, even if tragedy is an impossible measure of it. If asked, it would respond that tragedy is too high and noble for its "lower regions," but in reality the despair that lives there is a different song, a different quest: a highly fragile word, merely possible, evanescent in its possibility, almost negligible, too discrete, in near perfect silence, but as such cut off from all that can be weighed, handled, and judged—a word apart, departed, "mad."

The act of serving manifests this madness above all. It is found in the *Dieneridee* [idea of service] that dominates Walser's entire work. The theme of submission, of obedience performed with joy and conviction, is on the face of things tied to the theme of humility. It is tied to the tragic form's pure hopelessness and to how it prevails over free existence. One does not often notice the contradiction between the themes of the *Un-grund*, the absence of foundation, and of *Dieneridee*. Why must flight from *religio* express itself in the figure of the assistant, the clerk, the waiter? Too often we are constrained to repeat Walser's words, which appear to be so simple, "*ich bin noch nichts*" [I am still nothing]. ("I am a man, you should know, who does not deserve to be known"; "I am poor, and everything I say sounds impoverished.") Simon does not attach humility to service. The motifs of submission and obedience appear in various contexts, with the themes of abandonment and departure ("A Painter"), with themes of wandering and the woods. What upsets their quiet appearance is that the "servant" is a seducer. The "servant" knows how to execute a detour. That is, the "servant" knows how to take the lead down unfamiliar roads, along a thread of words whose secret he alone, almost unaware, seems to possess. There are people who defend themselves from seduction and others who, like Klara, abandon themselves to it. But service always indicates—or rather lets itself show—the possibility of a radical detour. That is how the servant seduces: because the servant already seems fundamentally, wholly, absolutely seduced. He is the most easily seduced, the ingenue par excellence. His condition proclaims how simple seduction is: how imminent, how close the possibility for our method to drive someone crazy, to seduce someone. That is why the servant is the other side of pure madness.

A work that can be linked to Walser only as its opposite can help to understand this nexus in which the figure of the servant directs. It would seem that nothing contrasts with Walser's *wandering* more than Herman Hesse's *pilgrimage*.[83] Pilgrims have a destination, and the destination continues to speak to pilgrims in their exile, as they resolutely inhabit their intention. Even if they moved without concern, pilgrims would still be directed. Their journeys stretch out in time, through impenetrable twists, toward the destination that has always existed. The star of redemption guides them, whether their path turns to "the East, land of light," land of esoteric traditions that Hesse brings together, or whether they answer the voices of the antique land that call them from their extreme poverty, as with the Baal Shem Tov. "Where are we going? Ever home." In Hofmannsthal, too, the journey is toward home. It is a pilgrimage, except in his last works, *Andreas* and *Der Turm*, where the pilgrim wakes up suddenly a pure traveler, and the landscapes no longer come to meet his soul, which had always lived in expectation of this happy visit. Hofmannsthal, in his last works, truly does not deserve Walser's fierce dig that Canetti so enjoyed: "Can't he forget being so famous for just a little while?"

It is in the course of a pilgrimage that a character of Hesse's reveals the hidden side of the servant in Walser. The account of the journey to the homeland is well known, "the soul's youth" that takes place in the magic circle of the unification of time and place. In that story, we meet names we already know, from the restless Hugo Wolf to the painter Paul Klee, whose Bible was *Don Quixote*. All the characters rotate around the servant Leo, whose sudden disappearance down the throat of Morbio makes them lose their faith in the journey and breaks up their group. They cannot endure the trial, and "a thousand tangled threads that a hundred hands would take years to sort out" hold them prisoners in exile. With Leo's disappearance, the journey animated by a pilgrim's clear intention is superseded by stumbling about in the labyrinth. Pilgrims of the

League turn into solitary vagabonds (whom Hesse had already softly sung in *Eine Fussreise im Herbst*: "To live is solitude. No one knows the other. Everyone is alone"). How can the disappearance of a simple servant determine such a downfall? What secret is hidden in serving?

Leo is a perfect servant. Whenever he presents himself to H.H. to drive him up to the cathedral, they cannot help but notice his "elastic, patient stride, all driver, completely dedicated to the task at hand, all function." During the happy days of pilgrimage, Leo had spoken to H.H. about the law by which an artist's image seems more alive than the artist, just as a mother passes her own beauty and energy to her children. "'The law?' I asked with curiosity. 'What law is that, Leo?'" The law of serving, Leo answered. Whoever wants to live a long life must serve. Whoever wants to rule does not live long. Only the servant endures, whoever loves serving endures. The others, those who want to become bosses, "all end up in nothing." They are sick. "'In what nothing, Leo?' 'In rest homes, for example.'" The need to rule signifies an essential void, a fundamental poverty. Penia is a ruler. Whoever wants to become a boss is empty, lacking, woefully imperfect, weakened by their incompleteness, and destined to vanish (the pointless war of Basilius, in the words of Ignatius). Serving, rather, is inexhaustible. It is Poros, fullness of being, a well whose source never dries up. It is unending *dépense* [expense]. Whoever commands must use other people, imprison them, and transform them in order to survive. Whoever obeys the law gives life, expends endlessly, is consumed for other people, is renewed by this, and so endures. The boss, who merely acquires and produces, gets sick and dies.

In these words we rediscover intact the dialogue between Simon and Klara: "I do not place great value on my life, but only on the lives of others, and nevertheless I love life, but I love it because I hope it gives me the chance to dispose of it decently . . . , and so I give myself to you because I know no better gift. . . . This gift that I give you is unstable and eternal: because even the simplest person is eternal. I shall belong to you still when in a short while I will no longer be anything, not even a speck of dust: because the gift always survives as long as the one who receives it can mourn the

loss of its possessor." Life is given to Simon to be spent; in fact, to
be given as a gift, since only the gift is eternal. Through giving,
the memory of those who know how to give also survives, since
those who know how to give, give themselves. "I was born to give.
I have always belonged to someone. I was disappointed if I went
an entire day without finding anyone to whom I could offer myself." Wandering consists in seeking someone to whom to give
oneself, in consuming oneself by giving oneself. Those who know
how to serve are in search of those who know how to listen to the
law of serving. The servant puts the law to the test and with it seduces. That is the source of the uneasiness of the characters around
Simon's crystalline *Klarheit*. He literally hates to receive gifts! "You
shouldn't love those who want to love, otherwise they would be
disturbed in their devotion." The utopia of a relationship where
one only gives, without ever "acquiring," emerges from the words
of the perfect servant. And it is the same motif as in Musil's
Geschwisterliebe.

Certainly, Simon is unlikely in the role of the supreme leader of
the League, "in solemn and magnificent attire." The transformation is impossible for him, no less than the faith of the zaddik is
impossible for him. But he, too, is one of the masks of the servant,
one of the forms in which the foolish wisdom of giving is refracted. He is perhaps its most profanely enlightened form, without any miraculous gleam, far from any ex-static initiation (and
further from any burst of literary decadence, which thrives in
Hesse's theme concerning the relationship between character and
author). Simon is also one of the cured, one of the awakened. Like
Leo, he can go along singing and whistling, playing with animals
and things, learning their languages. His madness is the sign of
reawakening, and of healing, that follows the dark Venetian night.
This night is not madness, as Benjamin said, but rather despair.
Despair does not ever appear directly in Walser's works, since he
assembles his characters after they have reawakened. We learn with
bitter distinction about their past, about this memory of theirs.
But the story speaks only of the madness of the reawakening and
of its relationship with the cases of the world in the light of the
golden teaching of wandering and serving. On this side of despair,

Leo explains, live the children, and beyond it live the reawakened. The way to despair traverses "every serious attempt to comprehend and justify human life," every search dedicated to judging cases according to value. H.H. is in the middle of the realm of despair. The work that he desires to write testifies to this. Works of despair are worth nothing. They suffer only from their own poverty. They do not know how to give themselves. Simon is not desperate. Nor is the child. Simon has crossed through despair, and he is finally able to feel the joy of serving and giving. The brother, a painter, is still a child. (Coincidentally, the art of Karl Walser, who illustrated a few of his brother Robert's works, partially to help stimulate their distribution, is an art of simplicity that renders interpretation superfluous. It is a playful art without system or law, a gently ironic art with flashes of Rococo and Biedermeier.)[84] The brother is a child who resists despair. Simon, on the other hand, confronted despair and traversed it. But this decisive experience is not utterable. Simon manifests it only in the two great forms of existence, his wandering and his serving: his opening up to receive the case as a divine singularity and the giving of himself. This double form merely indicates the possibility of a healthy permanence, of not ending up in the void, of not passing from nothing to nothing.

Simon does not teach this possibility. Simon is never the teacher, unlike Leo the servant, who in the end becomes one. Like his infinite capacity to give, Simon's enigma sustains itself and remains. However well he knows how to seduce (just as Leo the servant is a seducer), this seduction does not ever transform itself for him into power, into art. This is the peculiarity of Walser's style (which recalls Wittgenstein). The reawakened one is not a teacher; that experience cannot be taught. To teach is impossible. Only those who have undergone the experience understand it. This madness lets itself be understood by those who hold out their hand to it. In some way, like Klara's God, the madness is content with this gesture—it is content whenever people listen to it and attempt to utter it, because it is in that instant that they give themselves.

The Art
of Archery

The impossibility of teaching is connected with Wittgenstein's response to the idea of solution[85] and with Schoenberg's "didactic principle." Teaching is an indefatigable act of re-covery that ought to clarify the infinite complexity of languages and traditions that constitute their specific *Tatsachenraum*, an act never at home and never in pilgrimage. This is equally true of Walser's writing.

The cultural coordinates of the grand form have been up to now only partially investigated. Its radical difference from the "style" of contemporary European culture, from American-European civilization, is usually assimilated into the problem of an internal discord whose terms would never exceed the sphere of that civilization except in elusive motifs. But to the extent that this discord is never explicitly acknowledged, to the extent that the discretion and modesty of misfits is stronger and more refined than ever for the possibility of their own language, such an "excess" takes place. A possible path has already been indicated (we will return there) in the matter of the critical presence of *Ostjudentum* in the culture of the *Donaumonarchie*. Another is represented by the peculiar nostalgia for the East that runs through the sphere of American-European civilization almost continuously, even if it only reveals itself fully in sudden moments.

This attraction, which has solid and well-known roots in German culture, received a new impulse with the translations of Bud-

dhist writings by K. E. Neumann for Piper Verlag (not acciden-
tally the publisher of Wilhelm Worringer and the "Blaue Reiter"
group, of Schopenhauer's works, and of deluxe books in homage to
Mahler in 1910 and to Schoenberg in 1912). While the German
"pilgrimage to the East" was clearly influenced by Schopenhauer
and focused on the most "systematic" aspects of Hindu and Buddhist mysticism, Vienna at the turning point was galvanized by the
"undogmatization" that runs through the Chinese and Japanese
Zen Buddhist traditions.[86] The German Orient appears as a Tao, a
Way, both logical and ascetic, involving painful sacrifice and de-
nial of the world of appearances in search of the full light of the
nullification of being. The Viennese eternal travelers do not dare
utter the Way. On the Way, everything happens as a function of
the destination. Everything aims toward the end. The value of each
step is measured only by its progress toward separation from being. This in-tending to separate, this relationship between Way
and destination by which every being along the Way is nullified as
a function of the end, which is itself the condition of non-exis-
tence, constitutes a profound motif of the Viennese critique of the
subject-object relationship and of the concept of substance or essence. The history of this critique cannot be encompassed within
the "internal" limits of contemporary European culture, and even
less by reducing the relationship with *this* Orient to an exotic fascination. Such a relationship happens by fixing on and measuring
the abyss that opens out from the eye of the Zen monk, the eye
that sees the solution. (They asked Joshu, "What is my essence?"
And he responded, "The tree bends, the bird flies, the fish leaps,
the water is muddy." And again, "What is my self?" And he, "The
oak in the yard. *Look at it!*"). A critical and nostalgic comparison,
inextricably entwined, follows the direct look, the gesture of Chu
Hsi that Hesse praised. ("About enlightenment or about the beginning and end of the world, he kept silent. He only raised his
finger and lightly pointed. And the wisdom of that silent-speak-
ing finger became ever more eloquent and profound: it spoke, it
taught, it praised, it punished, and it guided thus uniquely to the
heart of the world and of the truth.") Siddhartha's ascesis is also

completely imbued with it. It leads to the veneration of the Buddha who enlightens every rock, every plant, and every animal to the perfection of every instant, to the sanctity of every being. *Love* is the force that compels us toward this destination, love as the quintessence of the *person*, of seeking, of in-tending—of metaphysical separation from being, since "the moment you aim toward something, you have already lost it." To express in terms of love and seeking the direct look at the divine value of the self is intrinsically contradictory. The very awareness of it—of the otherness of that look as opposed to reflection—renders the Viennese "seeker" like Hesse's Siddhartha in every other aspect, a coarse figure, not disposed to giving literary consolation. Zen motifs, common in Viennese Central Europe, are distributed within well-defined limits of critical and nostalgic consciousness.

This also happens to the figure of the teacher. We have already seen how, in Walser, reawakening is the living negation of teaching, and we find an identical repudiation of it in Wittgenstein, in Schoenberg, and in Freud's confession that teaching is impossible. The Viennese non-teachers do not preach, do not judge, and do not show the way. There are profound echoes of Zenjitsu in their counsel, of the ancient T'ang dynasty master: "to live in the world and yet not join the world's dust . . . ; a noble heart never shows itself . . . ; criticize yourself, no one else. Do not discuss truth and error." The idea that judging (as if one were in possession of values) is indecent belongs not only to a radical and paradoxical perspective on evangelism (Vannini) but also to *this* Orient. "I consider judgment of good and evil like the serpentine dance of a dragon, and the coming and going of beliefs like nothing other than the traces left by the four seasons." Zen masters wait for those who know how to listen to them, they do not ever seek them out. They "do not preach models to follow, do not believe in the edifying power of words" (Herrigel). The teachers never explain, but only point. Their relationship with those who listen to them is never discursive or agonistic; they are not out to convince. As the image of steps in the *Tractatus* undoubtedly alludes to a discourse of the Buddha, so it is impossible not to discern the Zen "style" in the first line of the Preface. ("Perhaps this book will be understood only by someone who has himself already had the thoughts that are expressed in it—or at least similar thoughts.") A Zen style runs through Wittgenstein's writing in general: in its attempt to render the problem plastically intelligible, to reduce it to a *case* for meditation, to articulate the argument in dialogue. The very roots of Wittgenstein's critique of Western *ratio typisch aufbauend* should also be seen in this perspective.

What all this is getting at is precisely the transcendence of the dual notion of reflection, of the a priori condition of constructive reasoning that consists in separating the thing from the self and in attributing substance to the self. It is perfectly clear to Wittgenstein, when he declares himself alien to the spirit of this civilization, that nihilism and the constructive power of nihilism reside precisely in this metaphysical separation. To tend, to in-tend, to ex-press, and to pro-duce all belong to such constructiveness and to its nihilism. Their action presupposes a fundamental separateness and, at the same time, the readiness of the thing, reduced to a phenomenon, to be reached, joined, transformed, and consumed. There is no *intentio* where "the perceiver is beyond the subjective and objective . . . , has the impression not of being the one to perceive things but of being perceived by them, has the sensation that they take advantage of the perceiver's senses in order to be and in order to reach the maximum fullness of being" (Herrigel). The text of *Zen in der Kunst des Bogenschiessens*[87] is throughout a limpid sign of this critique of intentionality as the key category of nihilism. The practice of archery does not help to develop attention to the "other," to the target (to learn to see the target, the "enemy"), but exactly the opposite, to reach a state that is free of intention, to become empty of the constructive and intending self. It is a doctrine that denies the presence of "a self-substance in the spiritual life of humanity" (Suzuki). The right shot at the right moment only happens when the archer is removed from any attachment to the old self, whether spiritual or physical, and remains surprised by the shot itself. "To the extent that she reveals herself more willing to learn to shoot a sure arrow and to hit the target,"

Herrigel's archery teacher explains, "she will be that much less able to succeed in the one thing and that much farther from the other. The obstacle is her will, which is too eager." One can never be one with the target where will controls the archer's hand (and will hangs upon power over the target). Thus the readiness should not be understood as intentional waiting and not as a simple absence of seeking, but as perfect presence: living in the present, in the moment, ready for enlightenment, just as without looking the archer hits the center of the target. The technical Mahayana term to define this state of illumination (satori) is *paravrittis*, which means to turn back or re-turn (Suzuki). It is a looking into oneself as remembering (*anamnesis*), a fundamental identity between the one who hits and the one who is hit.

Regardless of how useful the way of Zen may be for understanding the critique of Western civilization by the great Central European Viennese, that is not why it was proposed as a model. It is, in fact, practically never explicated. The impossibility of even discussing its Westernization is widely admitted. No one can traverse the inexorable lexicon of metaphysics by simply ignoring it. The Zen Way remains a great metaphor for this fundamental "ignorance," for ignoring the lexicon of metaphysics, and the caducity, the transience of nihilism that composes it. By this comparison (which remains critical) constructive reasoning is deprived of its "obviousness," stripped of the teleological and progressive basis that had legitimized its prevalence. Criticizing it does not by any means amount to traversing it and perhaps does not even constitute a first step. This is made very clear by a passage in Herrigel (even though he does not seem to realize its importance). To his archery teacher, who wants to show him how the bowstring is hung in the same way that an *infant* pulls the finger of someone who offers it, Herrigel asks, "Should I then intentionally do away with my intentions?" The master cannot understand this compound question-confirmation and does not know "the right answer." To typical Western sophism, the Zen way cannot answer. Non-intentionality is intentional for the West. What Herrigel is up against isn't the problem the Zen archer cannot answer, but the very life that problem reveals. For the West, any interior void is examined, attended with intention. Any ecstasy is pro-duced, brought forward. This condition precedes any dual-reflective self-articulation of thought. Thought can reach a point of seeing the other by itself, but never of being struck by it. It can reach a point of having a reflective idea of satori, of enlightenment—an idea, that is, that negates the very essence of enlightenment. Herrigel himself explains Zen in relative terms—by negation with respect to the reflecting *intentio*. This takes us to the paradox of a discursive explanation of satori. Precisely because of its intrinsic baselessness, such an explanation helps us understand which aspects of the Zen Way had a signficant influence in Central European culture around the time of the First World War: a vision of things as having the seal of the absolute, a vision of the origin of things as being without form and inaccessible, an intimate contact with them, to the point of having the sensation that "the thing is directed not toward the one who sees it, but toward itself" (Herrigel). The explanation of satori is wholly relative to the typically Western problem of traversing and surmounting nihilism. The term "satori" is used to mean the equivalent of non-discursive, non-logical experience, of a perfect liberation from reflection, and of immersion in the center beyond all contrasting. Thus Pai Chang responded to a question on enlightenment, "Once confirmation and negation, pleasure and displeasure, approval and disapproval, all the various opinions and the various feelings reach a terminus and cannot bind, then one is free wherever one may go; that person is called bodhisattva, with a new awakened mind that rises immediately to the arena of Buddha-hood." The idea of this enlightenment acts, in Herrigel, as the idea-limit of evident Kantian ascendance. Thus even in Viennese culture the Zen Way is an object of nostalgia. It involves an awareness of detachment, of unresolvable difference, and yet an attempt to utter it, to live it—an attempt that is bound to relapse into "unredeemable" intention. This gives way to an extraordinary, labyrinthine reflection on language. Zen teaches that experience is superior to thought by as much as thought is superior to language. Experience, however, has here become an idea-limit that is continually renewed, as such, in reflective thought. Thought inclines toward experience, but it is structurally impossible to reach it and define it. The limit of language here means much more than the reassuring image of an "endless search," of a generic and judicious task of disestablishing dogma. It shows the poverty of reflection at the peak of its civilization, in comparison with experience as experience.

It does not seem that this aspect of the Viennese critique of language can be found in Karl Kraus. His linguistic hygiene is mastery, and the magic of language *compos sui* consists in pitting it against the corrosive effect of time. Language emerges as "the true enemy of time." Kraus believes in the word, and specifically in the word as an instrument by which one can immerse oneself in the center of Being. "I can always count on words, / they know how to take me from appearance to essence." The correct words express the correct concept. Kraus finds himself in the correctness of language. He teaches it and he is its custodian. Beyond language thus defined there is nothing but "journalistic" events, the day to day *samsarian* life! No one reduces the real to the correctly utterable more completely than Kraus does, and no one therefore makes the utterable so completely real. His effort is entirely dedicated to restoring an ontological dignity to language, liberating it of any conventionality and artificiality. He wants to get himself "out" of this world of relativity, within whose limits, by contrast, Zen seeks nirvana. "Whatever may be your effort, nirvana should be sought in the middle of *samsara* (the transpiring world)" (Suzuki).

There is a distinct contrast between Kraus's position and the development both of Wittgenstein's intellectual perspective and of Fritz Mauthner's, whose reflections on language certainly influenced Wittgenstein. Mauthner considered incredible the idea "that language reflects and represents the constituent elements of a unique and universal reality, and that therefore from the existence of words can be inferred the existence of corresponding extra-linguistic entities."[88] Language is nothing but *bildliche Darstellung* (Wittgenstein's *Bild*)—a conventional form—even if the desire to become substance lies in the depths of the convention, the desire to hypostatize the *Bilder* that constitute it. By making language the enemy of time, Kraus reveals this desire, the superstitious need to possess, in language, Being itself, *Wesen*, and to use language (which is an instrument of nihilistic reflection) as a means of prevailing over events. Thus he would remove the unresolvable tension between words, thought, and experience—that is, between words and their silence.

At the peak of this tension stands Webern's music. Chinese texts develop, in Mahler's Lieder, in Berg, and in Webern, an essential function, precisely because they disclose the value of silence in compositional structure, which every interpreter has maintained. In Webern the pursuit of this value is programmatic. The musical propositions, abbreviated to spasms, scanned from lull to lull, isolated in their singularity, radiate with crystalline purity from the silence that encircles words and that words cannot subsume. The perfectly isolated sound that cannot be repeated (since the case is unrepeatable and since every being in its singularity is unrepeatable and eternal) is fixed in the silence within us, the void within us, that we made in ourselves in order to listen to it and take it in. To make silence within us is also the final key of Mahler's *Das Lied von der Erde*. Mahler's cycle seems to conclude with a gesture like that of Haku-in, who used to hold his hand up high and invite his disciples to listen to the sound of it. The power of this void appears great. Infinite sounds of exquisite purity emanate from it, and it receives infinite sounds in return. Entire orchestral scores are invaded by its might (Boulez). It is a generative void, but not in the productive and constructive sense of the term. The cases that break out from it, like forms of listening, are not fixed on a scale of evolutionary and progressive coordinates, by which the one completes the other or expresses its meaning, its destiny. Every sound is unique and unrepeatable. The composition demonstrates that sounds are unrepeatable. Their purity is exalted by not repeating them. "When Kakua went back to Japan, the emperor heard about him and asked him to teach him Zen. Kakua remained in silence before the emperor for a long while. Then he pulled a flute from the folds of his robes and he played a single, brief note. Bowing deeply, he left."

The principle of brevity and of absolute clarity concentrates the content of the utterable into a single point of unheard tension. When *Klarheit* is complete, a white, perfect serenity prevails. A Zen master named Seikyo, during the Sung dynasty, illustrated the states of spiritual purification through the symbol of the gradual "whitening" of an ox (Suzuki). One of the pictures is *white on white*. "Everything is empty: the whip, the yoke, the man, the ox. . . . When this state prevails, the spirit of the ancient master is manifest." The same tension without in-tention in the *white on white* (one of the most esoteric and yet traditional aspects, there-fore, of contemporary avant-garde art) dominates in the silent art of Japanese theater, "frozen dance, dance without dance" (Her-rigel), and above all in Zen painting. In Zen landscapes, unmoving space full of infinite breath encircles the observer "who is at the center without being the center; who is within, at one with the pulse of things" (Herrigel). "One lets nature draw its own images without reference to people. It has its own moods, expressed through rocks, mountains, rivers, tree trunks, birds, human beings, and plants" (Suzuki). The relationship between drawing and void is here as critical as that between words and silence or between sound and pause or lull. All senses of the landscape are compre-hensible only to the extent that they are woven with void and si-lence. The void unites the isolated images and permeates them. It does not express them in their immediate isolation, which any per-spective could measure. The void makes every image leap into presence, into its own space without foundation and without tonality. The problem of this void obsessed Viennese thinking about design and architecture. Klimt struggled throughout his en-tire work with the relationship between void and image, but his background remained too "rich" and resonant to be truly detached from the West's *horror vacui*. A landscape by Schiele, on the other hand, one of his last, *Häuser und Föhren* (see Figure 16), seems truly dedicated to clarity without an atmosphere of Zen seeing. The void invades this brief sketch, as it does Webern's. Unique and eternal cases unlock themselves there into existence, cases that a profane enlightenment succeeds in grasping as such. I am reminded of the little painting that Hesse's character Klingsor wanted to give to his friend Louis, "the most Chinese painting ever painted, with the pagoda, the red pathway, the jagged trees in pale green." Wherever it is possible to see and clearly describe the visible, there the void that encircles it, its foundation of silence, becomes manifest—and nothing is lost.

Zen poetry is based on the same principles that continually return in Wittgenstein's "aesthetic" judgments. Responding to Basho's haiku, "Old marsh! The frog jumps! Splash of water!" Herrigel comments, "That is all. And yet, does it not contain the entire universe?" Conversely, the in-tending toward essence, the shouting at the unutterable, the romantic and expressionistic *Streben* does not merely have the effect of producing compositions dominated by *horror vacui*, that is, by fear of silence, of a pause, of a lull, and powerlessness to stand the void. It also has the effect of reducing any single existence to details, to *a* detail. For the tired eyes of seekers after essence and the "most profound," of those who in-tend toward the beyond, all that exists is nothing but *a* detail. On the other hand nothing is detail, *a* detail, for the great Viennese thinkers on language. In other words, for them, God is in the details. Details must emerge the way mountains, woods, trees, flowers, and animals emerge in a Zen landscape, with absolute *Klarheit*, without ornament. Loos's critique, on the contrary, which is still interpreted as a sort of functionalistic ascesis, practically as an epigone of nineteenth-century progressiveness or a fetishist image of technology,[89] confirms precisely the essential nature of details, the deep aspect of appearance. It is possible to "decorate" only what is held to be insignificant. The "tattoo" quality of ornament would lend harmony and form to a mere particle, to the marginal, and would redeem the supposed vulgarity of detail. But when details are seen with *Klarheit* and heard in the utmost concentration of the void per se, then that is all, or all is manifest in that. The Zen story of Rikyu is literally identical with Loos's and Wittgenstein's behavior with the craftsmen (when Wittgenstein built his sister's house). Rikyu, a master of the tea ceremony, asked a carpenter to help him hang a flower pot, and he advised him during the job ("higher, lower, more to the right, more to the left") until he found the right spot. The carpenter, just to make sure, marked the spot and then pretended to have forgotten it. "Was it here," he asked, "or rather here?" But the master indicated exactly the spot he had chosen before. So too the story of Loos's soap exhibits exact correspondence with the anecdote of the young student who brings a pail of water to Master Gisan and spills a few splashes. "Idiot," screams the master, "what right do you have to spill a single drop inside this temple?" Thanks to this reprimand, the disciple attains satori and from that moment on is known as Splash.

Love of details and care for material are in Loos, as we have seen, one and the same. The figure of the craftsman is exalted through this motif, whose metaphysical roots necessarily elude aesthetic and literary, as well as historical and sociological, interpretation. Loos's craftsman is an expression of the point at which technical capacity becomes spiritual, at which concentration on material and tools is already part of the work. Thus for a painter using india ink the act of drawing the image on rice paper, all the work that went into preparing the stylus and colors, and the hours of concentration and marshaling forces during which the artist is unreachable, all this "precipitates" as if from afar. Thus a master of flower arranging begins his lesson "cautiously choosing the string" that ties them and, "after carefully rolling it up, puts it aside" (Herrigel). This is not a matter of simply putting "small things" in order; it is a matter of essential moments in the work itself, since the work is a metaphysical consonance of art and craft, material and spiritual, subjective and objective.

Walser's idler knows the art of Zen painting and flower arranging very well. From his first work, *The Themes of Fritz Kocher*, the method of an authentic "small" master is described with minute attention, along with "reverential respect for everything that exists" (and with the profound nostalgia that necessarily results from this in the *Abendland* that ignores it). Consider the praise of calligraphy in "The Class Theme Paper," the recommendations on how to sit quietly in your seat and on what paper to use. Consider the recurrent motif of *courtesy*, of fascination with the norm that prevents "originality," and the imperceptible changes in the ceremony. Consider, finally, the part on winter that combines, again, Webern with Kakua's flute: "I like things that are one color, one tone. Snow is a single song on a single tone."

Master of this brevity, of this simplicity which is *Klarheit*, Peter Altenberg could be called in to tie together all the motifs analyzed to this point. Like Fritz Kocher, Altenberg is incapable of those flaming colors that are like "a song of too many voices singing too high." In the extreme discretion of his language it is as if all the others were retracted into a dimension of pure memory, into a perfect no-place. This distinction takes the form of irony, but it is the irony that follows awakening—the awakening that, in its turn, followed despair. It is the irony of the awakened, of those who know that the idea of their waking is a perfect no-place in the *Abendland*—that this idea is only "interior." Altenberg's *kleines Leben* [ordinary life] is encountered not only after despair, like Walser's, but also after the awakening. Its impulse to see is not a tenacious refusal of judgment. It is the condition of full awakening, of a daytime without emphasis, without blinding light, that thus permits every single tone to exist and be seen. Their *Ansichtskarten* [picture postcards] are perfect examples of this impulse, and thus Berg and Webern understood the truly Wolfian "little things" of his genius *ohne Fähigkeiten* [without technique]. The concentration of style, in some of his pieces, is next to enlightenment, and the suspended tonality that vibrates there is comparable only to the waiting without intention of Zen poetry.

Those who recognize essence as a property of such waiting also feel its absence. Altenberg's irony clarifies the intention that dominates this form in spite of everything. It explains how intention prevents any fullness of the present, how it subdivides time into memory and future, and makes the moment volatile. The moment's flight is the sound that Altenberg transcribes in its singularity. This pursuit, which amounts to a pursuit of self, always returns anew to the forms of recollection, of passing away.[90] The torment of the interminable quality of this pursuit does not recognize the "fallen" of Hofmannsthal's misfits. This torment too is *seen*, is one of the facts of life, one of the cases that it is necessary to learn to see with unencumbered eye. It is one of the cases in life where seeing is actually an attempt to see, where speaking is nothing but an effort to speak. It is one of the cases in life whose awakening cannot be experienced except in reflection and otherness. And still, the "miracle" to be achieved consists in understanding all of this in the form of *Klarheit*. It is not the "miracle" of the priest who succeeded in writing the holy name of Amida in the air or of the monk who walked on the waves of a river and to whom Huang Po turned and said, "If I had known you would invent miracles, I'd have cut off your legs." Neither can it be the full miracle of Bakei, who eats when he is hungry and drinks when he is thirsty, since we are powerless to become one with the target, to immerse ourselves in ourselves free of any intention. It is a matter of a "miracle" for our interminable intending, discovering all of its poverty, the perfect form of that eating and drinking. Since this and no more manageable object is the scope, Peter Altenberg is one who pursues himself without ever being able to find himself. Nor does he have Govinda's gift ("'I am old, it's true,' said Govinda, 'but I have never paused in my pursuit, which seems to be my destiny.'") of deluding himself at the end on the perfect smile of Siddhartha.

A Dark Alley
in the Old City

Peter Altenberg's Ersucher shares nothing with diffident Ulysses, who fears "that Calypso may be a trap," who lacks tact and suffers from a persecution complex typical of intellectuals, who tries to eliminate risk. Bazlen drew a ruthless portrait of him.[91] Altenberg's Ersucher represents Bazlen himself, in his novel, in his readings. Viennese Central Europe is completely at home in the Trieste of Bazlen and Saba. Indeed, Trieste at times took Vienna's enigma into account with even more sobriety and detachment, if that is possible, and with greater intelligence. On Trieste, Bazlen's *Intervista* is unequaled. A bourgeoisie "that believes they milk the wolf in Rome to feed the family" and whose thought takes on golden wings when they show *Nabucco* at the theater collides with impartial Austria, full of the tolerance and dignity "of the dying snobs." At home this bourgeoisie encounters a bureaucracy more liberal than the irredentists, obliged to prohibit something every so often, but ready to sack the telephone operator who had incautiously "intercepted" a patriotic conversation of Svevo's daughter. This bourgeoisie, if it had to escape, would have broken the ghetto book stalls under the weight of Carduccis, D'Annunzios, and Sem Benellis, while the Germans departed "leaving a great unofficial culture behind them, important and hardly known." Yet this bourgeoisie gave birth to Italo Svevo and Umberto Saba, Scipio Slataper, Roberto Bazlen, and Carlo Michelstaedter, and took Ferrucio

Busoni on his first steps. It could happen (and it did to Ladislao Mittner in another Babel not far away) that the father could be a Hungarian with a German name, but fascinated with Italian culture, and the mother could be an Italian whose ancestors were Croatian, with an irredentist uncle wearing German insignia, and another uncle a Bohemian but loyal to the Emperor.[92] "I am anything but a melting pot," Bazlen justifiably observes. "I am a crossroads." At the crossroads, the different roads do not fuse into a single highway, but all possible directions remain open. The impulse to learn them and travel them all arises from here, an unused restlessness, that impresses whoever is born at the crossroads and whoever celebrates their epos in Theodore Däubler.

Among these diverse, possible directions, alongside Ibsen's Nordic and expressionistic direction, alongside Michelstaedter's tragic and classical direction, alongside Svevo's protagonist of European decadence (decadence, according to Bazlen: "the last European movement in which literature might have made a living contribution to European culture"), there is the Vienna that is defined by Hofmannsthal's misfits and Altenberg's and Musil's man without qualities, that lives in Loos's "details" and in Webern's pauses. Bazlen and Saba are deeply connected to Vienna, and every attempt to understand them solely within the scope of twentieth-century Italian culture is a priori destined to fail. Nor are they connected to the empire as peripherals. Saba takes the problem of compositional clarity, brevity, and comprehensibility to a level of exceptional prominence. Bazlen advances a new critical perspective of *Einfühlung* [empathy], alien to the intentional and reflective paradigm, and far from the pseudo-creativity of homogenizing the work under consideration.

Bazlen's critical perspective involves reading, not interpretive teaching. It does not furnish the key to mastery of the work, but it shows the work, indicates it, and reveals it. These are glosses, comments, and footnotes. "Almost all books are footnotes swollen into volumes (*volumina*). I only write footnotes." It is a genre to which the best things of Altenberg and Kraus also belong, as well as Saba's *Scorciatoie*. Nietzsche's influence is evident throughout Bazlen's

Note. He considers Nietzsche's first and most important creative renewal (along with Saba's, as discussed below). Goethe's criticism is Nietzschean. "Goethe's perfection: not in the statuary clarity (what does it mean?) but in the rhythmic equilibrium between clarity and madness." And again, "The harmony of Goethe's life: not Apollonian, but the most beautiful, the most rhythmic alternation of form and chaos." His "genealogy" of morals is Nietzschean. "Socrates is the West's first plebeian. . . . Drinking the hemlock in that satisfied manner with no edge of agony, like a businessman, with the sure conviction that 'up there' all is still happier." He also considers a Nietzsche rewritten in the "low" measure of the footnote, in which motifs remain hardly mentioned, stripped of any evangelical or prophetic pretense. The *measure* of Bazlen's Nietzsche (who comes from a bitter experience of submission and linguistic asceticism) is not, however, in Kraus's sanctification of language, but rather in the "profane" awareness that language is a precious and irreplaceable gift and at the same time limited, weak, always on the point of vanishing, delicate in its mechanisms. One turns to this Nietzsche, however, with patient irony. He is not a new idol, nor should he believe himself to be so. It is necessary to teach him to distance himself from his misery, to see it critically. It is necessary to educate him about this, not to lose him to the despair and anguish that, as we know, precedes the awakening. In irony, language finds an affinity with its limits, learns to recognize them and become, *in* them, self-possessed.

The "philosophy" of the footnote, of submission to the *volumina,* is not a matter of falling to ones knees before fetishized language, but of preserving it as a weak and precious gift before the attack of the great intentions, the visions of the world, the judgments. ("Teach nothing to people: they are capable of learning on their own"; "the exaggerated veneration of intelligence is left over from the age when it was difficult to be intelligent," which could be, literally, an aphorism of Wittgenstein or a phrase from Musil's *On Stupidity.*) The footnote is also an adventure, a risk. It gives itself over to the text entirely. It is listening, ready for surprises, profoundly curious. It loves temptation, yet it is difficult to please. Apparently adventure is centrifugal, as Calasso has noticed, and it turns about an empty point, a pause, a silence. Because listening is full, it must create the void within itself. It must always return to this "interior" adventure, the kind most alien to Ulysses' "prudence." The adventure is essentially concentration and immersion: to put all content (to tempt it) to the test of the interior void, to see if it can manage the silence. The arrow of the footnote is shot at that target, at the heart of the archer himself.

One comes alive when this exercise succeeds. ("Born dead, some succeed, little by little, in becoming alive.") Saba is a great and subtle master of this. He flings his shortcuts (*Scorciatoie*) like a shot from a sling. His writing is full "of parentheses, dashes, quotation marks, and italics. . . . I do not know anymore how to speak without abbreviating; and I could not abbreviate otherwise." The telegraphic style of the soul invented by Altenberg finds, in footnotes, in souvenirs, in Saba's short stories, one of its most perfect realizations. Shortcuts save no time. Brevity is difficult, impervious ("paths for goats"), when one seeks *Klarheit* with every step "in God's honor." Shortcuts are not the shortest path, but the path of concentration and of maximum density, of radical *dépense*, without Penelope in waiting. Not even a path, but a crossroads again, a contrasting complex of voices that never join, but that are compound, that require composition of their rigid differences.

Bazlen, in a fragment of his unfinished *Capitano*, defines the principle of this composition thus: "I could tell you that you are still very young, and that the great sorrow is small sorrow, and the great happiness is small happiness. Perhaps, though, I am as young as you, and I believe in a time in which voices remain equally clear in happiness and sorrow." In *Parole*, Saba had imagined this principle in the same terms. He seeks "a corner of the world" where words could be cleansed "of the falsehood" that blinds them. Tears (the divine value of tears) can restore the word to a clarity "where the heart of humanity was reflected, / naked and surprised, in its origins." The voice of awakening does not ignore despair and is not an ecstatic dismemberment. It remains limpid and clear in exhibiting the same sorrow. The voice should always remain limpid and clear, as in one of Wolf's Lieder, as if tense without intention in composing the differences between words and silence, between sound and pause. It is not yet time for this voice. The footnotes, the shortcut, Altenberg's *Extrakte*, all clearly indicate a void here, show a no-place. Saba points it out in Nietzsche, too, in "my good Nietzsche (not the other Nietzsche of others)," who is capable of speaking of the soul and of things of the soul "the way Carmen spoke of love to Don José." In his "poor and dear Nietzsche," Saba finds "a nearly complete sublimation of Eros," that would have rejected the soul if it had been found with Doctor Rosenberg and would have strangled his dirty sister with his own hands (and Saba wrote these things in 1945!). Saba points out the possible Nietzsche of the dance who attempts to traverse nihilism, who tries to utter its problem, and whose rhythm Bortolotto heard again in Wolf. It is the same Nietzsche found in Savinio's *Encyclopedia*, lyric and "generous," astonished, in pain and despair finally, when confronted by the "darkness people" who inquire about his purposes, his supposed hidden sense, his practical responsibility. "Do not let the darkness people mix with the people of light, and do not let them use their 'incomprehensible' words." It is the Nietzsche who sings "my simplicity" over "learned" texts, whose innocent "little tricks" would weave "pants for the spirit."

Even if a voice such as the one Nietzsche dreamed about, so eternally clear, cold, and concise, could never be; even if the voices "become hoarse . . . because they still have an entire life ahead of them, with heavens and hells and purgatories" (Bazlen), it is necessary to be prepared every day for that clarity, to fling words into the center of it. The fact that we are bound to in-tend this clarity lends credence to our critique of everything that arises in our time like an indestructible idol. We are therefore always infinitely distant from it. This fact has not even reached the bottom level of despair—indeed, it strives to remove it. The things of the past that do not want to die are liquidated, and the most fleeting fruits of time that would redeem us from time are liquidated. "The danger here is not in the solution, but in the palliatives that slow it down." In the end, Saba "the conservative" invites a parricide. It is Bazlen: "whatever does not wish to die must fall apart." This not wanting to die is the perfect sign of the world of the dead.

The Star
of Narration

Claudio Magris has pointed out the development of a Hassidic *pietas* in storytelling that informs not only contemporary Yiddish literature, but Joseph Roth himself. I think, however, this development is not so "remote," and an examination of its cultural terms may help to understand the motifs of Vienna at the turning point in a new perspective.

It could not have happened otherwise, since the dissolution of Eastern European Jewish culture, *Ostjudentum*, is an integral part of the *finis Austriae*. Its *Heimat* is both the shtetl *and* Vienna. I doubt that anyone experiences Vienna as a "familiar synthesis of a harmonious multiplicity" (Magris). I would repeat rather Bazlen's statement about Trieste: neither melting pot nor harmonious synthesis, but crossroads, a dramatic intersection of various events and different directions. The crossroads consists of a multiplicity of directions that mysteriously and momentarily meet and combine. The *Vaterland* is one route, the master avenue, designated as destiny in the rhetoric of solution. *Heimat* remains only at the crossroads: the realm without qualities of possibility, the place where possibilities meet and cross and blend and become one another. The real does not come out of this meeting of possibilities. Other, new directions emerge from it and leave those crossroads behind, venture out to find others. Narrative narrates the past, the absence, exhausted by now, of the crossroads of *Heimat*.

The *pietas* of narrative consists in preserving the past. Preservation is possible only through and in narrative. Narrative takes on the color of what it preserves, and so narrative and *Heimat* blend (a crossroads of possibilities that still know how to resist their *reductio ad unum*, yet they live in full awareness of their final day). Narrative becomes the only possible homeland. Narrative narrates itself, and what counts in the end is not its object, but the fact of its existence. The great collections of Martin Buber, Samuel A. Horodetzski, and others bear witness to the extraordinary fabulistic energy of the Hassidim. For them, it is a blessing to *narrate* the stories of the blessed and the events of their lives, even if not everything they tell really happened. The "what" of the story is not the blessed and true, but the intention of the narrator who narrates his spiritual *Heimat*, an intention that assumes the unblendable, very real matters of *Ostjudentum*.

The power of the book also reveals *pietas* through the power of narrative per se. No one can sit on a bench if a book is resting on it. Never leave books upside down. "If a book falls to the ground, we pick it up and kiss it."[93] When a book becomes completely worn out and unreadable, or ruined by fire in a pogrom, then the sextant buries it in the cemetery, running a risk like Shemarja in Roth's *Tarabas*. Certainly it is a matter here of veneration for Hebrew script, whose every letter is a name of God. In addition, there is the resonance of praising the symbol that permits the protection of the *Heimat*, the possession in some way of the tragedy of existence. The object of veneration in the book is its *words*. It is that the book can be read continuously. It can be experienced and transformed into stories, and into stories about anyone. Whoever knows something good about a righteous person (and it does not matter if it is not all "true") should tell it without delay, even if the story is already familiar to the audience. It is therefore the opposite of a logocentric sanctification of books. Words are real here in a sense distinct from a univocal correspondence to the reality of facts. Words are reality, are "things" in themselves. This sense of reality is available through hearing. One must prepare oneself to hear it. Words produce themselves magically as reality does, and humanity must become all-hearing in order to understand them. Perfect all-hearing individuals appear as the zaddikim in their stories.

This strong symbolic quality of Hassidic narrative (which is coded in the noun *d'var*, meaning both word and thing) comes apart in Roth, just as it does, in spite of linguistic continuity and a certain formal resemblance, in Isaac Bashevis Singer. *Heimat* here is only past and absence. The narrative narrates an absence. The narrative preserves things and words in the invisible. In *Shosha*, Singer warns about the radical groundlessness of the passing away of things into absence. "The history of the world was a book that man could read only going forward. He could never turn the pages of this world book backward. But everything that had ever been still existed. Yppe lived somewhere. The hens, geese, and ducks the butchers in Yanash's Court slaughtered each day still lived, clucked, quacked, and crowed on the other pages of the world book."[94] Would this "intuition" make sense if it were spoken to someone other than Shosha, the "idiot," the "pure fool," a fundamental figure in the Hassidic tradition? Shosha is the last survivor of those who know how to listen to tales. She is the last all-hearing figure. Her extraordinary powers of listening characterize her as the "fool." Her faith is seated, physically, in her sense of hearing. Without listening, without its power, narrative is meaningless. No one can narrate except to Shosha. At the center of narrative form is the form of listening. An identical *pietas* involves both dimensions. Those who know the language of stories listen. Those who already know the story listen. Those who can participate in it, correcting it, enriching it, reliving it, those who live in it listen. Shosha is a survivor of listening, and Tsutsik has not finished listening yet, because his roots are in narrating, in the Hassidic *pietas* that accompanies it. These roots are buried now, and the city where Tsutsik lives has no "circle" that listens.

In Roth, this process is complete, and listening completely disappears. His peculiar language would itself prevent listening. Narrative folds in on itself and tends to change into soliloquy. The silence of listening expresses the irreversible loss of *Heimat* and the impossibility of going home again. An attention to words as an end remains, since they are forever "the abyss over which every speaker treads" (Buber), but this attention is a desperate exercise. It is still necessary "to speak as if words opened the heavens: to speak as if words did not come from inside your mouth, but as if you went inside the words." The "as if" that appears in the Hassidic text with the immediacy of a symbolic relationship "falls" in Roth under the principle of Hans Vaihinger. (Feitelzohn, the extraordinary character in Singer's *Shosha*, would edify his entire mock temple with ideas in the name of Vaihinger.) It is necessary to continue to narrate *as if* there were still listeners, with the same simplicity and the same absence of "special" pathos, with the same *pietas* for words, even if they have nothing left of *d'var*.

If in reality narrative narrates *Heimat*, if narrators are narrated by *Heimat* (which is land, language, and legend), then now that *Heimat* has been transcended, narrative itself becomes an absence, a no-place. If narrative no longer has the foundation of *Heimat*, its words launch into a mad dance where they tear off their own limbs and throw them into the air, as happened to Rabbi Jacob Joseph, when he refused to recognize the sanctity of the Baal Shem Tov. "The propositions stood up saying they no longer wished to serve an unknown end overarching them, but rather they wanted to live by themselves for themselves." The discipline of *as if* would prevent this final diaspora: the narrative must have the same simplicity and clarity it would possess if that end still existed. It would be a false nostalgia to ignore the decline of discipline and therefore to pretend that language itself was not now an absence. Words must be forced to name it with the same clarity with which they narrated the *Heimat*.

Even in Hassidic narrative the motifs of home and of listening do not appear in terms of a happy synthesis or of a realized truth. A parable obsessed the Rabbi of Kotzk. When God was about to create Adam, Love got into a quarrel with Truth. Love said, "Let him be created, because he will perform many acts of mercy." Truth said, "Let him not be created, since he will be a liar." To listen to Love, God must bury Truth underground. Truth, then, abides in the tomb, or, as the Baal Shem said, Truth "is driven from place to place, and it is compelled to wander the earth." The vagabond of the Eastern lands that Roth mentions is, in his folly, a living symbol of Truth. The world, its creatures, their beauty—all of it is possible because Truth is not there. God would have destroyed our world, too—as he destroyed innumerable others before ours—if he had listened to Truth. In the interregnum, in the time that separates us from the coming of the Messiah, Truth is inaccessible. The impossibility of going home again (of *Heimkehr*) appears as the symbol of inaccessibility. At home, too, speaking and narrating are other than Truth. At home, too, truth lies entombed. In this sense, the nation of Israel has been *heimatlos* from its very beginning. There has never been a home for it. Its exile began with its origin in Egypt. That first, foundational, and essential laceration constitutes the dominant theme of Rosenzweig's great work, *The Star of Redemption*. It involves the loss of the motherland, fleeting and transient, of *Ostjudentum*, of the Hassidic shtetl. Then a second laceration divides us from words that live and renew themselves in listening. The characters in Roth and Singer represent both of these lacerations. They have ancestral knowledge of the abyssal difference between words and truth. They are children of the diaspora and exile. They can never adore words as a new idol, but at the same time they must wander to where language is everything, since earth is no more and since home has become nothing. It lives only in the pages of the book of the world.

Words are authentic when they know themselves within their limits, that is, when they know that Truth is underground. Every story is thus wrapped in the silence of Truth. The silence of listening is the last figure of the diaspora, whose roots are the silence of truth. Since nothing is comparable to the possession of truth and since truth is now silence, the greatest secret will definitely reside in silence. The silent foundation of words, the pauses that distinguish them, the void from which figures emerge, count more than any story. The most lofty secret "is submerged in the white sea that surrounds the letters on every side. The secret of the blank parchment around the letters is so immense, that all the world is not broad enough to contain it. . . . No one knows how to read it. No one penetrates it. Only the future world will understand it. And then what is written in the Torah will no longer be read, but what is not written in it, the blank parchment" (Langer). The blank parchment that embraces the letters (again the relationship between life and death, reason and folly) represents the silence of Truth. A time will come, though, of apocalyptic beauty in which it will be possible to understand it and read it. When the Messiah comes, the truth that the blank area of the book now preserves in the invisible will shine forth. It will be the time in which the Torah can be forgotten, in which the law will be put aside.

The struggle against law that renders Roth's writing so dramatic is the struggle against a kind of law that endeavors to phagocytize the sacred "white letters," the blank area of the book, and thus eliminate all space that preserves the possibility of redemption. To invade every page of it, prevent the repetition of words, mark every one of them with an appropriate pause, abbreviate their breath, this is what binds Roth to the great Viennese thinkers on language with their supreme indifference to *horror vacui*. It is his desperate exercise to keep words in the presence of the possibility of that time or, better, to keep words as purely within their limits as if this possibility were still open. The book's logocentric dominance is doubly overcome: by words that live only in listening and by the white letters, the blank space where truth is buried and where its secret is kept.

We find these relationships again in Canetti, not in Kraus. For Canetti as for Kraus, the integrity of words is sacred. ("I don't like to let myself get involved with words in perverse adventures. . . . There is enough to trouble me contained *in* words, in their hearts, and I do not wish to extract it from them as if I were an Aztec high priest. I despise such gory ways.") No amount of integrity, however, can ever make of words a perfect image of truth. Kraus's ascesis turns to integrity and *seems* to end there. (We shall see the "secret" hidden in that integrity.) Canetti's ascesis begins in such integrity, but turns immediately to listen to the silence embracing it

and carrying it forward. ("Every one ought to reach their fundamental ascesis. Mine would be the discipline of silence.") In Kraus,
words struggle against the blank area of the book in order to engulf
it, and they do not feel themselves integral outside of this struggle. Canetti is too keen a reader of Kafka not to abandon this pretext. For Canetti, words are too "modest" to presume to maintain
essence as opposed to appearance, to represent the immortal and
defend it from time. Integrity of words consists for Canetti, as for
Kafka, in clearly expressing the problematic nature of a world that
survives and renews itself thanks to the burial of truth. Doubt is
"natural" in this world, and no philosophical game of words is
qualified to resolve it. The philosophical "rite" of doubt does nothing but re-dress it continually. There is no answer to a question if
the answer is not already implicit in the question itself. It is therefore pointless to ask if asking is not already superfluous per se.
Kafka in his *Diary* cites the paradox of Rabbi Nachman, and this
can perhaps constitute a secret basis for Wittgenstein's tautology
as well.

The burial of truth in Hassidic narrative does not become indifference or hatred for life. It is here that the principles of this
narrative incline more towards Walser than towards Roth. The
Jewish will to live and the desperate attachment to life even at the
peak of suffering that we find in Canetti and Kraus, and that so
fundamentally separate both from Heidegger, spring from a vision
of the substantially unfinished quality of the world. The work of
creation is not over. It will end only in the time of redemption. In
waiting for its completion, Jews must preserve their essence in any
way they can. Jews must fight to survive by any means (Rosenzweig). Every moment of life, for them, is a blessing.

The Baal Shem praises God because God has buried truth and
thus has rendered the world possible. It is impossible to praise the
creator and despise his creatures. It is a sin to hide oneself from
one's own flesh (Isaiah 58:7). Those who despair over the burial of
truth and suffer from their own flesh preach death. The "modesty"
of Canetti's language is, ironically, a strenuous resistance to death,
the absolute master. Language that is less than modest strives for

and desires truth, so it desires to surmount and negate all appearances, everything finite. The truth of the finite resides, for this reason, in its vanishing. Such strong language causes the death of appearance, of life as a changing totality of appearance. "Philosophers who want to give us a dowry of death" embody power, whose utopia has always resided in reducing every life to a *state* and in liquidating any "resistance" to the state. Canetti responds to this "philosophy" with Kafka's typical figure of the animal. Swallowed, digested, assimilated, and thus bound to an unending conflict with death, the animal rises to the order of symbol of the resistance. Not by chance are dialogues with animals a recurrent motif in Hassidic tales, along with preaching to birds. All material is full of spiritual sparks of divine holiness that are heard and redeemed. Buber explains that ponds, rocks, plants, and animals are alive with waiting for the redemptive hour. To listen to the "spirituality" of material, however, also means to know how to enjoy it, to love life and cherish it, in whatever mask it presents itself. The pure simplicity of the Baal Shem's constant emphasis on joy is not in Canetti or Roth. For them, the earth can no longer be a cradle, or the sky a mirror and an echo. The power of death has closed the gaps and silences of *Heimat*. Life's resistance to death is refigured in the undefended "modesty" of narrative, and in the image of writing uncontaminated by power. This writing (for Canetti, it was in Kafka and Walser) preserves the past of Hassidic joy, as it preserves the blank area of the book of Truth. Even if the time of redemption has become the object of an impossible faith, it is necessary to narrate *as if* we were waiting for it, with infinite care and patience. All of which frustrates the tone of lament, of accusation and of resentment, since the vain mortification of the flesh (De Menasce) and sins against the body generate sorrow.

The irony in Hassidic stories comes from the tension balanced between joy transformed into blank silence and the *as if* of waiting. It is the opposite of Kraus's irony, which derived, inexorably, from judgment of opinions and appearances that senselessly stimulate daily life. Canetti's irony comes, rather, from communion with life. It does not sentimentalize, but it lives the life of the other. It lives the sorrow of its characters and succeeds in demonstrating to them the deep roots of their contradicting themselves and their passing away. Pursuit of a spark of the common soul is in every gesture and in every word. The idler leads this basic pursuit, unaware and almost speechless. Irony informs its interminability and the complex, limpid reserve of its words. It is the negation of sermons preaching ascesis and silence. The ego *judges*. Kraus's irony is the product of the absolute contrast between the values of the ego's honest *logos* and the debased values of the sick chatter of the masses. The ego is also the subject of philosophy. The ego swallows, digests, and assimilates the animal. Canetti's resistance to death contradicts, therefore, the entire framework of Kraus's discourse. How would it be possible to live the life of the other, outside Schopenhauer's compassion (which is critical in Kraus), if one were to confirm the full identity of one's ego? One day the Jewish community of a town came out to follow the carriage of Rabbi Reb Melech, to gain merit for honoring his wisdom. The zaddik thought about this a great deal and suddenly said, "If this is the case, I, too, want to follow their example." He got out and joined the throng behind his now-empty carriage. Another story tells how one evening a student felt a great desire to hear Rabbi Aaron recite the Book of Lamentations. He knocked on the teacher's window, saying, "Aaron! Open up! Open the door for me!" The teacher said, "Who's there?" "It is I," said the student, but Aaron neither answered nor opened. The student cried and called, "Aaron, why don't you open the door for me?" Then the Rabbi said, "Who is it who dares to say 'I,' as God himself said on the day he gave us the Law in the midst of thunder and lightning? No one born of a woman has the right to call himself so!" To show the unpronounceable nature of "I" is also the focus of irony. The meaning of characters like the fool, whose blithe humor unseats grave sobriety, resides in non-modesty of the ego. According to the Baal Shem, the only people who have already earned their places in the next life are two fools. "When people are depressed, we restore their good humor." The fool shows that "My very own I, with nothing in its way, was taken away by a little child, and it looks back at me disturbed, silent and alien as a dog" (Hofmannsthal, *Terzinen*). With a truly Hassidic gesture, Canetti transforms what Hofmannsthal expresses in the forms of *Trauerspiel* (in this passage, that reminds us of Rilke, that seems to come straight out of the *Duino Elegies*) into the very reason for putting up resistance to the subjugating subject of philosophy.

That is not the only reason why we ought to invoke the figure of the fool (and of his inseparable friend, the animal). God participates in the misadventures of his exile. When Jews suffer in their fundamental alienation, God takes part in their suffering. The Hassidim need to know how to console him. The greater their misery, the more their blessings on life should soar, and their happiness for life. In the midst of the most atrocious suffering, they need to show themselves *happy* before God, to sing and dance for him. Earth's melancholy has no hold on them. The force that allows them to experience the suffering of the other is the same one that makes them participate in God's suffering, in divinity's very exile. This is their highest "office": to console God for the diaspora that he cannot prevent and joyfully to assume the burden of it; to free God of it. One must turn into a fool in the presence of a suffering God.

Ostjudentum does not know the ghetto. The shtetl is in a certain sense the opposite of the ghetto, of its "totally unnatural" quality (Mandel). Hassidic tales overflow with colors and landscapes. The Hassidim wander "the beautiful roads that lead through this land of a thousand colors," and even more vividly they announce the cry of the land of the Messiah in waiting. These descriptions seem to contrast fundamentally with the desert that spreads out before Jiri Langer. "Far and wide, there is not a tree or hill, only an endless plain. On the horizon a small bridge leads to a sparse field, the only parcel of nature, my only relief in this desert." The only thing the two passages have in common is the absence of the ghetto. The extraordinary journeys of the Hassidim, which in a few moments traverse infinite distances, express how their existence cannot be confined within the limits of the ghetto.

If, however, the desert is without limits, then the eternal fountain of creation that the Baal Shem praised as "a river that never ends" cannot be announced there. The paradox is easy to explain. The multicolored riches of the desert are, to Hassidic eyes, the embodiment of the blank area on the page. All the forces of the living, all secrets from creation to redemption, are told in that blank area. The desert is animated by creation's "river that never ends." Hassidic landscapes abound with objects, animals, and villages beyond any spatial or temporal "coherence," like air full of burgeoning seeds. The vivid colors are not descriptive, but they capture the sparks of the universal soul inhabiting the desert. In the desert, no visible color acts as an obstacle or screen to the splendor of sparks, just as in the infinite plains no border hinders the lightning voyages of the Baal Shem from shtetl to shtetl and from town to town. The figure of the eternal wanderer floats out from the chimneys on the roofs of the shtetl, shrouded in white. Around him fly the sparks of the souls of objects, animals, and houses. Every hour of the day in every season of the year has its own spark. Sparks renew the struggle against the darkness of night and bring forth the light of the living. This is the meaning of the rooster, the rooster crowing at daybreak, the day's first caller, who praises the palingenesis of light, the splendor of the landscape of the living.

The figures in Hassidic landscapes turn out to be Chagall's. Even in Chagall they are already filtered through the narrative of memory. In no other artist is memory capable of such visionary force, finding itself so securely among the symbols of the past and recognizing them, intuiting them, reliving them. In others, nothing remains of the complex Hassidic landscape except for the steppes, the desert, the absence. Only Chagall still knows the secret that animates the desert with colors, that makes the hidden sparks fly, and that seeds the air with figures. Roth joins shtetl and ghetto. The shtetl takes on the colorlessness of the ghetto. The infinity of its landscape represents the infinite abjection of the ghetto. In Chagall, however, the shtetl is a living no-place, a utopia of Hassidic springtime. He permits the festival of one moment in the *Heimat*, pictured in memory, in the invisible, in pure story. At the rooster's crowing, all the beggars, merchants, clowns, fools, and animals gather as simple implements and objects charged with history and memory. They meet on the roofs, in the sky, on the streets. With the last sparks of the soul they shine through misery, and they light up whatever exists there again in the splendor of ephemeral and eternal singularity.

The doubleness of the Hassidic landscape matches the doubleness of *galuth* (diaspora, exile, persecution). It means not only the time of damnation, but the space necessary to prepare oneself for redemption. The method of redemption is in *galuth*. Its road supports our steps for as long as the end is deferred. The Jews are a naked and wandering mass.[95] The exodus from Egypt repeats itself for them with inexorable regularity. In the desert, as Schoenberg bears out in his *Moses*, the Jews are invincible. It is in the desert that "the people see themselves united" (Canetti) and concentrated. There they receive the laws and define the goal. If redemption is not conceivable except by means of exodus and desert, then the desert itself is home. The desert becomes transfigured, as in Chagall the immense steppes and the muddy villages are transfigured. This transfiguration of the desert is the strength of the Hassidism, but that does not mean one can dismiss and eradicate messianism. Such a dismissal takes place wherever this tradition comes alive in a solely critical sense, as it does in contemporary Yiddish literature and in Roth. Certainly, Hassidism reacts to the great messianic hope that the Kabbalah nourished in Hebrew mysticism down to the seventeenth century, and "eliminates" its centrality (as Scholem explains)[96] in religious life. But the idea of redemption remains fundamental in it, a redemption that is prepared daily and deferred in the precarious state of exile. Thus it is not a simple "peace" with exile, and even less a resigned peace or the simple end of messianic hoping. It is, rather, a new vision of the desert of *galuth*, exempt from any mortifying lament or vain sorrow. One can say that in Hassidism the theme of traversing is privileged over that of transcending. The great messianic hope of the preceding ages sought forms of transcending the desert. For the Hassidim this is a vain presumption. Since we have not yet learned to walk, we are infinitely distant from learning even the right steps that would allow us to begin to cross it.

No zaddik calls himself "Messiah" or defines the time of the Messiah's coming. Yet the Messiah lives, "who knows where, isolated, unrecognized by anyone" (Langer). It is because of our guilt that he cannot reveal himself. He comes to every generation, but we have not even begun to cross the desert of exile. If the world were to finally recognize him, then the devil would oppose him, which is what happened to the Messiah of Belz. The devil changed into a beautiful woman and, disputing with the Messiah, succeeded in provoking him into such a state of fervor that he forgot the words of the Talmud that forbid men to remain alone even for a moment with a strange woman. Was not the Baal Shem bound to flee just as he came into sight of the Land of the Lord that had called to him so powerfully? He called out to the ancient land, where he would want at that point to lie down and die, raising his voice to a volume that covered the territory, saying, "No, my dear friend, I will not die. Do not be angry with him whom you have called. He is born to return, and the hand of God is on his roots, to lead him in his time, to lead him to his time, O my dear friend." In the end, the Messiah's earthly wandering repeats itself, only renewing the strength of waiting and listening. This renewal overturns any failure.

A Messiah that actually comes will come too late. Earth will already be a cemetery, and everyday language "a continuous, involuntary, funereal metaphor" (Magris), expressing desolate despair over Hassidic *kavanah*, over its possible resistance and survival. Even at their most somber, the words of Hertz Yanovar under Nazi bombs turn Hassidic faith upside down: "Death is the Messiah. That's the truth. . . . Only the old tomb in the cemetery bears witness that the Messiah, Reb Aaron Messiah, once lived in Belz." The tomb of the Messiah is again the blank part of the book, and things still swell from the parts of its secret. Even if the element of faith is not missing, in Yiddish literature stories are constructed around it in negative. Stories narrate loss and the absence of faith. Extreme silence is the silence of faith; the extreme desert is none other than the nothing of the hope that established it.

Only Canetti's "resistance" still preserves, perhaps, the possibility of hope. Canetti also speaks of and in the desert of pure crossing. No messianic prophecy could limit it, not even that which overturns the Messiah in death. He reveals himself in the minute analysis of forms of crossing, in their "modesty," and in their structural powerlessness. There is nothing but crossing. Canetti recognizes no power, state, or god ("and whoever has him is his prophet") who may be a power in the desert. "That which is merely *recorded* still contains a grain of hope, however grand the despair from which it comes." The Hassidic god is accompanied through uninterrupted wandering narrative, because he is not a power. The Hassidic god fails with his Messiah. He suffers endlessly with his people. For the Hassidim, the sorrow that comes of the idea of God's suffering is terrible, and it would be even more terrible if his people were to accuse him. An extraordinary and overwhelming *generosity* toward God in exile spans Hassidic wandering narrative. "All the sorrows of humanity are also the sorrows of *shekhinah*." Heschel adds that the consolation of knowing the divine presence shares the burden of one's own agony is total consolation. The emphasis is not so much on demanding consolation as on giving it. The negation of any triumphalistic theology is basic here, but the secret of negation lies in rupturing the binomial power-divinity, the fundamental theological symbol of power. Wandering is not the only aspect characterized by powerlessness of the divine. Powerlessness is a thing to be preserved and cared for. Even if God were able to break forth miraculously in the middle of suffering and exile and decree the end of it, this intervention would only be possible if his zaddikim called for it, if they forced God into it. One day a disciple came to the Rabbi of Kotzk asking him to bless a Hassid who had fallen into poverty. The Kotzker replied, "How can I contradict the will of heaven?" Yet this God who cannot work miracles (and miracles are, as we know, the quintessence of power), suffering in his exile, consoled by the songs and dances of the Hassidim, perhaps stricken (as Feitelzohn believed) by a kind of amnesia "that made him lose the sense of his creation," this God is not at all *otiosus*. His figure concentrates in itself, at the peak of tension, every sense and every direction of exile. Not his "otiosity" or indifference, but his nearness, his sympathy for every aspect of exile is disturbing. Essential, not otiose, is the symbol of powerlessness that expresses itself in him.

Rosenzweig explains the sense of the "eradication" of messianism that ends—inverted—in Roth's and Singer's despair. The Messiah cannot express the idea of becoming, of developing toward redemption. Christians develop; Christians *become* Christian. Jews think of themselves as eternal. One enters into Christianity; one is Jewish. Jews are eternal in their present, and eternal from the beginning, from Genesis. Their language is the language God spoke.[97] Waiting for the Messianic hour should not suffocate this present eternity, this ability to see in the present none other than the denunciation of the non-fullness, of the emptiness and silence of God. The wandering of the Jews is doubled, since in their wandering the waiting plunges into the eternal roots of their body and blood. "This matter of taking root in us and only in us guarantees our eternity" (Rosenzweig). Wandering is not mere movement, a development from years of condemnation to the fullness of time. Jews have no roots in the earth, but nevertheless they are "profoundly rooted in themselves." This eternal root expresses itself precisely in their wandering. "Die Macht der Weltgeschichte"— the force of world history, of becoming, of things coming to be and passing away into nothing—shatters against it. Jews exist in time, but they have been in time *eternally*. Time and eternity are confused in their eternal wandering. The Messiah is expressed in this symbol, in its currency, and not in the future of a redemption that removes the present condemnation. The aim of the Jews is, rather, as distant as it is present: "was *immer* ist, ist nicht zeitlos; was sich immer *bleibt*, ist nicht zeitlich"[98] (whatever has been *eternally* may wander on eternally in time, but whatever remains eternally fixed in its roots cannot be consumed by time).

These last considerations shed new light on the structure of narrative. It is not the failure of messianic hope, already "eradicated" in Hassidic mysticism, or the loss and absence of *Heimat*, of the seat of *Ostjudentum*, which had played such a large part in the crossroads of the Empire, that resulted in the despair of Roth and Singer. It is rather the sterilization of the eternal roots of Jewish selfhood. Not having roots on earth and the eternity of wandering per se could not provoke despair. The agony is the silence of roots in self, the silence of one's body and blood. When the agony becomes aware of itself, then wandering will be transformed into becoming, will exist only in time, and time will not consume it. Narrative must follow destiny. It is no longer possible to show the eternity of the roots that sustained it. The symbol is shattered and only one part of it remains, solitary: the interminable absence of dwelling on earth. This means no longer being able to be at home with oneself.

To try to express all of this with the clarity of Hassidic tales, to say it without lament, without pointless accusations against agony, is a grand form. Roth did it in his last days, in "The Legend of the Holy Drinker." It is a story of the repetition of disaster on the path of restitution. This path, which leads to those who know how to give, is closed off until death. In life, the voice that calls us back to it is repeated incessantly together with voices that "seduce," that lead elsewhere, and that get confused with it. Yet no other way is presented. An irony that comes up whole forms the most profound communion with the suffering, forms a language that has its equal only in the finest Hassidic tales. Roth's "Legend" is modeled on tales like that of Rabbi Nachman's "The Seven Beggars," whose end we will not be worthy to hear until the Messiah comes, "may God speed that day and make us its witnesses."

Kraus's Ideogram

There is another form of nostalgia for the East in Vienna at the turning point. I have already commented what a reductionist mistake it is to concentrate all the multiple perspectives from Steinhof into Karl Kraus's "juridical mode" of discourse. In March 1907, Schnitzler and Hofmannsthal, Schoenberg and Freud, Klimt and Moser signed the manifesto inviting Mahler to remain in Europe, but Kraus did not. Later, around the time of his collaboration with the *Blauer Reiter* almanac, Schoenberg wrote in his diary: "Kraus knows perfectly well that he belongs to hated journalism, even though he does everything he can to make people think he is an artist. . . . He intends to impose the idea that he is not only an artist, but he is *the* artist, the only true artist of our times. To a journalist without scruples, nothing is impossible."

In the beginning, but only in the beginning, Kraus had faith in language. He placed it under close examination then, studying the meaning of the subjective genitive, developing an idea of thought embodied in language, and articulating language's self-reflexive nature. Like all beginnings, Kraus's was profoundly tied to the past and baffled by the new. What remains essential in Kraus's work, though, lies in the ethical and discursive basis that he lends to the critique of artistic facts and to the analysis of language. The unity of ethics and aesthetics rests in a still more basic origin, such as nature and language. Language is the basis of ethics and aesthetics, just as nature is the basis of all creation. Kraus produces no critique of the idea of origin, although that is the center of the Viennese turning point (around a "Nietzschean core.")

From *Sittlichkeit und Kriminaltät*, a collection of essays written between 1902 and 1907, Kraus attacks the quotidian (idealized in the daily press) and the times (summarized as too *wienerisch*, too Viennese). Both charges are leveled in name of a morality that Kraus hardly subjects to even a minimal dialectic consideration. Kraus is ethical in exactly the same way as Weininger, whose influence pervades the work of the eruptive author of *Die Fackel* without ever being acknowledged. Take this fragment from "The Persecution of Women" for example: "Whoever has come to recognize the ethical indifference of women's souls will break up in laughter over the indignation of the petit bourgeois who calls for police protection and involves the aid of psychiatry against his lover for lying."

Kraus's critique of Heine and appreciation of Johan Nepomuk Nestroy demonstrate definitively that this ethical and aesthetic attitude represents the past (the necessary past) of Wittgenstein's Vienna. The theoretical impossibility of wholly embracing the European tendencies of nineteenth-century German literature combines here with a repugnance (like Weininger's) for Jewish *Heimatlosigkeit*, for the Jewish culture of exile. Consequently not Heine, but Nestroy: the *Burgtheater* of the healthy Viennese tradition that fills Kraus's *Schauspielkunst* (plays). That also explains his attacks on Max Reinhardt: actor and word, not direction and action.[99]

Kraus's attitude to Dollfuss goes back to previous conditions. It has deep roots in his life and work. "He would talk about the polar ice caps to anyone who felt a little cold." He "tried to prove how good counts for nothing without understanding it, or how desire is incapable of truth without knowing what is true" (Brecht). Again in *Sittlichkeit und Kriminaltät* Kraus presents himself "as the one who struggles for the survival of conservative forces against an erupting horde with no traditions; as the one who prefers the police state included, not only for aesthetic reasons, in supporting a despotism of journalists." In spite of such pronouncements, Kraus

was a great celebrity to critics who made him the embodiment of
"grand Vienna." In contrast to them, he knew how to recognize
his historical and spiritual situation. He knew that it was not possible to stem the tide of the age. He was the first to decide against
everything that broke with tradition. "I am not an imitator living
in the crumbling old slum of language," he wrote in one of his best
poems, adding, as a true protagonist of the Viennese turning
point: "mein Grab ist leer"—"my grave is empty."

Kraus's later defenders can hardly imagine how far back his case
on language may reach. Calasso laments it,[100] in the tradition of
Heller and Benjamin. Benjamin called Kraus's work "a war dance
over the crypt of the German language." But in 1931, in both a
conference and an essay, two critics found in Kraus the drama,
rhythm, and style of classical Chinese. Kraus kept this secret hidden even from himself. Awareness of this affinity with Chinese was
unavailable to a criticism that exalts only the most fleeting aspects,
yet it saves his work in an authentic dimension of timelessness.
What seemed a mixture of ethics and aesthetics is transformed in
this very dimension into a utopian harmony between words and
things, between words and actions. The order of words acquires a
cosmic significance, transcending the linguistic dimension of its
formal relationship with the universe of situations and facts. Words
should define thoughts with precision and sincerity, so right actions may follow, so justice may reign in the land. "Heaven hates
disorder," it says in the *Shih Ching* [The classic of songs],[101] and
for Kraus, disorder in language is a sign of great disorder in the
cosmos.

The first emblem of Kraus is the ideogram of man attached to
word and faithful to it. The word appears at his lips, but has its
roots in his entire being. The sense of belonging to a tradition
(more powerful when more dedicated) transcends historical and
linguistic dimensions. The continuous exercise of a reanimating
memory that can salute the dead as if they were living and listen to
their music as if it were being played here and now looks to the
center, to the invariable. What seemed the true, unmoving axis of
discourse is transformed into the utopian mixture of foundational

harmony between words and being, between human and divine Tao. Classical Chinese education orients itself directly toward this center. A close study of the *Shih Ching* is necessary for learning how to use words well. Using words well means centering oneself in the invariable. The *Shih Ching* says, "This is my sorrow: that there are men who have no desire to understand the beauty of ancient things." The book continually cites this beauty, as it incessantly repeats the ceremonies and rituals of justice "that govern a monarch as if he were enlightened." Kraus's principle of quotation belongs to this time of ritual and public prayer.

Kraus's integrity of words (something that should "surge from the ground in harmony with earth and sky") is also direction, process, and energy, even when it seems to flee before any originality, seeking refuge in the soil of its tradition, of its classicism. Kraus's second emblem could be the sign of footprints leading to intelligence or one on the virtue of work after having gazed directly into the heart, or knowing oneself. For this, Kraus's Confucian brushstrokes can seem, as they did to Benjamin, motivated by "mad laughter." The mask of whoever seeks the classical rhythm of quotation is obligated to struggle against quotidian profanity, though the end result may be the disfiguring of one's own brushstrokes. What are we still capable of quoting? *Die Fackel* is a dead sea, almost a document for paraphrasing what Theodore Adorno said of Berg, that it is impossible to abandon the already-said and that one must assimilate it and get nourishment from it. In Kraus's style of quotation the standard of classicism that provides words with order is inseparable from the demons that destroy tradition and memory. Kraus gazes too directly to have missed this struggle and to have turned away from the adversary's pressing force. The principle of quotation expresses unvarying humanity, and that is why it lives in language, while it testifies to the dissolution of classical beauty. The principle of quotation admits no exceptions. The classical tradition endures indirectly in the voices that deny it and negate it. Quotation turns into a reflection of disorder that "flows like water coursing in spring toward the valley, overflowing its channels, lost in pools." This dramatic change is seen straight on, without illusion or nostalgia, in *Die letzten Tage der Menschheit*.[102] It shows an apocalypse in which "the most incredible things were said, and the most macabre things were quotations. The specters and ghosts that haunt us have the names of living people" (Kraus). Quotation is condemned to repeat the tragedy that destroys humanity. The protagonists in this tragedy are "characters from operetta." The destruction of humanity is a laughing matter. It is comedy. "Life dies, and the killers dance a tango"—"Das Leben starb. Die Mörder tanzen Tango"—Kraus wrote in a poem in 1913, during a night awake over Musil. It is necessary to learn to laugh at the killers. Kraus in his authentic mask (his Chinese mask) protests the difficulty of this art, and since he continues to carry it, with fatigue, he protests the necessity of weeping.

Profane Attention

Almost at the end of *The Man Without Qualities* appear the chapters on "the expression of the idea of emotion." They are among the last parts Musil revised before his death. The reassuring image of a "tangible likeness between reality and the idea we make of it" had collapsed. It was no longer possible to assume that "emotions discolor the exact image of the world, that they deform it and misrepresent it." Gone was the myth of the "original" to which the idea of possessing a "true" reality would have conformed. The unreality of the "subjective" opposes "true" reality. Subjective reality is an unreality that analyzes the world in diverse images composed of emotion's various grades. Ulrich certainly "did not have the least intention of mistaking awareness for an error or the world for an illusion." The predominant force that causes us to better adapt ourselves to reality appears as a grade of emotion, confused with representations of various depths. This passage, in which Musil brings Mach and Nietzsche into critical confrontation, introduces the problem of an "unfounded" reality. Through infinite procedures, we clarify its image "under the urgency of life," a problem specified and developed in "Ulrich und die zwei Welten des Gefühls." It is not a matter here of a broad "division of labor" between emotions, but of the possibilities of development within every emotion.

Emotions appear to Ulrich in two fundamental types: those that develop in an exterior sense and those of an interior sense. Certainty—*Bestimmtheit*—characterizes the former. Exterior development (*äussere Entfaltung*) of emotion always directs itself toward something, has something in sight, leads to an action or a reasonably univocal resolution (*Beschluss*). The interior mood (*Stimmung*) seems, by contrast, inactive, as if it were limited to witnessing events "from behind tinted glass." Yet, fixed emotions, emotions that tend toward resolve and that behave like imprisoned energy, restrict their destinations one by one until they are gone. They discharge their strength at their targets. On the other hand, the *Stimmung* that flows over every object "without any effect on anything," transmutes the world incessantly "with the same indifference and disinterest with which the sky changes colors. In this way things and events are transformed like clouds in the sky."

Defined emotions are like a substance with outstretched arms— "ein Wesen mit greifenden Armen." They pass from object to object, from destination to destination, without power to stop. Defined emotions have an indefinable need to change allegiance, while emotions that remain indeterminate, that have nothing in their sights, seem to endure "like a family or species."

Emotions may develop, therefore, into voracious and acquisitive elements. Emotions approach things to know them, possess them, and dominate them. Their resolve always leads into blind alleys. The thing possessed and dominated turns out to be nothing, and the intention is bound to feel loss and approach something else. It is an interminable interval, composed of intention, waiting, satisfaction, and loss, studded as it may be with attempts to "radiate," with nostalgia for the interior development of emotion, for its "indifference." People in whom the exterior development predominates "voraciously seize everything that they meet and are ever on the attack." Their passions are as strong as they are mutable. Against this "Faustian" type we can juxtapose the contemplative, whose emotions are, indeed, introverted, turned inward. Musil calls this type "oriental," capable of "concentrating oneself within, to the point that mind, heart, and body are all one silence."

Ulrich warns that such definitions may be unfounded. These

"affected, stylish phrases" only deliver a tiny part of the thoughts and "deep respirations of a summer day." Certainly "he saw a great difference" between the two described types, between those who put their entire beings "at peace" and concentrate themselves in a place where things "happen without anything happening"; and the wandering thought that leaps from problem to problem, that, as Evagrio said, "leads the mind from city to city, from village to village, from home to home," engaged in long discourses. "A fundamental difference in life" seems to express itself between these two types, developed to their extreme limits. Musil flees, though, from a distilled phenomenology of emotions or from limiting himself to macro-classifications of visions of the world. The last part of the novel certainly constitutes a powerful re-cognition of the transcendental conditions, so to speak, of nihilism. The analysis of acquisitive emotions is an essay in Nietzschean psychology on the foundations of nihilism. Ulrich tries to probe these foundations in the "sacred dialogues" with his sister. This is not, however, the proper place for the last part of the novel. It is not an awareness that detachment from nihilism should be arrested upon its re-cognition. Nor is it a realization that ex-stasis from the foundations of nihilism is an extirpation and cannot attain that brimming silence, radiant, capable of burning in itself any acquisitive intention, whose every word is a reminder that utopia is unattainable. The extraordinary *Klarheit* of silence is a story that by definition cannot be told. The story that is told is the infinite probing of nihilistic emotions—a story that is necessarily unfinished.

Musil's essay touches all these elements without drawing a circle around them. If his tour had a center, it would be the essential impossibility of deciding between the two worlds of emotions. Musil's essay is not motivated by the analysis of the two worlds as such or by the unattainable nature of what we can define as hesychastic. This drama motivates it: in the state of being "without qualities," we cannot decide between the two worlds of emotions, in spite of their radical differences. They fall into reciprocal equivalence, constantly exchanging places and reversing themselves. This does not deny recognition of the conditions of nihilism or the idea of a pos-

sible turning of emotions toward the diaphanous clarity of the gratuitous. It denies rather the possibility of an exclusive choice between the two worlds. These worlds do not fall within the realm of
choice. In the state of being "without qualities," these emotions
come, become, from time to time, as the case may be. They happen, they fall on man. Thus he does not have a sense of nostalgia
for the contemplative, and he apparently lacks a virile acceptance
of Faustian destiny. Our world exists in the insurmountable indifference of this difference. The metaphysical quintessence of the
"man without qualities" is a recognition of undecidable differences
that are therefore indifferent or equivalent.

The twofold essence of all emotions furnishes a "possible explanation that is too simple." Its "pretentious and arrogant" concepts
can give "great satisfaction" to Ulrich, but the two-fold essence remains a tight knot. It is as if the concept did not give way to judgment, to *Ur-teil* (separation, distinction, fundamental decision).
The essay does not lack a concept, but it lacks a capacity for judgment, a power to decide—*Urteils-kraft*. The "man without qualities" expresses, in fact, a superabundance of concepts. He seems to
offer several means to penetrate into the most secret "types," but he
cannot pass judgment among them. Thus all the manners of emotion that he discovers signify only one kind of man, the kind that
understands in himself the most radical differences without being
able to decide upon the "quality" of any of them. He is a nihilist
who nevertheless "dreams dreams of God." He is an impatient activist, who is far from taking any pragmatic action in spite of his
impatience. Ulrich and Agathe recognize each other as nihilists and
activists (and, we might add, as hopelessly contemplative and acquisitive): "und bald das eine bald das andere, je nachdem wie es
kam"—"now as one and now the other, as it happened, as the case
may be." This is their key. The relationship between twins belongs
to that constellation of indivisible things that can nonetheless
never be united. The twins (Gemini) are indivisible in their insuperable difference. This is not a sign of synthesis or harmony, but
a sign of the unreconcilable and double, in which projects are
planned "like pure unreality" and one tries to act in a spirit "that

was the magic spirit of inactivity." In this constellation the ways of emotions follow each other and cross over each other, happy/unhappy, as the case may be. The time of conversation between the twins is the time of the case.

This awareness of time derives almost necessarily from the "expression of the concept of emotions." It is the secret "gift" of the man without qualities and the structure of the utopia of "essayism." Where emotions happen, and only the idea of them appears, then *Ur-teil,* the divisible linearity of time, remains clean and unbroken. When emotions take place in the constellation of the twins (Gemini), they do not congeal into a point on the line that leads from a beginning to an end. No temporal absolute underlies them. Musil underscores the *case* of the beginning ("Über dem Atlantik . . . ") with all the force of his irony. The *Stimmung* of "Into the Millennium" fathoms a silence that is never perfectly attainable, as in certain of Mahler's finales. Musil's *Erlebnis* of time resides in his concentration on the case at hand throughout the narrative, down to the most intimate fibers of narrative material, and his ability to incarnate himself in it. Every instant of the novel, every mood, every gesture reaches fulfillment and has its moment in time. These are not moments that express various isolated situations that, in turn, can be measured and analyzed interchangeably. This is a matter of an undefinable multiplicity of moments, each with its independent fact. They are moments/facts that collect together in bunches, that make and unmake "families," and that form unrepeatable events.

Through an *Erlebnis* of time Musil expresses the crisis of narrative. Narration is possible where time develops an "explanation" for events, determining their relationships, indicating a beginning and an end. Time here maintains a secret idea of self-redemption stemming from an ancient and nearly always forgotten eschatological beginning. In secularized eschatology, human relationships in their diverse languages develop according to a plan and manifest a sense of direction. The fundamental structure of this concept of time remains unchanged even if the direction leads to nothing, to the abyss, and not to the good. Even if eschatology reverses its promise, its form still dominates the narrative. The current possibility of sending such a form into crisis, however, constitutes the unique, decipherable "sense" of Musil's novel. Time explodes into a myriad of moments that accompany, upon complete disenchantment with any eschatological perpective, maximum attention to the *fact*, the event, the moment: maximum attention to this singularity. The perfect form of attention clothes every word, mood, thought, and gesture in diaphanous clarity. It breaks every continuum, every simple linearity, and repeats itself in various forms, *wie es kam*, as the various facts present themselves.

Musil "smilingly" presents this feeling of time through a long quotation from Swedenborg. The quotation creates an effect of distance, almost of resigned irony, as if this feeling of time should necessarily flee any attempt at a precise definition and as if it were possible to register it only through the "extravagant" words of a visionary. The motto of the meditations that Ulrich develops is a contemplative's dream, and it could not be otherwise: that only the absolute time of narration can be judged systematically. Essay time, on the other hand, declares itself only in the manifestation of the cases that incarnate it. It cannot be extracted from the *Stimmung* of the moment. The image indicates its possible place, registers its character, without attempting its solution.

Angels "do not know what time is, because in heaven there are no days or years. There are only changing moods." Angels "have no notion of time, unlike humans. . . . If they hear someone speaking about time (God has always supplied angels to keep humans company), they understand it in terms of moods and the determination of moods. . . . In the spiritual world, angels appear as soon as they feel a need for their presence, because then they are transported to that mood; and inversely, if they feel aversion they go away." Ulrich "felt true delight" in evoking these images out of "old metaphysics," in the capacity to speak of angels with the accuracy and precision of an "engineer," in a dry and dispassionate manner. The explosion of time into moments and moods is fundamentally distant from turning completely away from the exte-

rior emotions, from the acquisitive, for the voracious resolve of the
Faustian. The "setting sights" of the acquisitive would be inconceivable apart from a basis of linear and eschatological time, however secularized the eschatology may appear. A concept of time
that abstractly excludes the acquisitive, however, is unsuitable to
the infinite variations of mood. Such variations fit the constellation of facts at the crossroads between nihilist and activist, between
contemplative and acquisitive.

God has always supplied angels to keep humans company, so
that they may speak of these possible times and moods. They are
the no-place that attends humanity's actual space and time. *Essay-
istically*, a *decision* between the two dimensions is impossible. It
would mean either living in heaven or idolatrously endorsing time
as the only conceivable reality. That is why Musil/Ulrich can only
speak "smilingly" about the "angelic ingenuity" of the old metaphysics, so dear to Goethe and Kant (who actually believed in its
vision of a correspondence between time and interior state and
who spoke of it "as if it were a matter of Stockholm and its inhabitants"). Yet "angelic ingenuity" exposes how unfounded is the pretext of time as an absolute, with its spaces and distances. It reveals
the character that would become the absolute and utter master because it rules over absolute time: the acquisitive, omnidetermined,
and nihilistic. The collapse of this vision connects to the entire infinite complex of possibilities of living, to the difficult *ars combi-
natoria* that knows how to seize the quality and moment of every
possibility and how to make it resonate. Thus the problem of time,
rediscovered at the end of the analysis of emotions, passes into the
problem of "heuristic ethics." This is "an ethics endowed with real
growth power," not subject to "periodical catastrophic defeat." It
rests "not on a hierarchy fixed for all eternity but rather on the uninterrupted activity of a creative imagination."[103] This problematic
ethics corresponds in Musil to the problematic appearance of a
moment that bunches single moods, that illuminates them and
embraces them as, in a hundred places in Hieronymus Bosch, great
glass halos both separate and hold together the enchantment of
lovers who cannot unite, yet are never divided.

It is not possible here to fully investigate the problem of the essay in Musil. It would be enough to have pointed out its incorporation into the pattern of analysis that we are attempting to identify. The essay is certainly not the expression of an age in which "insecurity" comes back into fashion, in which people from "slightly uncertain professions: poets, critics, women, and 'junior' professionals" loudly demand new faiths and basic values. The essay holds suspect any pretense of center, of order, of unshakable foundations. Its prohibition against "believing things finished" is not in itself provisional or accessory, as if it were a matter of "discarding" lost *Weltanschauungen*. The essay form appears rather as a definitive life style and style of thinking, a broad assumption of responsibility over any decadent insecurity and any perennial philosophy. The essay is not a free-roaming intelligence, impressionistic writing, or merely a form of suspended judgment, as if it were lying in wait for new systems. It is truly the writing of interior moments and states as something removed from the continuum and from narrative. These are things that cannot be reduced to a system, but are no less capable of being described analytically, precisely, *microscopically* in their distinctions. The polarity of irony and utopia[104] (the essay's elements of style) is also the polarity between dissolving the continuum (the turning point of narrative) and the no-place of the angelic state, "ironically" described through Swedenborg. The infinite grades of reality's participation in utopian nature (the novel's very content) also express infinite possible relationships between time and fact, infinite possible meanings of events. This is no allegory, "where everything means more than what it can honestly claim," but, nonetheless, there is the greatest *attention* to all of these possibilities. There is also *surrender*—exempt from any hesitant pessimism—to the inability to finish the itinerary, resolve the utopia, make of the world of facts a spiritual world where no distance impedes the transformation of emotions.

NB

The essay form, according to Musil, neither gravitates around a center nor announces nor alludes to a future system.[105] Thus its moment is not repeated in orbit after orbit around a center that attracts it and that always retreats from it. Nor does it charge eschatologically toward the new message, the new order. Rather, the moments of the facts are what captures its attention. That is what essayistic attention considers. The essay writes out these moments and considers them, with greatest attention to the world as a whole, a protean "totality of facts." Attention is critical distance, *irony*, the opposite of impressionism or any vitalistic *Einfühlung*. Irony is transfigured when it crystallizes the utopia of the twilight of time onto the rugged, hard, profane surface of the case. Irony has the ability to manifest the utopia of the immediate and perfect transpiring into space of the interior state.[106]

The final part of *The Man Without Qualities*, dominated by infinitesimal attention to moods, is also where Musil's idea of the essay finds fuller expression. The essay appears as attention's own form. For such a form there are no "details." There are only irreducible singularities. Every "detail" connects, as soon as attention focuses on it, to unforeseen and bottomless abysses of singularity. The tone of the final part brings out the extraordinary tension that unites brother and sister, as if they could be united only on the edge of the most fundamental separation. The uninterrupted meditation (not stream of consciousness, but stream of meditations!) generated by such a state is its proper form of attention. The tone resembles the mystical *prosoché* [attention] of those who seek silence. Ulrich shows himself to be aware of this, even if there is no method, no technique to teach it. Ulrich's attention cannot be pure in the sense of being free of thought or imagination, free of intention or will. Attention is not a perfect method for contemplation. Its purity belongs to the moments of its own essayism. It is paradoxical from the mystical point of view inasmuch as it is attention turned to "profane" moods, attention that is developed along a non-liberating *ex-stasis*, but that leads back with more force and passion to these moods, to their "details." The paradox of Musil's attention lies in its turning toward the profane, to infinite grades of reality's participation in utopian nature, *as if* it suffered from divine things (*theia pathein*), *as if* it were a matter of describing changes of mood in a purely spiritual world. The dissolving magic of *ironic* recognition still returns for that "as if" at the outer limit of the novel's contemplative and meditative force, the inflexible protector of that force.

Simone Weil says, in *La connaisance surnaturelle*, "God is attention without distraction."[107] The great mystical theme of an inexhaustible force of intuition, of reaching a dimension of ecstasy that renders oblivion impossible (thus the opposite of the common currency of the term "mystical"), returns therefore in the *cases* of Musil's novel—that is, in the situation most abandoned by God: the state of being "without qualities." To construct the essay form as attention without distraction, to make the essay into an unseducible intuition, is the great *complexio oppositorum* that ties together the novel's events and its *Erlebnisse*. The wandering thinking of the essay succeeds in acquiring, in an inexhaustible traversing of cases, the tone of *prosoché*. None of the cases is so removed, so forgotten. Attention penetrates to each and reveals of each an *abyssal* dimension. The essay form's thinking wanders abyssally, and not from surface to surface anymore or from moment to moment.

There is even greater evidence of the paradoxical nature of attention according to Musil if we reflect on the essay as a fundamentally non-predicating form of writing. To preach is to judge *divisio primaeva*, to possess or want to possess the essence of a thing as a priori distinguishable from its "appearance." The case of Musil does not tolerate such differentiation. The essay that waits for moments that are named for the different facts that happen in them does not have their true names. Essays are dispossessed writing.[108] The greatest force of attention that this writing can develop requires not excluding or forgetting the impossibility of judgment and not allowing oneself to be seduced by *preaching*. And if the essence of preaching lies in the verb "to be," essayistic writing is disconnected from "being" or confirms "being" only by ironizing its groundlessness. The most profound connection between Musil and Nietzsche lies in their critique of the category of "being," of any pretense of confirming a distinction between essence and appearance through preaching.[109]

Derrida's comments about Levinas could easily, at this point, be repeated about Musil. For Musil, too, a "non-violent" language would be a language deprived of the verb "to be." "Since the verb to be and the predicating act are implied in every other verb and every common noun, non-violent language would be, at most, a language of pure invocation, of pure adoration. It would utter only proper nouns to invoke the other from far away."[110] The dialogue between brother and sister comes to realize a similar language unintentionally. Ulrich and Agathe "invoke" each other from afar. They are, *so far apart*, the indivisible one who can never be united. This language is the most extreme utopia conceivable. It is the last dimension of the reality's participation in utopian nature. Precisely because a perfectly non-violent language would be, at most, pure invocation (it would speak the mystical language of the heart's silent prayers), the dimension of distance is natural to it. This language can do nothing but call from afar. It is distant. The essay form corrodes and criticizes the violence of preaching to the point of calling from afar the utopia of language dispossessed of all "being." It can reach this point, not beyond. This language would be, in reality, a form of listening, as happens for Kierkegaard in true prayer, in which pure attention to conversation with God is freed from any seduction, from any pretense, and from any question, and stands in pure listening.[111] The essay reaches the point of making "a gesture" toward this form of listening. The divine state of it, though, is necessarily denied.

The pinnacle of attention would be, therefore, a language deprived of "being," resolved in listening. Musil's essayistic attention demonstrates this utopia, with irony and surrender. A language that speaks without "being" would be the equivalent of an ethics that acts as a "creative imagination," without obligation, to a love that neither demands nor possesses, but is free, non-exclusive, non-acquisitive, only giving, pure *dépense*. This is, perhaps, an attempt to give voice to the silence that embraces all preaching, all *Ur-teil* of the language of "being," irreducible to preaching, whose road Wittgenstein prohibited at the end of the *Tractatus*.

Notes

Notes

1. Foolish things have been written about Otto Wagner's St. Leopold am Steinhof. It seems that starting with J. A. Lux and H. Tietze, whose monographs (1914 and 1922 respectively) spoke of a "blessed delight" at the sight of the church, of the interior as a "festival chamber," "a kind of church for non-practicing people," and so forth, the only things that attracted the attention of historians and architects were the comfortable footstools and the hygenic fonts for holy water.

2. W. Jollos, *Arte tedesca fra le due guerre* (Milan: Mondadori, 1955), p. 65.

3. See Robert Musil, *Selected Writings*, ed. Burton Pike (N.Y.: Continuum, 1986), pp. 315–16.—TRANS.

4. See M. Rosso, "Introduction," in L. Wittgenstein, *Osservazioni filosofiche* (Turin: Einaudi, 1976), p. lxxii. [All citations from the *Tractatus* are from *Tractatus Logico-Philosphicus*, new ed., trans. D. F. Pears and B. F. McGuinness, Introduction by Bertrand Russell (London: Routledge and Kegan Paul, 1971).—TRANS.]

5. R. De Monticelli, "Frege, Husserl, Wittgenstein," *Nuova Corrente* 72–73 (1977). I am grateful to Roberta De Monticelli for numerous ideas and suggestions.

6. See my *Krisis: Saggio sulla crisi del pensiero negative da Nietzsche a Wittgenstein* (Milan: Feltrinelli, 1976), pp. 85 ff.

7. Regarding this critique, I base my remarks on G. Franck, "Fondazione della conoscenza e fondamenti dell'operare," *Nuova Corrente* 72–73 (1977), and on many recent studies by A. Gargani, from his "Scienza e forme di vita," also in *Nuova Corrente* 72–73, which is entirely

dedicated to Wittgenstein, to *Il sapere senza fondamenti* (Turin: Einaudi, 1975); from "Tecniche descrittive e procedure costruttive," in U. Curi, ed., *La razionalità scientifica* (Abano Terme: Francisci, 1978), to *Wittgenstein tra Austria e Inghilterra* (Turin: Einaudi, 1979).

8. See on these themes, in addition to the "encyclopedic" work of A. Janik and S. Toulmin, *Wittgenstein's Vienna* (New York: Simon and Schuster, 1973), W. M. Johnston, *The Austrian Mind* (Berkeley: University of California Press, 1972); and the important studies by Enrico Bellone, *I modelli e la concezione del mondo nella fisica moderna da Laplace a Bohr* (Milan: Feltrinelli, 1973), and *Il mondo di carta: Ricerche sulla seconda rivoluzione scientifica* (Milan: Mondadori, 1976) [in English, *A World on Paper: Studies in the Second Scientific Revolution*, trans. Mirella and Riccardo Giacone (Cambridge, Mass.: MIT Press, 1980)].

9. L. Wittgenstein, *Vermischte Bemerkungen* [in English, *Culture and Value*, ed. G. H. von Wright with Heikki Nyman, trans. Peter Winch (Chicago: University of Chicago Press, 1980)].

10. L. Wittgenstein, *Über Gewissheit* [in English, *On Certainty*, trans. Denis Paul (Oxford: Blackwell, 1969)].

11. Wittgenstein, *Culture and Value*.

12. The scope of this essay does not permit me to develop Benjamin's concept of *Trauerspiel*, but I have analyzed it in "Di alcuni motivi in Walter Benjamin," *Nuova Corrente* 67 (1975) and in "Intransitabili utopie," in H. von Hofmannsthal, *La Torre* [*Der Turm*], trans. S. Bortoli Cappelletto (Milan: 1978).

13. L. Wittgenstein, *Della Certezza* [*Über Gewissheit* / On Certainty], trans. M. Trinchero (Turin: Einaudi, 1978), pp. 110, 70.

14. R. Bazlen, *Il capitano di lungo corso* (Milan: Adelphi, 1973), p. 208.

15. G. Colli, *La nascita della filosofia* (Milan: Adelphi, 1975), pp. 85 ff.

16. G. Colli, *Filosofia dell'espressione* (Milan: Adelphi, 1969), pp. 191–92.

17. I have relied for this discussion on ideas contained in the essays of E. Severino, from *Essenza del nichilismo* (Milan: Adelphi, 1982) to *Gli abitatori del tempo* (Rome: A. Armando 1978) and *Legge e caso* (Milan: Adelphi, 1979).

18. From a letter from Roberto Bazlen to Eugenio Montale, used as an epigraph in O. Manoni, *Fictions freudiennes* (Paris: Seuil, 1978).

19. Wittgenstein, *Culture and Value*; the "aphorism" is taken up again in his *Remarks on the Foundations of Mathematics* [English translation, rev. ed. (Chicago: University of Chicago Press, 1986)].

20. Thus also S. Quinzio, *La fede sepolta* (Milan: Adelphi, 1978), p. 92.

21. M. Vannini, *Lontani dal segno: Saggio sul cristianesimo* (Florence: La Nuova Italia, 1971), p. 14.

22. To understand this "reversal" of a Heideggerian concept, formed on a famous text of Hölderlin, see my essays "Eupalino o l'architettura" and "Die Christenheit oder Europa," both in *Nuova Corrente* 76–77 (1978), an issue entirely devoted to Heidegger.

23. P. Boulez, *Par volonté et par hasard: Entretiens avec Celestin Deliege* (Paris: Editions du Seuil, 1975).

24. M. Bortolotto, "Altra Aurora," in F. Nietzsche, *Scritti su Wagner* (Milan: Adelphi, 1979), p. 55.

25. M. Bortolotto, "Le vin du voyant," in *Adelphiana 1971* (Milan: Adelphi, 1971).

26. L. Nono, "Text-Musik-Gesang" (1960), in J. Stenzl, *Luigi Nono: Texte Studien zu seiner Musik* (Zurich-Freiburg: Atlantis, 1975), p. 44.

27. M. Bortolotto, *Introduzione al Lied romantico* (Milan: Adelphi, 1984), pp. 162–63.

28. See A. Schoenberg, *Fünfzehn Gedichte aus dem Buch der hangenden Gärten für eine Singstimme und Klavier, Op. 15; Texte von Stefan George* (Vienna: Universal Edition, 1914).—TRANS.

29. T. W. Adorno, *Impromptus: Zweite Folge neu gedrückter musikalischer Aufsätze* (Frankfurt: Suhrkamp, 1968). In this passage Adorno retraces, on the same basis, a parallel between Berg and Schoenberg.

30. G. Manzoni, *Arnold Schoenberg: L'uomo, l'opera, i testi musicali* (Milan: Feltrinelli, 1975), p. 42.

31. R. Musil, *Mann ohne Eigenschaften*; in English, *The Man Without Qualities*, trans. Sophie Wilkins, editorial consultant Burton Pike (New York: Knopf, 1995).—TRANS.

32. E. Lemoine-Luccioni, *Partage des femmes* (Paris: Seuil, 1976), pp. 125 ff.

33. E. Castrucci, "Ekstatische Sozietät: Note filosofico-politiche su Robert Musil," *Rivista Internazionale di Filosofia del Diritto* 2 (1977): 4.

34. J. Derrida. *Eperons: Les styles de Nietzsche* (Paris: Flammarion, 1978), pp. 86–92.

35. C. G. Jung, *Psychology and Alchemy*, trans. R. F. C. Hull, 2nd ed. rev. (London: Routledge, 1992 [1968]).—TRANS.

36. For this section see the fundamental essays of R. Klein, "Spirito Peregrino" and "L'immaginazione come veste dell'anima in Marsilio Fi-

cino and Giordano Bruno," in *La forma e l'intelligibile* (Turin: Einaudi, 1975). [In English, *Form and Meaning: Essays on the Renaissance and Modern Art*, trans. Madeline Jay and Leon Wieseltier (New York: Viking, 1979).]

37. H. von Hofmannsthal, *Der Schwierige*, ed. W. E. Yates (Cambridge, Eng.: Cambridge University Press, 1966).—TRANS.

38. E. Staiger, "*Der Schwierige*," in *Meisterwerke deutscher Sprache*, 2nd ed. (Zurich: Atlantis-Verlag, 1948).

39. H. von Hofmannsthal, *Der Turm: Ein Trauerspiel* (Frankfurt: Fischer, 1992).—TRANS.

40. Cf. H. De Lubac, *L'alba incompiuta del Rinascimento* (Milan: Jaca Book, 1977).

41. F. A. Yates, *Shakespeare's Last Plays: A New Approach* (London: Routledge and Kegan Paul, 1975). After one has arrived at an understanding of this part of my work, it is recommended that a comparison be made with Yates's other books, *Giordano Bruno and the Hermetic Tradition* (Chicago: University of Chicago Press, 1964), as well as *Theatre of the World* (Chicago: University of Chicago Press, 1969), which treats John Dee, protagonist of Meyrink's *The Angel of the Western Window*. About Dee, see also F. Jesi, "John Dee e il suo sapere," *Communità* 166 (1972).

42. C. Loos, *Adolf Loos Privat* (Vienna: W. Bohlau, 1985), pp. 103–4.

43. L. Andreas-Salomé, "Zum Typus Weib," in *Das "zweideutige" Lacheln der Erotik: Texte zur Psychoanalyse* (Freiburg: Kore, 1990).

44. R. M. Rilke, "Puppen," in *Gesammelte Werke*, vol. 4 (Leipzig: Insel-Verlag, 1927).

45. M. Eliade, *Mephistopheles and the Androgyne: Studies in Religious Myth and Symbol*, trans. J. M. Cohen (New York: Sheed and Ward, 1965).

46. G. Agamben, *Infanzia e storia: Distruzione dell'esperienza e origine della storia*, 2nd ed. (Turin: Einaudi, 1971 [in English, *Infancy and History: The Destruction of Experience*, trans. Liz Heron (London, New York: Verso, 1993)]. Walter Benjamin, "Erfahrung und Armut," in *Gesammelte Schriften* unter Mitwirkung von Theodor W. Adorno und Gershom Scholem, herausgegeben von Rolf Tiedemann und Hermann Schweppenhauser (Frankfurt, 1980) vol. 2, part I, p. 218.

47. On Simmel's influence on Benjamin, see my *Metropolis* (Rome: Officina, 1973).

48. C. Magris, *Il mito absburgico nella letteratura autriaca contempo-*

ranea (Turin: Einaudi, 1963), and *Lontano da dove: Joseph Roth e la tradizione ebraico-orientale* (Turin: Einaudi, 1971).

49. J. Roth, *Werke*, 4 vols. (Cologne: Kiepenheuer und Witsch, 1975–76). The Overlook Press, Woodstock, N.Y., has undertaken the project of publishing Roth in English translation. See *Confession of a Murderer Told in One Night* (1985), *The Emperor's Tomb* (1984), 'Hotel Savoy,' 'Fallmerayer the Stationmaster,' and 'The Bust of the Emperor' (1986), *Job: The Story of a Simple Man* (1982), *The Legend of the Holy Drinker* (1991), *The Radetsky March* (1994), *Right and Left* (1992), *The Silent Prophet* (1980), 'The Spider's Web' and 'Zipper and His Father' (1989), and *Tarabas, a Guest on Earth* (1987).—TRANS.

50. G. Baget-Bozzo and E. Benvenuto, *La conoscenza di Dio* (Rome: Borla, 1978), p. 98.

51. F. Rosenzweig, *Der Stern der Erlösung* (Frankfurt: Kauffmann, 1921) [in English, *The Star of Redemption*, trans. William W. Hallo (Notre Dame, Ind.: Notre Dame University Press, 1985)]. High-quality studies of Rosenzweig are not common; see N. N. Glatzer, *Franz Rosenzweig: His Life and Thought* (New York: Farrar, Straus and Young, 1953). For the relationship between Rosenzweig's Jewish mysticism and Christian concepts, it is interesting to regard the letters between Rosenzweig and Eugen Rosenstock-Huessey, in E. Rosenstock-Huessy, ed., *Judaism Despite Christianity: The Letters on Christianity and Judaism Between Eugen Rosenstock-Huessy and Franz Rosenzweig* (Tuscaloosa: University of Alabama Press, 1969).

52. M. Heidegger, "Language in the Poem: A Discussion of Georg Trakl's Poetic Work," in *On the Way to Language* [in English, trans. Peter D. Hertz (San Francisco: Harper & Row, 1971), pp. 159–98].

53. See A. Kubin, *Mappenwerke, Bücher, Einzelblätter aus der Sammlung Hedwig und Helmut Goedeckemeyer* (Göttingen: Kunstgeschichtliches Seminar der Universität Göttingen, 1980). See also Kubin's autobiography, *Dämonen und Nachtgesichte* (Munich: R. Piper, 1959), and the catalogue raisonée, A. Marks, *Alfred Kubin* (New York: Praeger, 1969).—TRANS.

54. E. Jünger, *Strahlungen* (Tübingen: Heliopolis-Verlag, 1949) [in English, *The Paris Diaries, 1941–1944*, trans. Michael Hulse (New York: Farrar Straus Giroux, 1989)].

55. E. Jünger, "Die Staubdämonen," in *Alfred Kubin: Weltgeflecht, Schriften und Bilder zu Leben und Werk* (Salzburg: Galerie Welz, 1978).

56. A. Kubin, *Die Andere Seite*; in English, *The Other Side: A Fantastic Novel* (New York: Crown, 1967).—TRANS.

57. W. Schmied, *Der Zeichner Alfred Kubin* (Salzburg: 1967), p. 36 [in English, *Alfred Kubin* (New York: Praeger, 1969)].

58. On this resemblance see A. M. Ripellino, *Praga magica* (Turin: Einaudi, 1973), and R. Barthes, *Arcimboldo* [English translation, New York: Rizzoli, 1980].

59. E. Jünger, *Auf den Marmorklippen* [in English, *On the Marble Cliffs: A Novel*, trans. Stuart Hood (New York: New Directions, 1947)]. The book, whose first copy reached Jünger October 6, 1939, reflects in a very transparent way the cultural and political positions of the author with regard to the Nazi regime, positions of almost desperate detachment that seem to plunge roots into the most aristocratic and esoteric aspects of the "conservative revolution" of the 1920's. In his diary of 1939–40, *Gärten und Strassen*, it is possible to follow the draft of the novel and see the importance that Jünger attributed to it: "I think I have succeeded, in this work of fantasy, in writing pieces that can sustain comparison with the best that has been produced in our language."

60. M. Blanchot, "Un oeuvre d'Ernst Jünger," in *Faux pas* (Paris: Gallimard, 1943). G. De Chirico, "Betrachtungen über eine Ausstellung deutscher Kunst" and "Max Klinger (1920)," in *Wir Metaphysiker: Gesammelte Schriften* (Berlin: Propylaen Verlag, 1973). On Klinger, and in particular on the *Glove* cycle, see A. A. Dückers, *Max Klinger* (Berlin: Rembrandt-Verlag, 1976).

61. J. Lezama Lima, "Classical Myths and Fatigue," in *Las eras imaginarias* (Madrid: Editorial Fundamentos, 1971).

62. Cf. G. Briganti, *I pittori dell'immaginario* (Milan: Electa, 1977), pp. 248–49.

63. E. Bloch, "Herbst, Sumpf, Heide, und Sezession," in *Literarische Aufsätze* (Frankfurt: Suhrkamp, 1965), pp. 439 ff [in English, *Literary Essays*, trans. Andrew Joron and Helga Wild (Stanford, Calif.: Stanford University Press, forthcoming)].

64. J. J. Bachofen, *Il popolo licio* (Florence: G. C. Sansoni, 1944). (See also Bachofen, *Gesammelte Werke* [Basel: Schwabe, 1943–67].—TRANS.)

65. On this passage, see J. Lezama Lima, *Introduccion a los vasos orficos* (Barcelona: Barral Editores, 1971).

66. J. Evola, "Introduction" to the collection Bachofen, *Le madri e la virilità olimpica* (Milan, 1949).

67. G. Colli, *Dopo Nietzsche* (Milan: Adelphi, 1974).

68. E. Jünger, *Annäherungen: Drogen und Rausch* (Stuttgart: Klett, 1970).

69. J. Evola, *The Metaphysics of Sex* (New York: Inner Traditions International, 1983).—TRANS.

70. A. Savinio, *Vita di Enrico Ibsen* (Milan: Adelphi, 1979), p. 51.

71. G. Bataille, *Laura: Storia di una ragazzina e altri scritti* (Rome, 1976), p. 119.

72. V. Rozanov, *Foglie cadute* (Milan: Adelphi, 1976), p. 136 [in English, *Fallen Leaves*, trans. S. S. Koteliansky (London: The Mandrake Press, 1929–)].

73. This is how Schiele expresses himself in his "manifesto" *Neukünstler,* now collected with his other writings in C. M. Nebehay, ed., *Egon Schiele, 1890–1918: Leben, Briefe, Gedichte* (Salzburg: Residenz, 1979).

74. Dylan Thomas's line comes to mind: "My hero bares his nerves along my wrist . . . "—a line that could serve to explain not only Schiele's self-portraits, but also those disturbing self-portraits of another *ewiges Kind,* Richard Gerstl, one showing a standing nude (1908), streaked, screaming, fatigue *expressed* in every fiber, and with the most desperate "I must." [See D. Thomas, "My Hero Bares His Nerves," in *Collected Poems, 1934–1953,* ed. Walford Davies and Ralph Maud (London: Dent, 1988).—TRANS.]

75. R. Walser, *Der Spaziergang* (Herrliberg-Zurich: Buhl, 1944), *Geschwister Tanner* (Frankfurt: Suhrkamp, 1967), and *Fritz Kochers Aufsätze* (Zurich: Suhrkamp, 1986).

76. C. Magris, "Davanti alla porta della vita," in R. Walser, *L'assistente,* trans. E. Pocar (Turin: Einaudi, 1978).

77. M. Buber, *Legend of the Baal Shem* [English translation, New York: Harper, 1955]. I will also refer to Buber's other book, *Die Erzählungen der Chassidim* (Zurich: Manesse Verlag, 1949) [in English, *Tales of the Hassidim,* trans. Olga Marx (New York: Schocken, 1947–48)].

78. R. Calasso, "Il sonno del calligrafo," in R. Walser, *Jakob von Gunten,* trans. E. Castellani (Milan: Adelphi, 1970).

79. J. De Menasce, *Quand Israel aime Dieu* (Paris: Plon, 1931), pp. 139 ff.

80. R. Walser, *Kleine Dichtungen* (1914) in *Das Gesamtwerk,* (Geneva: Kossodo, 1967–75), vol. 2, p. 6.

81. E. Canetti, *La provincia dell'uomo* (Milan: Bompiani, 1978), pp. 304–5.

82. R. Walser, "Hölderlin," in *Poetenleben* (1918), in *Das Gesamtwerk* (Geneva: Kossodo, 1978), vol. 3, pp. 116 ff.

83. I cite Hesse, *Morgenlandfahrt* (Berlin: S. Fischer, 1932) [in English, *Journey to the East*, trans. Hilda Rosner (New York: Farrar Straus Giroux, 1956)]; *Siddharta: Eine indische Dichtung* (Berlin: S. Fischer, 1923) [in English, trans. Hilda Rosner (New York: New Directions, 1951)]; and *Klingsors letzter Sommer* (Zurich: Fetz & Warmuth, 1958 [in English, *Klingsor's Last Summer*, trans. Richard and Clara Winston (New York: Farrar Straus Giroux, 1970)].

84. K. Scheffer, "Karl Walser," in *Talente* (Berlin: B. Cassirer, 1921).

85. *Tractatus* 6.521: "The solution of the problem of life is seen in the vanishing of the problem."—TRANS.

86. The citations that appear in this part of the book are taken, essentially, from the following works: D. T. Suzuki, *Mysticism: Christian and Buddhist* (New York: Harper, 1957), and *Essays in Zen Buddhism* (London: Luzak, 1927); E. Herrigel, *Der Zenweg* [in English, *The Method of Zen*, trans. R. F. C. Hull (New York: Pantheon, 1960)]; Yuan-wu, *Pen yen lu* [in English, *The Blue Cliff Record*, trans. Thomas and J. C. Cleary (New York: Random House, 1977)]; Shih Chao-shu, *Radical Zen: The Sayings of Master Joshu*, trans. Yoel Hoffman (New York: Random House, 1974); and P. Reps, *101 Zen Stories* (Philadelphia: David McKay, 1940).

87. E. Herrigel, *Zen in der Kunst des Bogenschiessens* (Weilheim: O. W. Barth, 1981) [in English, *Zen in the Art of Archery*, trans. R. F. C. Hull (New York: Pantheon, 1953)].

88. F. Bellino, "Wittgenstein e Mauthner: la filosofia come Sprachkritik," in *Studi e ricerche dell'Istituto di Filosofia* (Bari: L'Istituto, 1977).

89. Thus M. Müller, *Die Verdrängung des Ornaments: Zum Verhältnis von Architektur und Lebenspraxis* (Frankfurt: Suhrkamp, 1977), pp. 99 ff.

90. See M. Gelsi, "Peter Altenberg e la sacralità del quotidiano," *Nuova Corrente* 79–80 (1979).

91. R. Bazlen, *Note senza testo* (Milan: Adelphi, 1970), pp. 79 ff.

92. L. Mittner, "Appunti autobiografici," *Belfagor* 4 (1975), and "Randglossen zur Kulturgeschichte der Donaumonarchie," in *Jahrbuch der deutschen Akademie für Sprache und Dichtung* (Heidelberg-Darmstadt: Edward Roether, 1973).

93. J. Langer, *Nine Gates to the Chassidic Mysteries* (New York: Behrman House, 1961). Apart from works of Buber, De Menasce, and Langer cited above, I refer here to A. J. Heschel, *A Passion for Truth* (New York: Farrar Straus Giroux, 1973); A. Mandel, *La voie du hassidisme* (Paris: Calmann-Levy, 1963); M. Buber, *Schriften zum Chassidismus*, in

Gesammelte Werke, vol. 3 (Frankfurt: Fischer, 1963); and G. Scholem, *Judaica* (Frankfurt: Suhrkamp, 1963), pp. 165–206.

94. I. B. Singer, *Shosha* (New York: Farrar Straus Giroux, 1978).

95. E. Canetti, *Massa e potere* (Milan: Adelphi, 1972), p. 192. We have already seen how Wittgenstein might express the identical judgment in *Culture and Value.*

96. G. Scholem, *Major Trends in Jewish Mysticism* (New York: Schocken, 1946), pp. 329 ff. Scholem also dedicated his great work on Sabbatai Zevi to the theme of Messianism, *Sabbatai Zevi, the Mystical Messiah* (Princeton, N.J.: Princeton University Press, 1973).

97. See J. Habermas, "Der deutsche Idealismus und die judischen Philosophen," in *Philosophisch-politische Profile* (Frankfurt: Suhrkamp, 1971), p. 49.

98. K. Löwith, "M. Heidegger und F. Rosenzweig, ein Nachtrag zu 'Sein und Zeit,'" in *Gesammelte Abhandlungen* (Stuttgart: W. Kohlhammer, 1960).

99. H. Kohn, *Karl Kraus, Arthur Schnitzler, Otto Weininger: Aus dem judischen Wien der Jahrhundertwende* (Tübingen: Mohr, 1962), p. 59.

100. R. Calasso, "Una muraglia cinese," in K. Kraus, *Detti e contradetti* (Milan: Adelphi, 1972).

101. I extract Kraus's emblems from the explication of basic ideograms in Confucian texts by Ezra Pound. Pound prepared poems from the *Shih Ching* for Italian readers in the 1950's, including *Confucio: Studio integrale & l'asse che non vacilla* (Milan: All'Insegna del pesce d'oro, 1955; 2nd ed., 1960).

102. K. Kraus, *Die letzten Tage der Menschheit: Tragodie in fünf Akten mit Vorspiel und Epilog* (Munich: Kosel-Verlag, 1957) [in English, *The Last Days of Mankind: A Tragedy in Five Acts* (New York: F. Ungar, 1974)]. Kraus's supreme mastery in rousing the horror that Canetti so splendidly analyzed in *Potere e sopravivenza* (Milan: Adelphi, 1974) bursts into flame in this work, precisely through the device of quotation. Quotation became a means to stir horror. Unfortunately, now we can only quote horrors.

103. P. Zellini, *Breve storia dell'infinito* (Milan: Adelphi, 1980), p. 29.

104. See, in this regard, B. Allemann, "Robert Musil," in *Ironie und Dichtung* (Pfullingen: Neske, 1956).

105. In this, Musil's essay form is metaphysically distinct from Lukács's in *The Soul and Forms* (just as his irony is distinct from Mann's). It appears, rather, to hold a stricter affinity with that of Benjamin. See G.

Schiavoni, *Walter Benjamin: Sopravivere alla cultura* (Palermo: Sellerio, 1980), p. 35.

106. On the subject of moments, see my essay and others collected in M. Bertaggia, et al., *Crucialità del tempo: Saggi sulla concezione nietzchiana del tempo* (Naples: Liguori, 1980).

107. Quoted in A. Del Noce, "Simone Weil interprete del monde d'oggi," in *L'epoca della secolarizzazione* (Milan: Giuffre, 1970), p. 141; I have this essay in mind for this and other points in my work, in spite of (or perhaps as a result of) my enormous distance from its "conclusions."

108. Castrucci's interesting observations in "Ekstatische Sozietät: Note filosofico-politiche su Robert Musil" should be developed in this direction.

109. On the relationship between Musil and Nietzsche, an intelligent "summary" can be found in I. Seidler, "Das Nietzschebild Robert Musils," in *Nietzsche und die deutsche Literatur*, B,2 (Tübingen: Niemeyer, 1978).

110. J. Derrida, "Violence and Metaphysics," in *Writing and Difference* (Chicago: University of Chicago Press, 1978). F. Desideri rightly refers to this passage with regard to Benjamin, in his volume, *Walter Benjamin: Il tempo e le forme* (Rome: Riuniti, 1980), p. 91.

111. S. Kierkegaard, *Dagboger*, vol. 1 [in English, *Diary*, ed. Peter P. Rohde (New York: Philosophical Library, 1960)].

Figure Sources

Crossing Aesthetics

Library of Congress
Cataloging-in-Publication Data

Cacciari, Massimo.
[Dallo Steinhof.   English]
Posthumous people : Vienna at the turning point / Massimo
Cacciari; translated by Rodger Friedman.
     p.   cm. — (Meridian, Stanford, Calif.)
Translation of: Dallo Steinhof. Milano : Adelphi, 1980.
ISBN 0-8047-2709-0 (cloth : alk. paper). —
ISBN 0-8047-2710-4 (paper : alk. paper)
1. Vienna (Austria)—Intellectual life.   2. Politics and culture—
Austria—Vienna.   3. Vienna (Austria)—Social life and customs.
4. Vienna (Austria)—Biography.   5. Intellectuals—Austria—
Vienna.   6. Vienna (Austria)—Civilization.   I. Title.
II. Series.
DB851.C3213   1996
943.6′13—dc20   96-14952   CIP

Original printing 1996

Last figure below indicates year of this printing

05   04   03   02   01   00   99   98   97   96